THE FLORIDA ROOM

The FLORIDA ROOM

ALEXANDRA T. VAZQUEZ

DUKE UNIVERSITY PRESS *Durham and London* 2022

© 2022 DUKE UNIVERSITY PRESS
This work is licensed under a Creative Commons Attribution-NonCommercial-NoDerivatives 4.0 International License, available at https://creativecommons.org/licenses/by-nc-nd/4.0/.

Designed by Matthew Tauch
Typeset in Alegreya and Univers by Westchester Publishing Services

Library of Congress Cataloging-in-Publication Data
Names: Vazquez, Alexandra T., [date] author.
Title: The Florida room / Alexandra T. Vazquez.
Description: Durham: Duke University Press, 2022. | Includes bibliographical references and index.
Identifiers: LCCN 2021022854 (print)
LCCN 2021022855 (ebook)
ISBN 9781478015307 (hardcover)
ISBN 9781478017929 (paperback)
ISBN 9781478022541 (ebook)
ISBN 9781478092704 (ebook other)
Subjects: LCSH: Music—Florida—Miami—History and criticism. | Music—Social aspects—Florida—Miami. | Music and history—Florida—Miami. | Miami (Fla.)—Intellectual life. | Miami (Fla.)—History. | BISAC: SOCIAL SCIENCE / Ethnic Studies / American / African American & Black Studies | SOCIAL SCIENCE / Ethnic Studies / American / Hispanic American Studies
Classification: LCC ML200.8.M49 V397 2022 (print) | LCC ML200.8.M49 (ebook) | DDC 780.9759/381—dc23
LC record available at https://lccn.loc.gov/2021022854
LC ebook record available at https://lccn.loc.gov/2021022855

This book is freely available in an open access edition thanks to TOME (Toward an Open Monograph Ecosystem)—a collaboration of the Association of American Universities, the Association of University Presses, and the Association of Research Libraries and the generous support of New York University. Learn more at the TOME website, which can be found at the following web address: https://openmonographs.org.

TO AND FROM MY SISTER TORY

"In Lower Florida Wilds," by Juan Valadez, 2021.

CONTENTS

PREFACE. HEAD FOR THE BEACH · ix

Chapter One
THE FLORIDA ROOM
1

Chapter Two
MIAMI FROM THE SPOILS
46

Chapter Three
DRUMS TAKE TIME
81

Chapter Four
BASS IS THE PLACE
117

AFTERWORD
156

ACKNOWLEDGMENTS · 159 / NOTES · 165

BIBLIOGRAPHY · 203 / INDEX · 215

PREFACE

HEAD FOR THE BEACH

There is everything for you here. There is nothing for you here. As much can be said, and has been said, about a city like Miami in a state like Florida. The same might be said for this book. The logic of the case study requires evaluation and reward. (Why does this thing merit our attention? What sets it apart?) Its specialness separates it from the rest. If we can get out of that logic—*what's in this for me?*—there might be something else entirely given, here, in that place and in this book, that isn't bound up with taking or a summary "takeaway" from the local. What may be given is hospitality, a hardy encouragement to stay for a minute, even when it feels unfamiliar and disorienting, and especially when it resists easy import into your own story. Visits of any duration are most welcome to *The Florida Room*. To hold a reader's attention in the humidity of residential particulars is the challenge of writing about place for those who have not been there. The experience of reading will likely require more rest stops. For the initiates, it is the how and the mode of assembly of place in this book that might delay and make different the familiar and orienting. This may require other forms of refreshment. Miami, Florida, is a place that will never be clearly or fully written about. It will not offer neat arguments about something or someplace else. This is the difficult beauty and wonder of its laboratory. It is also what offers assurance: surely there is something for you here.

The Florida Room is a method, a spatial imaginary, a vestibule, an addition to the main house of writings about place. The chapters are temporary rooms for connectivity between seemingly disparate things and people, and thus make necessary movement between history, theory, biography, and—most of all—music. Music's making and magic make possible the geographic thought experiment and peopling of this book. For the ways it compresses place, time, communities, and their creative play, music allows *The Florida Room* to hear Miami as a place of and from many. We hear the

Miccosukee as founding its rock-and-roll aesthetics. There are more than a few archipelagic island groupings sounded here: the Lucayan that built it and the Caribbean, notably Cuba, Haiti, and Jamaica, that further contoured it. The mainland is here, too, especially southern Georgia, brought by those who moved in reverse of the Great Migration to "the bottom," as it is colloquially known. Miami's attachment to northern capitals such as New York and Philly is most palpable in music in recorded and live forms. If any consistent critique can and should be made of Miami studies, it is that it is always incomplete. Who and when is here partly reflects my generational experience and those whom I grew up with. Its datedness is an argument. Its partialness is an argument too: this place needs hundreds of theorists and storytellers, old and young. What is offered here is not an encyclopedic mission to include everywhere and everyone but an invitation to revel in its small reveal of how many versions can be told about this place.[1] In this book it may be even hard to detect how certain details tell Miami. They find subterranean company with others that have long resisted the appeal for Miami's spectacular inclusion as a modern metropole. Their subtle narrative tread grounds fantasies by those interests, from real estate to the arts, that would deny the histories of those who made and make it a place to live and do beautiful things.

Miami is saturated with torn experiences. Its myriad painful stories of separation, survival, and infuriation strongly tell over and over, despite its more than a century-long promise to a very select few of paradise and all that goes with it. Miami is a city considered foregone and far gone.[2] Much like New Orleans, rising sea levels have set the terms of its engulfment. It has long been primed for environmental disaster. The rapacious investments to make the land *settle*, to force its marshy volatility solid, and to insist that narratives about the city do the same have made Miami an experience sold in three speeds: fast, slow, stuck. Fast for the fever pitch of its development, slow for those left behind. Stuck, perhaps the most difficult gear, when trying to find other ways to live in and through it. The given Miami has never been stable. Its porous foundations have it in constant movement.[3] The enduring exploitation of this moving given to make a comfortable place for some has made disposable and displaceable a great many. They have been inconvenient obstacles for Miami's total development and amnesia for well over a century. This book adamantly lives in their stories told, broken and outright, whether in song, in paint, in writing, in conversation. Miami's environmental devastation is real, and it is urgent. Of coterminous urgency is the telling of those lives and all that living and making that have long been refused recognition. To dismiss Miami as forgone and far gone is to enact a double violence: a giving up on its fragile ecologies *and* a willful forgetting of its under-told stories. *The Florida Room* hopes to switch up the speeds of the city's telling: to stop the impulse to possess, to make fast and furious inscription of Miami's erasures, to break open the cemented resignation of no past and no future. It soaks pages heavily with the area's unremembered.

It is not just Miami's coastal position or its strange geographic contours that unsettle any sense of stability. The differences (peopled and placed) pressed into Miami's relatively short history have paradoxically primed it for lazy assessment. It is too often celebrated for an easy, suntanned brand of multiculturalism that ignores the deep inequities that run the city. It is outright dismissed as a bad object in national events, particularly elections, which makes its myriad populations, and even the populations within those populations, into a singular mass.[4] Miami thrives as an impossible heterogeneity that makes it an anomaly of the United States. And yet it is for many, as you will be told over and over again, a place without culture or aesthetic traditions. This repeated eradication of indigenous ingenuity and the contributions of Miami's Black and immigrant populations finds sanction in too many places. This book hopes to augment important historical studies of Miami with a plunge into its steadfast and brilliant cultural work as its basis, not as its afterthought. You will find guides for context in the notes section rather than the main body of the text because this book wants to lead with artists' stories, the things they make, the places they imagine. In Miami this is an activity that is always just beginning. The opening stanza of Lorna Goodison's poem "Deep Sea Diving" offers an invocation for both hearing and living it:

For the rare ones, the pieces only glimpsed at in dreams,
it is essential that you dive deeply.
On the surface all that you will see are objects discernable
to anybody, in colors between everyday and ordinary.
What a splendid spectrum ranges below for those
who dive deeply.[5]

The local offers its own models for critique; it doesn't need an outside apparatus. It does not require outside curators to bring it up to speed or to invite imposed rubrics in from the cold. What is already here, I ask, that wants to be *here* a little differently? How to hear the "splendid spectrum"?

PREFACE xi

Along with the Florida room as a locally articulated architectural phenomenon, the book insinuates other given models for its writing. The reading of each chapter requires willing entry into a mangrove tangle. The mangrove's shoots make it impossible to unravel neat lines of origin and influence. The details of their connectivity, somehow and miraculously, hold together and make home for a lot of life. They hold up in the fiercest of storms. Even when they are forcibly removed, the mangrove's propagules renew, somewhere else, perhaps close by their former home.[6] Other eco-conceptual models abound in here. *The Florida Room* borrows from their forms, demands, resilience, and especially their transitions. Severo Sarduy once called the thin bands that separate songs on long-play records *playas* (beaches). For Sarduy the spaces do not signal alienation but instead carry the warmth and salinity of the shore and offer a place for "a homage to the naked body and to the beachside panoply." With Sarduy we may hear these *playas* as thriving with activity, as transformative spaces between where and when one song ends and another begins. They are full of searches for aesthetic forms, for temporary partners, and the bands "have no final outcome."[7] Songs on the record object circle in parallel, and the beaches that link them help to make other kinds of connections between ensembles. I invite you to imagine the breaks within and between chapters as *playas*, as places for you, the reader, to bring what you need and leave what you don't.

Florida, with all its particulars, can't be told enough times. It's strangeness to the United States has long been a national given. "South America, take it away," Bugs Bunny famously said right before he animatedly sawed it off from the mainland. Some will pick up this book and hope to find "Florida"; others may want to go directly to "Miami." The writings on and around either are often kept apart, as are their authors. Here they share room. Throughout these pages, place will exceed official city limits and cross counties, sometimes for a longer ride, say to the Everglades. Places farther out and across time require other forms of transport, such as a record, radio, or drum. Because its precolonial and colonial histories do not align or are cut off from various critiques of the Americas, Florida demands other lexicons, adaptations, and, no less important, *styles* for its telling. *Write it*, as more than a few of my formative teachers used to say to encourage me to put together, in my own words and ways, what I thought was going on. The constant unrelenting education that is music, from remembered songs played on the school bus to the new worlds of cabaret performances in Miami's here and now, is my idiom. While music makes exquisite forms of camouflage, I insist on hearing the real decisions made by musicians and all those who in one way or another had some hand in their training. And therefore, a lot of biographical detail is laced throughout this book. The biographies included here are not told in full but in glimmers that tell a fullness of living. There is a lot of movement made in them, geographic and imaginative, and they cue capacious approaches to concepts of the settled and the arrived. By listening to their migrancy and to what gets picked up and left behind while on the move, I hear techniques of making-do with the at-hand and how this making do is aesthetically mobilized by the dispossessed. Although the book depends upon oral histories of some of its players, it thrives in the complexities of their creative worlds that are often unverifiable. People's partial stories in *The Florida Room* were either shared with me directly or left behind in interviews with others. The richness of their fragments carries the stakes of births and deaths, migrations, teaching, love. At times in direct relation to my own experiencing of these things, there is thus a lot of maternity in these pages that is often, though not always, suggested through biography. To honor all them and all there in *The Florida Room* is my written refinement of a deep love of where I am from.

Chapter One

THE FLORIDA ROOM

....

There is an actual place called the Florida room found in many of the state's homes. It is a room slightly askew of the house, usually offset a living room, that suggests another mode of *living room* specific to the infrastructure of the peninsula. The Florida room is neither officially inside nor outside, and although it feels like an addition to the main house, it is in the planned bones of the design to add more social life to the entirety. Screened in, or framed by glass jalousie windows (French for jealousy, from the Italian *geloso*), it keeps out the undesired to make way for the chosen, rain for dry, chill for sun. Even as mosquitoes are kept out, even as it exists in plain view, the room still allows for hiding out.[1] Extreme and temperate, it can be too hot, too cold, just right. It is being in the elements with some protective casing, a recognition of out there and in here that chooses neither. There is a decision made when one occupies it, an off-center choice that desires other than the overdetermined bedroom or dining room. It welcomes the makeshift, as it is often turned into that second or third bedroom needed when someone comes to visit, a quarrel demands separation, or an adolescent requires her own room, even if that space is visible to the rest of the domestic and the street. The advent of air conditioning couldn't kill off its purpose or feeling even when the rooms became permanently walled in. And when you enter it, you often must take a step down to the almost subterranean, as you would step into the ocean. You leave the sand for the water. It can go by other names. Descriptive: screened-in patio. Demonstrative: the extra room. Entrepreneurial: the home office. But it doesn't. The Florida room. It trades in gimmickry that you will likely internalize and make outwardly serious, a playful and difficult adjustment that thrives in the state.

As a title, *The Florida Room* began as an inside joke that, over time, became the outwardly serious gathering space for the following set of place-based works. The room is as actual as it is conceptual, as structural as it is imaginative. The lives in these chapters all pointed to being there, to wanting to be in the Florida room, if not quite together, then together in their need to be elsewhere than the main house. They resist union but evoke a shared dependence on this localized yet mobile place, its particular social living, a shared climate, and being inside and outside at once. *The Florida Room* lets everyone and everywhere in but does not stage or force encounters between people and things. It is a place for tender conjunction between stories that are kept apart, but its makeshift ethos also confronts the difficulty and constancy of being able to say and assemble them all at once. This is its risk in formation, of not wanting to create portable gauntlets that correct, fill in, or narrate its insides for an outside. What you will find here are people and places and music that need to heard together, even if they aren't all in the same room at the same time, era, or language. This book is steeped in painful histories; it airs some, keeps others private. Yet its myriad performances are brimming with potent sociality, making rich material for patio talk, contributing, as ever, to its open lilt while also revealing the long hangout time required to make beautiful composite together.

The entries to come all form some pulsating event, a kind of flip book. This introductory flip book depends on animation between the various scenes of and in Florida, movements slow and fast, that make adjustments of comprehension in the blink of an eye. Whether making motion with the pages from front to back or back to front, from some penultimate point, in medias res, the flip book can make stick some distinctive fragment from the rest and also hold a complete experience that hovers just above the object. The flip book relies on the help of a reader to make it move at their own pace, and invites all inclination to stop and start the coherence of the whole. The following drawings are not the gradual sort that shift one micro detail from a page corner to the next to easily lift the eye and ear through the transitions. But that is not to say they aren't deliberately placed.

The "Florida room" can be found in architectural digests or lifestyle magazines in and out of the state of Florida, with sudden floridity after World War II. It is a room that might not actually be in Florida at all but is a place exported to other climes and homes as far and as cold as New York, Indiana, and Ohio. Real estate advertisements, over time, have used the Florida room to highlight a listing's extra space, adding suggestive color with a hint of exotic transport. Even a complex across the Oxford Dictionary system has three separate entries for Florida room (all nouns): *Oxford Reference* has it as simply "another word for sunroom." *The Oxford English Dictionary* makes it "a room built at the back of a house and partly or wholly glazed, typically with a brick or tile floor and a drinks bar." And finally the *Canadian Oxford Dictionary* defines it as "a sunroom, usu. only partly insulated, enclosed in glass on three sides."[2] It has been the activating setting for everything in Richard Blanco's poem "El Florida" and Tarell Alvin McCraney's play *Head of Passes*, and it even unfurls the two-page short story "Wrong Number" by Roberto G. Fernández.[3] It is a song by Steely Dan's last remaining member, Donald Fagan (cowritten with Libby Titus), that advances its own description: "There's a room in back / With a view of the sea / Where she sits and dreams / Does she dream of me?" It then is made to function as a site of choral return: "When the cold wind comes, I go where the dahlias bloom / I keep drifting back to your Florida Room."[4] A return to a make-out session and/or perhaps a euphemism for a woman's body? "The Florida Room" was the title given for an "occasional feature" for more informal writing in the eminent *Florida Historical Quarterly* in 2003.[5] It has been used to name a bar at the Delano Hotel on Miami Beach and who knows how many informal others. It makes a parlor game out of a research question for any Floridian I encounter, in Florida or anywhere else: what do you think of when you hear "the Florida room"? To which I have received replies both familiar and stunning: that softy rattan sofa where my aunt stayed, windows with hurricane-tape marks. Regardless of the answer, there is never much of a pause. My friend Michael Aranov, raised in a townhouse in North Miami Beach, replied to the question this way: "I've never felt more like an Uzbeki immigrant before." Which brings up a central point: the Florida room, though a feature of the middle-class domestic scene, has been made beyond the glare of assimilated and impossible lifestyles out of reach for so many. It is less a sign of upward mobility than a yearning for a place, a place within a place. It is why one may be hard-pressed to hear or say the word without an accent. One finds them, or versions of them, in every neighborhood. All around Florida, and the radial outer Florida, you find people making them, regardless.

The Florida Room takes up this thing called "Florida" and all its in- and out-of-place people, the work they make there, or the work they make because of there. Let's begin with a few histories of assembly involved in it. In Florida, historical facts have long worked hard to make its mythologies real. For example, we find mention of the Florida room as far back as 1891, when Elizabeth Dustin described an early form of it in her "Doings of Women" column in the *Los Angeles Times*. Take in her account of an established trend, already made ripe for irony, a mere forty-six years after Florida's official statehood:

A FLORIDA ROOM

> If you can't go to Florida in Lent you can perhaps have a Florida room. The notion has been taken up hereabouts, and really there have been worse fads in decoration. The possession of such an apartment is a certificate that you have been south some previous year—or that some time you are going. In a dainty Florida boudoir the wings of the flame-bright flamingoes, which fly through the green gloom of the swamps like tongues of fire, make charming bits of color, thrust behind the corner of a shelf or mirror. Soft, coarse blankets woven from the yellow fabric of the Nankin cotton, and dyed in pale, brownish tan, are hung as portieres and thrown as rugs across divans. In a cozy corner stands a tiny tea table made from a palmetto tree, its top a polished disk of the curiously marked wood, its three legs long varnished leaf stalks, their joining hidden by fans of the young leaves. It's a queer, tropical-looking bit, and if your hostess serves you on it a glass of orange-flower syrup you are apt to think, as you sit and sip, with your eyes resting on some weird sketch from the lagoons, that, after all, if she would but pull down that skin of a rattlesnake, it's not, with its trails of southern moss, in the meshes of which perch tiny, vivid-colored Florida birds in all sorts of pretty attitudes, it's not such a bad room.[6]

And so the Florida room, even and especially in this early iteration (the fake before the real), plays several roles. Here it is proof of having been there, an imported sensibility, or a promissory note that says "sometime you are going." Its time for the outsider is a stimulating one entered during Lenten abstention. A reprieve of color and strange, a souvenir brought back after a visit. Its perfect situ for "queer, tropical looking bits," for objects that would otherwise feel off in any other room. Here they belong and have function. What Dustin seems curious about but can't quite place could be summed up by the questions: Where does this stuff and this place come from? Whose house, whose domain, does this room cite? Perhaps it was a vacation home or an established residence of a northern refugee needing sun on their lungs. Who are the influences on this unnamed decorator? And most importantly, where do such aesthetics come from? We are given all the signals for answers to such questions: the environmental, the myriad trades and trade that happen within Florida, and what's involved when all this is taken away and presented to an outsider: "If she would but pull down that skin of a rattlesnake . . . it's not such a bad room." But she doesn't, she leaves it, and in fact insists on that rattlesnake, unknowingly or willingly offending what we might shorthand here as northern sensibility. She ignores accusations of tacky that makes this little room the place she is so proud of, it is where she gathers her out-of-state self and company.[7] It is a portable reliquary and also more than. The Florida room's export, beyond being a holding pen for touristic curios, suggests a planned desire for social togetherness alongside out-of-place things.

We later find the Florida room in a *New York Times* 1953 feature written by Betty Pepis, future author of *Interior Decoration A to Z* (1965), titled finally, officially, simply: "The 'Florida Room'" (figure 1.1). It has graduated from Dustin's outlandish receptacle to America's modernist accomplishment. Pepis begins her article and inaugurates a trend at once: "Likely to leave its mark on other parts of the country, despite climatic differences. . . ." It is "a room in which indoors and outdoors meet," she explains, and the two-page feature includes large photographic examples by famed modernist architects such as Robert Little, Wahl Snyder, James Merrick Smith, and notably, Paul Rudolph, whose words and work are quoted in the three-paragraph feature. Rudolph was for much of his career known as a foundational figure in the "Sarasota School of Architecture" or "Sarasota Modern" well before he designed his more famous works such as the Yale Art and Architecture building (during his tenure as chair of the School of Architecture beginning in 1958).[8] Before all this, before he would become known as one of America's greatest architects (an architect's architect), was Rudolph's Florida period, where together with Ralph Twitchell, he would design and build such structures as the legendary Healy Guest House (also known as the "Cocoon House").

In her article, Pepis quotes Rudolph's lecture at the Coast Arts Center she saw just the week before. There he argued, "Any architecture in a warm climate has a peculiar responsibility because modern architecture in general is easier accomplished in a warm climate than it is in a northern climate." It is a revelation that the south, so long figured as backward or behind, is here configured as an ideal condition for modernist experiments with space. The interruption is heft with the weight of past history—we cannot *not* note his use of *peculiar*—and its already established blueprints, the plantation systems that disciplined the land for efficiency and extraction. Born in Kentucky to an itinerant Methodist minister, and eventual Harvard student of Bauhaus founder Walter Gropius, Rudolph put into his Florida period his childhood intimacy with innovative vernacular architectures of the south, and he lent warmth to modernist inquiries of the relation between

The "Florida Room"

By BETTY PEPIS

CLEARWATER, Fla.

LIKELY to leave its mark on other parts of the country, despite climatic differences, is the building boom currently taking place in this state. Outstanding among contributions is the concept of what is called the "Florida room," at present being incorporated into many of the modern houses rising here by the score.

This is a room in which indoors and outdoors meet—for part of the room is inside the house, part of it is protected from the elements only by the use of screening or, occasionally, a roof. In adverse weather, and only then, the screened area is blocked off by a device like a sliding door. Several examples of rooms like this are pictured here and offer proof that such an area would be acceptable during warm months in more northerly climes.

An explanation of why so much experimentation is to be seen in this area was offered by architect Paul Rudolph speaking at a symposium on Florida residential architecture held here at the Gulf Coast Art Center last month. "Any architecture in a warm climate has a peculiar responsibility because modern architecture in general is easier accomplished in a warm climate than it is in a northern climate," Mr. Rudolph said. That Florida architects are not neglecting this opportunity to produce new forms for more pleasant living was fully evidenced by the symposium and as well by the changing appearance of the Florida landscape.

STRAW, REED AND METAL are materials adapted to furni... pletedly opened up in pleasant weather. The bedrooms are o...

---

inner and outer space.[9] Rudolph renders the south as a place for exercising responsibility for aesthetic play even if its climactic ease enabled and enables so much violence. And so it is possible to feel Rudolph's sense of space as resonant beyond the good living promised by glossy architectural digests, beyond the false whitewashing premise of mid-century.[10]

The examples provided by Pepis's *New York Times* article all share the qualities of outdoor rooms made with pliable materials or with materials pushed to the limits of their pliability. We are given examples of not so much the adaptability of the south to the modern but something of a vice versa: of modernism's extending from the south. The article is an invita-

FIGURE 1.1 Betty Pepis, "The 'Florida Room,'" *New York Times*, March 15, 1953. ProQuest (12566107).

tion to return to Rudolph's Florida period in particular, which stuns for its demonstrative attunement to surroundings.[11] According to Robert Bruegmann, Rudolph disliked having his designs be photographed as a curated lifestyle (the well-placed pair of slippers, a stack of magazines, preciously posed fruit bowls) suggesting the promise of privacy, leisure, possession.[12] After donating his archive to the Library of Congress and insisting upon its most open access possible, Rudolph wanted his drawings to be as specific as to render themselves, without the lifestylic extras. His innovative execution of such drawings were also left behind, openly, for others to come along and take flight from. There are many other blueprints, other extant

THE FLORIDA ROOM 7

drawings to be felt within and prior to Rudolph's work. They hold robust, if neglected, evidence of what the south has given to the modern, and in particular, those vernacular architectures—even unseen ones—that schooled Rudolph and his contemporaries.

All aesthetics come from somewhere. They are developed and forged by people over long periods of time, via direct encounter or near misses. To move down into Florida's southernmost region, the radiant area that takes hold of the bulk of this book, we may speculate and extend far back some of the mystified undercurrents of Dustin's article and the material modernist experiments in Rudolph. Take the two-thousand-year-old "Miami Circle," remnants of an ancient structure of the Tequesta and their ancestors that stands at the mouth of the Miami River, with a pristine view of Biscayne Bay (figure 1.2). It became a press and scholarly sensation when its discovery became widely known in 1998.[13] Its origins, age, and function continue to be debated—in fact, it has inspired an extensive critical literature. The Miami Circle includes twenty-four basins carved into limestone in a circle that measures thirty-eight feet in diameter.[14] Thanks to the meticulous studies collated and written by Miami-Dade archaeologist Robert S. Carr, we learn that these basins were dug into the limestone to hold posts for a structure. Through radiocarbon dating of charcoal and the variety of ceramic shards found in the basins, Carr approximates its "calibrated age" to AD 50 (the Glades I period).[15] Among the recovered objects at the Miami Circle were the complete vertebrae from a rare "requiem shark," the skull of a bottle-nosed dolphin, and a loggerhead turtle's carapace, all positioned in an east-west direction. There has been much speculation about the presence of these animal remains, whether they indicate sacrificial rituals, what Erica Hill calls "ceremonial trash," or what Ryan Wheeler and Carr posit as the possibilities of "other cultural practices" or "the ontological concept as 'other than human persons.'"[16] But archaeology cannot ever tell us the whole story, as some of its practitioners themselves admit and embrace. I am less interested on the verification of their "actual" function and more drawn to how their intactness suggests them as something other than utilitarian items.[17]

What is most provocative to imagine, thanks to Carr's hypothesis, and especially in collaboration with Alison A. Elgart's findings, are that these animal interments date several hundred years apart from the other. In other words, whatever this place was, it remained a formalized and revisited site over extended periods of time. The structure, its position at the crossroads of water, and its placed acknowledgment—for whatever meaning—of

FIGURE 1.2 Aerial view of the Miami Circle. Photo courtesy of Miami-Dade County Office of Historic Preservation.

the faunic surround suggest how people have made living with meaning possible. And, of course, of great importance to the Florida room and *The Florida Room* is Carr's indication that the excavation of the Miami Circle revealed a large amount of "exotic materials." Through the work of geologist Jacqueline E. Dixon et al., we learn that these materials include basaltic rocks from all over North America (especially the Caribbean and the Piedmont region near Atlanta, Georgia), galena from Missouri, copper from Michigan, and chert from Central Florida.[18] These outsides brought and tucked into this structure prefigure and pretheorize hemispheric study or inter-American scholarship; it helps to imagine something of the activities of a global South without the governing protocols of European colonialism and empire. What the Miami Circle was or is, with its millennia-long accumulation of things from elsewhere, is the kind of inquiry I extend right through to the Florida room: What is this place? And how does the gathering of enigmatic things from all over invite us to proceed radially from the local out, and from the outward in? What we learn from this ancient modern circle, from this firmly rooted and ephemeral structure, is that migrancy plays in the heart of its development and adornment. The knowledge of the east-west sunset, over time, evidenced by the Miami Circle marks the land's first stewards and their centuries of earthworks. This all reveals an ancient practical know-how, a making-do and making green with the at-hand, but with *chosen addition* of the area's histories of migrancy. In the very bones of their infrastructure, the Tequesta and their ancestors insisted on incorporating signals of movement and the encounters had while there as both foundation and decor. So perhaps, in this moving genealogy of the Florida room, a renaming or, at the very least, a slowing down of the sign "vernacular architectures" is in urgent order. Perhaps we can call these practices prescient philosophies of living and being with that are innovative for their practicality and their beauty.[19]

Take the indigenous ingenuity of the chickee developed the i:laposhni:cha thli:, people of Mikasuki-speaking heritage in Florida who today represent the Seminole Tribe of Florida, the Miccosukee Tribe of Indians of Florida, and Independents. They have been historically grouped under the name Seminole. The people who "Seminole" describes emerge from distinct language groups and cultures. The histories of Seminoles are at once mercurial, untold, mis-told, fragmented, or confined to settler ways of telling. The non-native often grasps for firm places, names, place-names, static group identifications, and, through the idioms of archaeology or anthropology, tries hard to make the past and present fully transparent. There is always a violent reduction of these long histories—and the lives that lived them—when shorthanded for outsider context. Deeply resistive are the entrenched histories of people who have long made thriving multicultural communities even and especially when coming together as refugees. And given the depth of degree—in time and space—of displacements, bloodshed, and willful erasures, there is no "figuring out" or fast track to understanding all that rumbles under the sign of the Seminole in ways that will satisfy settler modes of inquiry. Rather than perpetuate the endorsement of such shorthand, I stay close to a small constellation of artists and authors, here and in chapter 2, to nuance and, more importantly, recognize and honor all those who have endured much more than any truncated telling will allow.[20] Buffalo Tiger (Bird Clan) offers this for those struggling with the disorienting particulars: "We know who we are and what type of language we have."[21]

The chickee (or "house" in the Mikasuki language) is the traditional home structure and powerful symbol for both the Seminole Tribe of Florida and the Miccosukee Tribe of Indians of Florida, and is featured in their official logos as an icon of gathering. The chickee is an open-sided dwelling, built to scale depending on its function, and has long contoured the horizon of the Floridas. The chickees were traditionally placed in matrilocal hamlet arrangements, with separate ones built for cooking, for sleeping, and more portable ones made for hunting.[22] Their frames are usually made with logs from pine or cypress trees, and their roofs are made out of overlapping palmetto fronds woven into structural ribs (figure 1.3). Sleeping platforms were elevated several feet off the ground for aeration and for protection from curious fauna. It is a reinterpretation of a treetop, a silhouette that textures the sky. The palmetto fronds offer both a form of protection from and a being with the surround. The roof protects people and things from the rain, and its pliability allows strong winds to flow through rather than against the chickee. The structure moves with the given. The chickee's adaptability enables it to anticipate and endure anything that may be coming. Bird Clan philosopher Daniel Tommie Ochehachee began apprenticing under his uncle Johnny Tucker (an expert chickee builder) in the craft of their building as a teenager in the late 1970s and early 1980s.[23] The first thing Ochehachee remembered learning to do was "how to carry a good-sized log by yourself," how to balance even a twelve-foot log by pushing it upward, finding its center of gravity, and gently balancing the log on the shoulder without an extra pair of hands. Those extra hands, in turn, would be freed up to move on to the next step. An efficiency for making home.[24] He describes the difficulty of the work but believes that chickee building was part of what trained his multifaceted sense of discipline and creativity to make things easier. This is a learned practice that Ochehachee describes as "working smart instead of working hard."[25]

As Ochehachee would watch and learn from his uncle Tucker and from his cousin, James E. Billie (Bird Clan), the influential chairman of the Seminole Tribe of Florida, he learned that for the practice of chickee building, "the key word that you need is compassion." What does it mean, and what could it mean, to build a dwelling with compassion? Note that he did not say compassion *for*, which would suggest a separate lived experience from others. What Ochehachee extends is a different cosmology for recognizing and *being with* feeling, be it happiness or sorrow or struggle or hunger, and how it may be met with integrity, honesty, love, and food. This being with is hard work and requires a steadfast dedication to remembering the past and a sense of responsibility to the future. Compassion is a keyword made into action, a necessary quality built into structure. It is also a structure of recognition—with and without material evidence—of deep ancestral techniques. When I asked Ochehachee what compassion meant to him, he beautifully pivoted to a story about his grandparents, Ruby Tommie (Bird Clan) and Jimmy Tommie (Panther Clan). His grandfather was an important

FIGURE 1.3 Jill Guttman, FS89394, photograph of James Billie's chickee—Big Cypress Reservation, Florida, January 1989. Folklife Collection, Series 1577, Seminole Project, no. 50, State Archives of Florida.

spiritual healer and bundle carrier who was afflicted with blindness. As a notable medicine man to their people, Ochehachee's grandfather would receive many visitors throughout any given day, and his grandmother made the infrastructure so that care was available to all. Ruby Tommie would be sure to prepare enough food to last throughout the day, which included meals for the family, for the extended family, and also for all the visitors who would come from all over to see them. This was when they still lived in the Everglades and would move their chickee from dry hammock to dry hammock. Ochehachee said that they could spot visitors on the horizon thirty minutes before they would arrive, and this would give his grandmother enough time to heat up food for them. The hospitality of Ruby Tommie is what Ochehachee calls "one of the many branches of compassion," and it is a material and spiritual component woven into the chickee.[26] As Ochehachee put it, "You're not supposed to be stingy with your food."[27]

To return to one of Ochehachee's teachers (and cousin), James E. Billie, we are given other theories behind chickee design and what it enables for a different interaction between land and home and an invitation to imagine certain functions in and of *The Florida Room*. Billie emphasizes all the chickee lets in:

It does not hold back the noises coming from the outside. It does not prevent spiders, cockroaches, mosquitos, rats or snakes from visiting. Wintertime you freeze, but in summertime you are cool and comfortable. Every morning we are awakened an hour before daylight by the cawing of the crow greeting the day. Red birds (cardinals), mockingbirds, woodpeckers and from a distance you can hear the whooping crane and all are singing their songs and looking for breakfast. Jets overhead seem like they are coming through the roof. *A chickee does not hold back noise.* Raining on the roof and lightning is especially nice but a little scary. But it's our house and we love it.[28]

Billie says it twice: a chickee "does not hold back noise." It is surround-sound living. He asks that we imagine the rapid changes in frequency as a plane passes by; the special South Florida kind of doomsday rain and lightning that gives aural cues for the seasons (sublime for sure); and the deep south birdsongs, those mingled cries of migration that feel prehistoric and modern all at once. All of this is part of the chosen design and the love of living in the chickee. Here Billie shows a structural habitus for listening in this book. It does not, nor cannot, hold back noise. Billie's description of living models an inspiring capacity for taking in all the elements. Although the Florida room (as an architectural phenomenon) may try to filter out the undesired for the wanted, Billie shows *The Florida Room* that nothing is in my control, and this is a house one can love.

Ochehachee states that chickees are now mostly, though not exclusively, built for economic reasons. For example, they are commissioned by hotels, golf courses, or private pool cabanas. The trade is brisk and important for the Seminoles and is just one small industry among centuries-long industries developed with visionary entrepreneurial spirit. This spirit and determination are forces the i:laposhni:cha thli: help me to imagine in more detail in chapter 2. As is customary in their longer arts and economies of fortitude and self-sufficiency, there is an insistence on passing down traditional ways of life to the new generations. When I asked Ochehachee about how one may detect the different signatures from chickee makers in their work, he is quick to answer: "It is very, very subtle and very hard to tell." The choice of wood, or the ordered placement of logs, for example, and also the particular size of the chickee can suggest its maker. These chosen aesthetics of scale and assembly, in other words, are part of what marks one builder's craft from another's. It would likely be difficult to tell unless you were trained alongside these architects. As for Ochehachee's practical and creative legacy, he has already started to ready his six-year-old daughter, Shonayeh Shawnie

FIGURE 1.4 Photograph of Daniel Tommie Ochehachee (Bird Clan), February 10, 2018, in Loxahatchee, Florida. Ochehachee offered this photo of himself in his Seminole War reenactment regalia for the book. "This is the image I want to put out there so people remember." Photo permission by Gordon Ollie Wareham.

Tommie, in the practice of chickee building. It is an activity that goes hand in hand with trying to teach her colors and animals in his first language, Mikasuki. She's a "perfect candidate," he says, who will later "show some of the guys what hard work can do." Ochehachee has begun by teaching her which sticks to save for certain positions in a fire and how to sort the scale of a tree's offerings for a future chickee. "I'm working on a foundation," he says of this education. "You might see her, next year, with a hammer in her hand" (figure 1.4).[29]

Deep knowledge of currents, of elemental pliability, of weather patterns hard lived and hard won can also be seen, foundationally, in Florida's Bahamian "Conch" houses. These innovative structures were named after the Bahamian settlers who came to Tarpon Springs, Miami, and Key West in the 1870s to work its nascent tourist economies and the sponge trades, and make new, single-family homes. They were built in such a way that the open front to the open back door of the house makes a single continuous circulatory breezeway. Bahamian ship carpenters are generally attributed

FIGURE 1.5 The Mariah Brown House. Courtesy of the author.

to be the earliest architects of this style. Characteristics include using wood joinery, raised foundations so as to allow for circulation, galleried front porches, and jalousied windows throughout, all designed with no lifestyling extras and to allow for maximum possible air flow.[30] One notable example of this Bahamian living philosophy is the Mariah Brown house (circa 1890) in historic Coconut Grove Village West in Miami, one of the oldest parts of the city. Mariah Brown, born in 1851 in the Upper Bogue, Eleuthera, left home to work as a washerwoman in Key West and was among the first Bahamians to migrate to South Florida to work at the Peacock Inn, one of the first lodgings built for tourists, in 1880.[31] Brown first lived at the inn but soon sought to make a home of her family's own. A founder in what Bahamians called Kebo, the first Black community in Dade County, Brown and early residents cut their own street off of the Main Highway and named it Evangelist Street (now Charles Avenue). The Mariah Brown House was one of the first homes on this cutaway (see figure 1.5).[32]

We don't know who actually built the Mariah Brown House, but we want and need to imagine its activity of way past and current present. Looking at this house, the scrappiest of fighters, there is an absolutely detectable flurry of activity, of life and the living, even in its abandonment, even as its front windows are boarded up. It emanates light and air. The historical imaginary made possible by this beautifully economical and compact structure, of the exits and entrances of Florida's early Bahamian residents, of how they made precious time out of the workplace, is palpable in the here and now. Note how the two front windows lend an experimental threshold to the front porch, portals that allow a person to be between, to be both in and of what is happening on the inside and outside of the house. This zone is a place of testing, of not being ready to leave or stay, and there is a kind of aerated comfort in that formally built transition. It is a proto Florida room.

The Mariah Brown House makes new gatherings even in its current condition. The Brown House, like so many other vestiges of Florida's Black histories—histories that rapacious developers have been fully invested in exploiting and then erasing—appears to be left somewhere in the limens of destruction and the false promise of preservation. "Awaiting restoration" is Florida real estate code that appeases outcries for conservation, usually important Black historical locations, before they corruptly cut out any opposition and tear them down. A wear down to tear down.[33] But there is, as always in Miami, so much more to this story. The fight on the part of long-standing Village West Grove residents is far from over; it still stands; it is still there. One among many fighters, the indefatigable Linda Williams was born and raised in Village West.[34] Her mom ("a Georgia gal") was the well-known Bessie Thompson Williams Haithman, a domestic worker who maintained the homes of some of South Florida's prominent families, including the Alexander Graham Bells, Fairchilds, and Pancoasts (figures 1.6 and 1.7).[35] As a single working mom, Bessie Haithman saved her wages to buy a home in 1964 in Village West, where she raised young Linda. Linda Williams came of age with Coconut Grove's trenchant racial boundaries that later became known as the Coconut Grove Village West Neighborhood Conservation District (NCD–2).[36] She is sure to distinguish Village West from Coconut Grove because the former was the place designated "for our folks to live," noting that one could not cross 32nd Avenue unless employed by a family on the other side. For Williams, however, Village West was self-sufficient, "we [had] shoe cobblers, fish markets, beauticians, barbers, mom and pop stores, etc.," which enabled families and neighbors to clothe, feed, and provide care for the beautiful and talented among a tight-knit community. Among the incredible details of her life was her position as the first Black corps captain of the majorettes at then newly integrated Coral Gables Senior High. She eventually married Alfred Williams who she met while he was working as a butcher/market manager at the Winn-Dixie

FIGURE 1.6 Bessie Thompson Williams Haithman. Courtesy of Linda Williams.

FIGURE 1.7 Linda Williams. Courtesy of Linda Williams.

grocery store. In one of the greatest lines of love at first sight, Linda Williams said to Alfred Williams: "I won't even have to change my name."

Williams had an incredible career as an administrative secretary for Lester Pancoast, as the school secretary at the Everglades School for Girls (prior to the merger with the Ransom Everglades School), and even as the owner of her own secretarial firm for approximately five years. After downsizing her business, she accepted the opportunity to work for lawyer (and former client) Howard Long Jr., which continued until her mother became ill and required her full attention and care. Following her mother's passing in 2006, Williams became galvanized by the encroaching development of Village West and the Grove, primarily the "big boxes" that would replace the historic Bahamian homes and community style and character. "I don't require air conditioning," she said as a way to signal the particular kind of pollutants coming into the neighborhood. Trees were cut down and/or destroyed, taxes were elevated, and more willful neglect came from outside landlords intent on furthering more development. Williams first showed up to meetings of concerned locals about Village West and Grove preservation, including the Mariah Brown House and the historic Coconut Grove Cemetery on Charles Avenue. "I took a lot of notes; remember, I was a good secretary," and she proclaims that this was the beginning of her central role in community advocacy. A recording artist. She was instrumental in getting Charles Avenue designated as a historical corridor, and her participation in the Negro Women's Club helped to raise scholarship funds "so some little girl could go to school."[37]

Williams now serves on the board of the Coconut Grove Historical Cemetery Association, which is deeded the property of the Mariah Brown House. It is in the process of trying hard to turn the home into a museum, especially for elementary-school field trips to visit.[38] But for Williams, the committee cannot proceed without the participation of one of Mariah Brown's ancestors. Enter Robin Gore to this story. Gore, who was born and raised in Liberty City and Miami Gardens, lost her father, the Bahamian Willie McKeithan, a Miami Metro bus driver, when she was five years old: "He was very, very much a part of my life, and still is."[39] Gore was a veteran Dade County school bus driver until retiring in 2017. Retirement freed up the time and space for Gore to research her father's family and background, and together with other family members, she picked up a few threads that led to Mariah Brown. She started going to meetings about the house and was brought into the acquaintance of Sandra Riley, a retired theater and English public-school teacher who had formed her own theater company, "The Crystal Parrot."[40] Riley has long been fascinated with Brown and has written articles about her and also a historical drama.[41] In 2019 Riley and Gore exchanged their mutual research about Brown's past and confirmed Gore's hunch: this was her family, and she was Mariah Brown's great-great-granddaughter. The discovery shook the sixty-year-old Gore to her core. What was that like? "I still get chills whenever I talk about her. A great-great-grandmother that built the first house in the Grove in the Black section, and her being a washerwoman? I was so excited and I still get very excited." What are your dreams for the house? I asked. "That someday kids can go there on field trips and learn about how she made coconut candy and almond candy."[42]

Aeration, as evidenced in the Brown house, is a strong current in Black aesthetic practices and formal invention in Florida.[43] The creation of new forms that allow for air and breeze, out of necessity and choice, is enduring work that does everything to blast open racist assumptions of stagnation. Even in moments of devastating displacement, as is and was the case of Overtown, another of Miami's historic Black communities that has long been on the front lines of violent urban renewal and aggressive gentrification, Black Floridians have made Florida rooms that give and get air.[44] These places have been dynamically conceptualized, as with the work of artist

FIGURE 1.8 Purvis Young and his *Good Bread Alley* in 1971. Photo by John Pineda. "Purvis Young's Murals Line Two and a Half Blocks of NW 14th Street . . . tumult of images look down on a 'mean,' trash-littered slum." *Miami Herald*, September 24, 1971.

Purvis Young (1943–2010), who moved the idea of the Florida room out of the individual domain or idea of private property in its entirety. Young, born in Liberty City, gained public attention after painting a series of large panels that he installed on the ruins of Overtown's buildings beginning around 1971. Inspired by a photograph of Chicago's Organization of Black American Culture's "Wall of Respect" (1967–71), Young made his own suite of works that are often referred to as *Good Bread Alley* (figure 1.8).[45] Young attached paintings onto the neighborhood's wreckage wrought by Interstates 95 and 395, at that point in the midst of completion after decimating the Overtown neighborhood, its cultural institutions, and the movement patterns of its people. A kaleidoscope of steadfast embers, Young's paintings were stacked high and low and were a vital form of social and political record keeping. His insistent brushstrokes pressed hard against their makeshift frames, all put together with found materials by the artist himself. They are peopled with gestures that run into the other. Eyes are to be found everywhere in them. Hands too. They reach upward in ascension, petitioning, affirming, drowning. Vehicles, in the real time and future time of the highway's aftermath, are piled up and fixed in contained panels. People who remained and were forced out from the neighborhood are here in abstract portraiture; we feel them at work, together for some gathering, and all the surround sound is hemmed into and above withstanding walls.

Because of a lack of a well-lit studio space, Purvis Young would make a studio of the outdoors. He would often paint outside in clear view of all of Overtown. While this work was done partly out of necessity, his work suggests a keen attention and interest in watching people in the *doing*. Young's people are in motion, not made to pose in standstill or for the oft-abject secrecies of the private studio space. His inspirations are on their way somewhere or on their way back from doing something, and they make wide and reflective room of the interim. Young models the outside, a social outside, not the pristine one made possible for a privileged few. And by doing so, Young inspires a primary aesthetic and scholastic mode for *The Florida Room*. The performers and artists to be discussed throughout recall Young's prolific mode of working—and of doing so out in the open—with a feverish urgency to create in order to live, and to keep making work so that others may also continue living. Although it is impossible to cohere his immense body of work (Young's known works are said to number more than three thousand), artist and curator Juan Valadez notes certain themes that run through it: devotion to pregnant women, enslaved people, people on boats, warriors, and holy figures, in addition to bugs, horses, and cosmic matters of planets and stars.[46] Young's flurry of documentation pauses on natality, the divine, mortality, the interplanetary. And not only the newness with which Young put them to canvas but also the very construction of canvas and frame themselves, as Gean Moreno observes, "announces rather than commemorates."[47] *Good Bread Alley* suggests Young's large-scale and community service–driven register. It is also compressed into his more specific works. Encounter one of his works on a wall, and you'll find the Florida room's place within a place. You are asked to come in and stay for a while, however pleasant or painful. Young's stand-alone works suggest a portal-like quality of a Florida room that can be made anywhere and of any scale.[48]

Purvis Young's biography is often overdetermined by racist fantasies of the otherworldly naïve artist, or he is used as an exemplar, function, or cautionary tale of the Art World given the flurry of commodification and

FIGURE 1.9 Purvis Young, *Untitled* (PY1067), 1980–1999, paint on wood and paper, 48 × 52 in., Rubell Museum Miami. Photo by Alexandra Vazquez.

market making of his work.[49] There is a common tendency to speak for or on behalf of the artist and how he chose to sell his oeuvre. These narratives tend to supplant careful and detailed reading of his actual work. What is required when taking in one of his works among the multitude, not to make individuated possession of it, but to enter it as prescient theory? To imagine the formal choices he made in a small space? Take in Young's *Untitled* (figure 1.9), for example, and his dexterity with found-chosen materials that make an undulant blueprint that contains (and decidedly doesn't) a series of rooms. The bottom left of the work is left wide open, a drain or a window, or more so, an airshaft that oxygenates the whole. It isn't possible to know whether this piece just fell off (a phantom joint) or whether Young meant for it to keep the painting open, but it is nevertheless *open*. The wooden pieces used to break up the scenes are organ pedals, ways to play notes that ground what may be happening in the keys up top. A large dulcet portrait of a face rests atop a truck; balls with chains recall details from Young's slave paintings; there are people socializing around cars, some with outward danceable gestures; and there is a small building, perhaps a home, with a truck waiting just outside, idling below, or driving straight through it. This makeshift structure—this incredible theorization and implementation of a Florida room and its gathering of great difficulty and pleasure, and the announcement of all the people who have lived and continue to live there—offers a different kind of modernism that may have eluded Paul Rudolph. One has the great privilege to wonder how Young decided to put together these ten different scenes in this way and why he brought these particular pieces together, in this particular place, with joinery both tight and loose.

Young's work, you will note, inspires cumulative description. This is not accumulation for possession but rather meeting his unrelenting sense of adornment with your own. Engaging the work inspires inexorable add-ons: and then he does ____, and then he makes ____, look at the ____, why this figure ____, and why ____ there? All this is doubled and tripled, especially at the moment you think you are analytically done. The density of his compositions offers onlookers activities for the mind, games that keep memory active, abstractions that beg for more questions. Through *Good Bread Alley* and *Untitled*, Young's work lends a concretized sense of the baroque to the Florida room, one that has been conspicuously suggestive especially in the Miami Circle and Dustin's chamber. Young's baroque stuns for its complete assurance that there is cohesive activity among the seemingly disparate objects assembled here, and it is this assembly that puzzles and beautifully strains the eye and ear for a singular subject, whether person or theme. The very fact of them being brought to this wall, this canvas, this set of panels makes them more than "just things." Far from haphazard, the wet mortar carries the histories of people's survivalist arrangements of their surroundings. The People's Baroque.

III. The foregoing entries are all material, implemented establishments of the Florida room. There have been visitations to places that narrate Florida-for-outside, methods that hope to bring Florida inside, and other built actions that don't care to narrate at all but instead like to dig in and emanate the local for the local. These canonical and lesser-known examples (depending on your regional orientation) all hold the twinned elementals of objects and activities. Turning now to a few other architectures that are slightly more conceptual, but no less structural than these other examples, *The Florida Room* will reveal its plans for further realization. The awe that is part of Floridian study, and who and what you'll find in the expansive Florida room, is the ever-ready surprise that somewhere, someone has already laid it out for you. The state (whether location or living condition) tries hard to pronounce its newness. Yet village elders abound. Benny Latimore, a musician who will soon take over this room, once said, "When I was coming up, you listened to older people, and you learned from them. They were able to talk about their experiences, 'cause many things go 'round and 'round, but it's never the same when it goes around. *It's more like a spiral; it goes around and around, but moves up as it goes. And if you listen to older people, you can learn.*"[50]

As part of her enduring project to transform ethnographic discoveries into experimental writing, Zora Neale Hurston spent her lifetime recording folkloric matter from the state and condition of Florida. Some of this material was gathered during her childhood spent in Eatonville and through her insistent visitations of the peninsula when she didn't reside there full-time. Some of this material was collected during her tenure with the Federal Writers' Project for its anonymous, group-authored state guide, in addition to other unpublished offshoots such as *The Florida Negro*.[51] Hurston's research itineraries, particularly in the middle to late 1930s, have a suggestive unknown quality. It is impossible to know whether some of her writings were set down in the real time of their dating or were delayed inscriptions of experiences past. As one of the most established writers on the Florida unit but one of the lowest ranked and paid, Hurston enlisted her long cultivated and instructive persona of being lost or found when she most needed to be either. When her WPA supervisor, Carita Corse, would not hear from her for several weeks, her inquiries would eventually be answered with large envelopes stuffed full of findings sent from Hurston's Florida address. As one of her coworkers, Stetson Kennedy, recalled, "We did not care how, where, or when Zora had come by them—each and every one was priceless, and we hastened to sprinkle them through the *Florida Guide* manuscript for flavoring."[52] Hurston's modification of others' truant version of her is notably philanthropic. That she responded at all to these disciplining queries, and with a bounty of materials, one wonders how and what she released to them, to their editorial control, knowing that she would be relied upon for giving the living, breathing feeling to the staid guide with no formal credit to her name.

In 1938 Hurston sent in a set of paragraphs recorded from turpentine workers living and working in the most brutal of conditions in the northern reaches of Florida. Assembled under the heading "Negro Mythical Places," Hurston transcribes and transforms some locational reprieves imagined by the turpentiners in order to stay alive.[53] They are not heavens per se. More like somewhere elses. And they always include the possibility of going there. "Zar," for example, "is the farthest known point of the imagination. It is away on the other side of Far. Little is known about the doing of the people of Zar because only one or two have ever found their way back."[54] Four out of five of these locations picked up by Hurston were included in "Tour 7" of the FWP Florida guide. The guide leads the traveler past the Glen St. Mary Nurseries and onward to the roadside attractions of "cabins of Negro workers" adjacent to a turpentine mill and quickly notes, "Negros have their mythical cities and countries which are discussed and referred to in everyday conversation as if they actually existed."[55] Despite the violence of this contextual framing, and the likelihood that this work was included as the folkloric flavoring coveted by her white FWP colleagues, Hurston nevertheless tells them and us all: something in this state is out of your reach. She directs us to unfindable places that are nevertheless there.[56] Hurston herself is like a mythical place in the FWP guide, both there and not there. One mythical place Hurston set to page is called "Beluthahatchee," "a country where all unpleasant doings and sayings are forgotten. It is a land of forgiveness."[57] Kennedy, Hurston's younger coworker and the later author of *Palmetto Country* (1942) and the KKK exposé *Southern Exposure* (1946), was so taken by the tale of Beluthahatchee that he named his northern Florida estate and wildlife refuge after it. Kennedy's Beluthahatchee was a cherished retreat for Woody Guthrie and offered creative grounds for roughly eighty of his songs and for the completion of his autobiographical *Seeds of Man*. I include this fascinating detail not to show, as many are oft to do when discussing the folk strains of Americana, how all roads lead to Guthrie but to reveal how all roads really lead to Hurston.

Hurston is one interlocutor who helps us to ask not only why Florida, but *how* Florida? How can Florida be approached, articulated, adapted? Her 1939 "Proposed Recording Expedition into the Floridas"—the dream corruption of the grant-writing genre and dream proposition for the Florida room—is a realizable score.[58] In this short piece, Hurston turns the grand land mass into the plural Floridas and appeals for resources for future study in the state by dividing it into four areas. She introduces each with a stanza of a regional folk song, prefiguring music as the governing structure and ethos for each area. The state's trenchant Gulf Coast, northern cracker parts, panhandle environs, and southern internationalisms are filled with Hurston's aphoristic descriptions that double as open instructions: "The material is plentiful." "Look for the roots of traditional sermons and prayers." Of South Florida she writes that "this foreign area really should be designated as a collection of areas" and describes its Everglades as "a hot mixture of all the types of material of the area. Worth the whole trip alone." Details such as her plainly put "Bahamian and Cuban elements in abundance" are especially enticing signals for any who care about the combination of those elements. This combination is particularly rich for future sections of *The Florida Room*.

Hurston's notes for research are baroque in the amount of promissory details and mystifying for the over-full gaps she leaves between them. She makes ecological, cultural, demographic, and poetic arguments for Florida's vitality, especially as a site of recording. Recording Florida is not about compiling data (although her grant-speak makes it seem like it is) but a way to move through it in a different kind a way, a way to hear it—and the whole Atlantic world—of the back then and not yet, together. Toward the end of her research proposal, she writes:

> Recordings in Florida will be like backtracking a large part of the United States, Europe, and Africa for these elements have been attracted here and brought a gift to Florida culture each in its own way. The drums throb: Africa by way of Cuba; Africa by way of the British West Indies; Africa by way of Haiti and Martinique; Africa by way of Central and South America. Old Spain speaks through many interpreters. Old England speaks through black, white and intermediate lips. Florida, the inner melting pot of the great melting pot—America.[59]

For Hurston, recording allows for time travel to the preconquest of the Americas, to who was here before, and to those people and locations before they were brought to the new world. Her proposal offers a space to imagine how they converged to make a new world sound. Drums—and I hasten to add, all the hands that have played them over time—are the conduits for time travel. This is not a clumsy, romanticized back to Africa but a nascent criollo theory of how all these locations were made "by way of" it, all of which lead to the Floridas. Hurston asks that, while listening anew, we come up with inventive modes and vocabularies to describe our experiences of Florida—and any and all experiences out of our reach, even from remote locations. This invitation is heartedly extended in the final, fund-me send-off when Hurston writes: "There is still an opportunity to observe the wombs of folk culture still heavy with life."[60] Her "still" is a sound figure that reaches through the book and finds especial company in the fourth chapter.

Heaviness with life is a condition that is not easy to carry. It pushes the limits of your mind and body. It can make you tired. It is a downward force that requires a more concentrated pushing back. And yet in heaviness is also a condition of exuberance. Of learning how to live with the too much. Of an after-birth. In this Hurston example, it is heavy in that it makes any dissection or separation of Florida's, or any soundscape's, various parts impossible. It is this inventive mode that Hurston establishes and so many in *The Florida Room* insist upon: a heavy school that offers other anticipatory modes of response to histories of conquest, displacement, and subjugation. This school requires that we take it all, and take it all in, all at once. Heaviness is a quality and qualifier that works across the senses. "Heavy" has different applications in and as sight, smell, taste, and touch. It proposes a difficult unspeakable and even lends a way of joining the unspeakable and the pleasurable at once, as its contemporary usage in the Hispanophonic colloquial has much to teach us. Reggaeton to cumbia to rock en español all aspire to being bien heavy. As a conceptual unifier of synonyms that include the "lowdown" and (as I'll soon reveal) aural synonyms such as Miami Bass, heaviness offers other ways of reading, hearing, and seeing the surfaces of soundscapes, ways that attend to surfaces and the gulfs that live underneath them.

If, as Hurston argues, in Florida there is "*still* an opportunity to observe the wombs of folk culture still heavy with life," it is up to us to try and take up her instruction proposed long ago. What might be made possible, or even better, impossible, when taking up Hurston's Florida as a primary architecture for the larger Florida room?[61] By directing us to unfindable, unfundable places that are nevertheless there, Hurston's work bears the complicated histories that made something like Florida possible, and her work proposes and designates Black life and Black feminist critical practices at the core of the aesthetics made up there. By releasing these offerings to wherever future winds would have or carry them, Hurston's Florida offers an expandable environment for the study of inter-American arts and letters, partly because of the locations it opens up to do so, but mostly because Hurston and Florida, and Hurston's Florida, help us to rethink the measured terms of location itself in our reading and writing practices. How, in other words, does Hurston direct us to *hear* location as a way of entering it? This is an invitation to listen to Daphne Brooks's luminous work on Hurston and her "musical cartography."⁶² Location thus incorporates a multitude of sensations that exceeds those coordinates that too often bind our understandings of "setting" as we read. Hurston's playful sense of location does more than merely document or create stages where fiction can be put on. It offers holistic sensory experiences for how stories come to be told and lush environments for their future tellings, readings, and writings.

Hurston's proposal offers a prophetic blueprint for *The Florida Room*. The state and its state are material and imaginary, sharp-edged and flexible, regional and expansive.⁶³ Hurston asks that we let go of our sense-making enterprise: she makes Florida run differently. It is a beginning rather than an ending. It is an actual location that you can go to and an imagined dwelling that affirms, even in conditions of degradation, heaviness with life. And because of all of this, all at once, Florida can be found and felt across geographical and temporal limits. Hurston advances Florida as a state and a condition that teaches us to "learn to see the living," as Camille Dungy once put it.⁶⁴ I adopt Dungy's phrase to suggest that Hurston's Florida trains us to boldly move into a mode of working—both resurrective and innovative—when writing out how things come to sound and appear.⁶⁵ I suggest Hurston as the originary figure for this work, for this training, and for her making emergent a point in history where writing, alternative ethnographic practices, and the advent of new recording technologies activate Florida as a new way of thinking about place, and in particular, that place we have come to call America.⁶⁶

III. *Florida's Famous and Forgotten: History of Florida's Rock, Soul and Dance Music* is a two-volume encyclopedic history on the history of Florida's musicalia published in 2005 (figure 1.10). It was devotedly and painstakingly put together by Kurt Curtis, a former DJ and researcher who spent a lifetime collecting what some might have discarded as Florida's aesthetic detritus—and more than twenty years searching out many mainstream and obscure performers for their side of the recorded stories. Floridians will surely appreciate that Curtis was once a DJ for the Flanigan's Bar chain. Working with and in Florida, one is confronted by many tragic artifacts, of which this encyclopedia is a prime example. Henry Stone's foreword tells us that on the very day it was supposed to go into press in 2004, its author died suddenly of a heart attack at the age of fifty-three and never saw his labor in actual book form. It was, however, sent with him to the afterlife: "A single copy was rushed to print and laid to rest

FIGURE 1.10 Kurt Curtis, *Florida's Famous and Forgotten: History of Florida's Rock, Soul, and Dance Music: The First 30 Years: 1955–1985*, vol. 2, M to Z (Altamonte Springs, FL: Florida Media, 2005). Collection of the author.

with Kurt in his coffin."⁶⁷ There is a pathos felt in the font and design of its paperbacked covers, yellow and yellowed by a man who intuited this work was necessary for some, if unwanted by others. The cheap paper may betray the book's production values but somehow adds to the tenderness that one develops in relation to this precious collection. There are so many laudatory things to say about these extraordinary volumes. Curtis's putting together of music and musicians from the outermost coordinates of Florida, across the color lines, across genre, across any arcane sense of the high and low, is breathtaking. Far from the collector's joy in the act of display, his research, and the ways it is put together in this way, *in the same place*, convey an avid and deep love of the music rooted in his childhood St. Petersburg. The Florida room he builds for all the musicians involved, the ones he could find and, just as vitally, the many others he couldn't, conveys Curtis's analytic seriousness. His more historically accurate way of showing how musicians cross paths and how their records actually circulate does much to reaffirm that there is no definitive data to be found on consumptive or listening habits or for how influence happens.

Curtis does not, in accordance with much of popular music criticism, make categories of generic groups of rock, soul, and dance music but allows them to coexist and involve and influence the other. And placing them together, which Curtis does *without justification or fanfare*, shows how they all inform and lap into one another. The Allman Brothers Band is set between late-fifties crooner Steve Alaimo and Sammy Ambrose, one of Miami's great soul singers and limbo practitioners. Citizenship papers were not necessary. For Curtis, musicians need not be born in Florida to be Floridian, but must have had significant Florida periods or lightening-strike impact at a point in their recording careers. As one example, polymath Clarence Reid (aka Blowfly, originally from Cochran, Georgia) and his innovative R&B are framed by an entry on RCR's tickly disco rock (featuring Donna and Sandra Rhodes and Charles Chalmers, originally of Memphis) on one side and the Rhodes Brothers (originally from Columbus, Ohio) with their Motown-influenced vacation sound on the other. Curtis's indefatigable modeling of performers first, his attention to the work of performers before and beyond their categorical siphoning, is especially quantifiable when turning to the "Personal Interviews" appendix in the text. Curtis spoke with more than a hundred artists to build not one-sided but symbiotic entries that bridge their and his versions of the larger musical story. Imagine the myriad challenges involved in his tracking down, and after a lot of sweat equity, managing to get an artist to agree to talk to him. As he says in the preamble to the list of artists, "Tracking down many of the following for their stories, at times, was an incredible feat and a test of endurance and patience. It was no doubt a long, exhaustive and expensive 21-year journey. I would like to thank the 'music spirits' for being my guiding force through the 30-year 'time tunnel' of Florida Rock, Soul, & Dance Music."[68] Like Hurston's proposal, musical study is the premier vehicle for time travel.

    This mode of transport is not undertaken without the risk of the social, risk for which one may appeal to the "music spirits" for guidance. To leave the relative safety of the writer/introvert's private space to the unpredictability of the social world makes musical study a physically and intellectually challenging practice. Seeing musicians or hearing music in the company of others—once commonly experienced as going to shows or concerts—is one way of opening up to other times and places, say by the (hopefully) multiple generations to be found there. While many critics (including this one) have had to fight hoops-off hard to argue for the life and living in archival recordings, *The Florida Room* advocates some renewal around liveness, not the liveness fetish we've had to fight against that would demand certain bodies to be on permanent and accessible display, the kind of liveness that doesn't believe in our dead, but rather a peopling-your-life liveness. This finds analog in what might be possible when you find a way (after a lot of homework doing) to speak to the musicians themselves, and if being in their live presence is impossible, then play in the interviews they've left behind. What Curtis advocates is not an ethnographic method but a social one. It is a social method that refuses the devouring habits of fandom or connoisseurship, and instead asks: "What can I learn from this person?" *The Florida Room* is based on many hours and years of trying to build a social world, and part of doing so was to speak directly with many of the musicians and artists included herein. When artists don't appear with primary source material, it was not for lack of trying.

In the final pages of his encyclopedia, Curtis offers a set of strange and wonderful appendixes that we want to get behind and emulate in all our work. They include "Florida/Florida-Related Recording Artists Excluded Due to Insufficient Data" that honors, even if it can't, the impact of people's sound. As Curtis justifies, "Many years spent researching the following proved futile." Other categories include "In Loving Memory," which pays homage to Tampa Bay–area teen gathering places, with special subsections dedicated to "Pizza Parlors" and "Secret Make-Out Places," which we all know to be extremely important data points. He makes room for "Florida's top 40 greatest dance classics," that for many of us insta-cues the great Latinate opening of Company B's "Fascinated." There is an appendix for "Florida/Florida-Related Top 200 Greatest Classics," helmed by The Impacs and their 1966 melancholic hymn "Forever and a Day." There is wide room for debate: as Curtis notes of this list, "If you disagree, that's your privilege." What feels important to say about these appendixes are the marked ongoingness and outgoingness of this larger Florida history, the Rudoph-style leaving behind of designs for future dwellings. Through these supplements, Curtis leaves us his own proposal for recording expeditions into the Floridas.

The Florida Room understands itself in heaven and earth conversation with Curtis's love for the dizzying over-fullness of Florida's Famous and Forgotten. Of particular interest is continuing his work that uses the peninsula's ecological diversity to index its music. For example, Curtis includes a collection of musicians and songs under categories such as "Florida Islands and Keys," "Florida Gulf Coast," "Florida Everglades," "Florida Waters," and "Florida Hurricanes." Curtis is not the first figure to link sound and surround, but he helps to give evidence-based backup to a listener of Florida, and for those very specific played and heard relations she hears between swamp and bass line, purple orange red sunrise and swelling chorus, brackish sensation and studio production. *The Florida Room* makes recourse, in peripatetic glimmers, to many of these environments. What are the challenges to how we come to hear certain places as having an identifiable sound and how we might write about it? We evoke the Miami sound, the Baltimore sound, the DC sound, the Atlanta sound with an anthemic pride for the local. But doing so can effect a taxidermying of its strange differences, of encasing those differences into a signifier that notates them in expensive ironic packaging. The categories become untouchable. The distancing is spiritual as much as it is material, for it is from the distances that our natal city sounds are being released from independent labels in Germany, Japan, and Great Britain. How might this elusive yet cohesive sound be written about a little differently, especially in the case of Florida and *The Florida Room*? To offer it temporary shelter after a long life on the commodified road?

If Florida study requires a willing adjustment to the unrecognizable and impermanent, I argue here and everywhere that any Florida sound is an elusive swamp of possibility that helps you turn away from the clean, detectable lines of the surveyor and collector. It invites a willingness to wade into the mangrove muck that anchors it and those difficult locations that give it life. "Florida," it must be said (again), has become contemporary shorthand for ecological disaster. It is a state of emergency. Yet this forewarning—rooted in global warming and centuries of land misuse and abuse—has the perhaps unintended effect of sensing only death and destruction. Florida's varied ecologies are almost always spoken about as tragedies and its coastal locations as fait accompli. *The Florida Room* does not want to cede all its room to talk of environmental destruction. To do so would be to relinquish all those performances that remain critically abandoned. To take in its wilderness means to refuse any nihilistic surrender to the disaster that it is being primed to be. I remain with the mangroves even when they are abused and littered. I stand with the Everglades as I would that most beloved family member who also happens to be sick. Part of what is astonishing about the natural world, especially the tropical or subtropical, is how hard it fights to be itself. And so together with our extant material structures and some supplementary conceptual ones, *The Florida Room* opens up, finally, to a song that encapsulates all of the above. The reliquary, the antiquity, aerated structures, speculative grants, outdoors practice, future plans, and, inside all of this, its varied landscapes are made and felt in the following greatest hit.

IV. To get more specific on how a Florida room can be built and heard and felt in song, I'll wade in, slowly, to Benny Latimore's "Let's Straighten It Out," first recorded in Miami for Glades Records in 1974. Latimore was born in Charleston, Tennessee, in 1939 and first came to Miami in 1961 while on tour as a backup singer for Joe Henderson. While there, Latimore entered a talent contest at the venerated venue Clyde Killens's Knight Beat at the Sir John Hotel in Overtown.[69] Killens was so impressed with Latimore that he offered him a steady gig playing the organ for the venue. Although interpersonal disagreements with the house band kept Latimore out of it, Killens offered him the opportunity to play while the house band was on break. Latimore reports that Killens told him, "You try this. If you can hold the people so I don't have to play the jukebox then you've got the job."[70] And so Latimore intermissioned with his organ between the official house bands. He lived just above the club in an efficiency with his rent included in the $110 weekly salary. His solo career thus began by making lush the interim, the inbetween, of the main acts. His performances eventually captured the attention of South Florida producer Steve Alaimo, who went on to produce his early recordings in Miami and Muscle Shoals, Alabama. These records enjoyed moderate success, but it wasn't until "Let's Straighten It Out" that Latimore had the number-one gold single on the *Billboard* Black music charts and eventually reached number 31 on *Billboard*'s Hot 100.[71] There are many different variations of the song out there, and although originally recorded in Miami, other versions were pressed and sent to France and other international markets. They all work for what I am talking about, but for the fun of following along (and hopefully you will), I'm listening here to the version put out on the original LP *More More More* (figure 1.11). For some, this song was long ago on repeat—for others, this will be their first time. Regardless, I invite the ear to tilt toward its experimentalism hiding in plain view. <u>Play it</u>.[72]

Listen to all the vegetation in this song! It straightens out nothing. The first thing we hear is a drumroll downward. It takes the listener by the hand to the subterranean, to take ginger steps into the muck, into land that gives. Entering soon after is the bass played by Ron Bogdon and Latimore on organ. There is verdant, thick surround. Some heavy kind of alterity is required. The action is not one of grasping or gasping, but a laying

FIGURE 1.11 Benny Latimore's "Let's Straighten It Out"—*More More More* (Glades Records, ST-6503, ca. 1974, vinyl). Collection of the author.

into it. Everything takes deliberate time. What one hears is not a deferral but an organization. The introduction runs almost two minutes long, long to the point where you really feel like you're entering something. A Florida room. Its dimensions give us enough time to get as comfortable as possible, for what lies ahead is some difficult conversation. There is something assured that tells us that what we'll find ahead is hard-won relief, not confrontation. The beginning of this song finds companionship in so much Floridian musicalia. These extended, place-setting intros carry transitions between the elements: dry to moist, clear to murky, wetland to pineland. You can hear the convention in guitar preparations by Daytona Beach adoptees Duane and Gregg Allman, in KC and the Sunshine Band's Florida highlife invocatory tumbles, as danceable clearing spaces in songs by Trinere and Pretty Tony, and in the slow-burn entries of boleros by Zoraida Marerro. In Latimore's composition the introduction is not necessarily a seduction—it does not make us wait for some ultimate reward of predictable (inexpert) liaison. Latimore has been called a "love philosopher," and we feel it in subtle, durational practice here.[73] The introduction is something that tells you that you have company; someone is here. Only after the listener feels assured of this carefully crafted companionship does Latimore sing: "Sit yourself down girl and talk to me, tell me what's on your mind."

There are so many ways to feel the Florida room–like qualities in this song. It offers the structure and the lyrics for so many possible visitations. There is its sound, which I've begun to suggest in the above, and there is the matter of the song's personnel.[74] In the Floridian music scene, especially in Miami, there is a dynastic quality to its musicians. Music stays in the family and, rather than being stultified by insularity, gives artists multiple opportunities to gather with different players (especially across its R&B and dance music genres). As happens also in Cuban music, there is something robust about these slightly out of reach, southern scenes of music that bands together those who chose to stay and make music rather than leaving for other cultural capitals such as New York or Los Angeles. The song's bassist, Ron Bogdon, was a Philly native and sailing buff who brought a fascinating itinerary to this scene of recording. Bogdon got his start by playing saxophone with a Philadelphia group called the Mummers, with whom he toured Cuba when he was eleven years old. He came to Miami in the 1970s to play with Sam & Dave and became one of the most sought-after session musicians in the city, playing or recording with some of the city's most important artists.[75] Bogdon passed away from colon cancer in 2015. In the aftermath of his departure, Mike Reinig, one of his recent bandmates, gave him this beautiful tribute: "There were times I'd rehearse with him where you wouldn't hear him play a note—the note just appeared."[76]

When you listen to Bogdon's work on "Let's Straighten It Out," there is this surprise-given quality. His notes are made instantly available for play, even if elusive about their provenance. The drums are played by Robert Ferguson, pioneer Miami percussionist and part of the foundational group Frank Williams and the Rocketeers, who were a crucial part of what made the Sir John Hotel's Knight Beat an institution. Forrest City, Arkansas–born guitarist Willie Hale, widely known by his nickname "Little Beaver," does not appear on the track though he claimed to have written its bass line. This claim is refuted by Latimore, but he was a crucial player on the rest of album. Little Beaver first came to guitar after seeing Blind Roosevelt play in a juke joint when he was six years old. A self-taught musician, Hale moved to Homestead, Florida, in 1964 to play with Big Maybelle, eventually became part of the Rocketeers, and has played guitar or composed songs for every important musician to emerge from the area.[77] Over his four-plus-decades' music career, Hale's work has been covered by or used as source material by such artists as Jay-Z, Monterrey Mexico rockers Banda Macho, and Spanish rappers Los Chikos del Maíz. In sum: Latimore's company on *More More More* era bien heavy. And if you think I'm making up any of the environmental sound attachment here, consider that Bogdon, Ferguson, and Hale also had their own group called Thunder, Lightning and Rain before recording with Latimore. Their hit "Super Funky," recorded for Frank Williams's Saadia label, opens with a long introduction featuring the repeated, hallucinatory chorus "Hey, can you feel it?"[78]

In an interview, Latimore reflected on his decades-long practice:

> When we did songs, it [was] like a story because you've got a beginning, a middle and an end—*well, a colon, not really an end*. It's the end of that particular segment, then there's another chapter here, another chapter there. But [it's] something that is memorable, something that goes on in your head, a melody that flows and goes on into the future. Now we got what I call microwave music—"Oh, it's great! It's hot! It gets right to the point! Right to the point!" *And there's no in-between*. It's either here or there. . . . We're living in a pushbutton, microwave world. But something that makes you think or causes you to think—that's something that we can live on.[79]

Latimore gives us a guide to listen to gems such as "Let's Straighten It Out." He also gives us a guide for making a song. If, for this scholar, "song" means "book," Latimore makes it possible for me to render *The Florida Room* as a way to tell a story with a lot of in-between. Latimore reminds us that songs are not containable structures but wave-like repetitions for public health. Here is colon's etymology in ancient Greek: "limb, member or clause of sentence, portion of strophe," and in rhetoric, "a member or section of a sentence or rhythmical period."[80] This punctuation mark is more than a metaphor; it is a way to mark out the in-between as a space to live, work, write. A playing space left open for lots of additions, contestations. It hopes to leave more "memory that flows and goes on into the future." Latimore's call for in-betweens gives all much to live on. Head to a live version of "Let's Straighten It Out," where, to his signature introduction, Latimore adds calls of "yeah yeah, yeah," of "yeah," over and over, singing the ultimate yes-and in a bright red suit.[81]

Latimore's compositional method refuses the final word, and "Let's Straighten It Out" is an invitation to move into another segment. It asks for augmentation, company, space for a lyric to become something else. To write a song for another to live on is conversational rather than reactive. It allows for important temporal disordering of who calls and who responds,

FIGURE 1.12 Cover of Gwen McCrae's *Let's Straighten It Out* (T.K. Records, TKR 82518, ca. 1978, vinyl). Collection of the author.

of who says or does something first and who follows. The ethos and aesthetic of the in-between makes it difficult to indicate the flows of influence with strict directionals. Sometimes these conversations happen outright. Let's tune into another limb, a partnering segment on another record that is Gwen McCrae's 1978 version of "Let's Straighten It Out," where she transforms the idea of the cover song into a reveal song (see figure 1.12). Nor does McCrae follow the conventions of the "answer song," the woman responsive to some man's call, but in any case, Latimore did not write it in a way that demanded a definitive answer.

McCrae's is another telling using the structure penned by Latimore. In her version the song is slightly brought up a key, and the effect is a subtle lift off of the ground. More space, more circulation. Her version used the same tracks used by Latimore, so the session was McCrae, the recorded presence of the original players, and the producer, Clarence Reid. As her daughter Leah Jackson informed me, "It was just her alone in a booth with a microphone and a producer."[82] Added to her version are some marshy opening strings and swells arranged by Mike Lewis. They add different currents to Latimore's original, a kind of velvet philharmonic setting for McCrae's entrance. The strings tell us to get ready in another way, and instrumentally at least, the narrative has already changed. When McCrae comes in with "Sit yourself down and *listen* to me," she gently takes the song by the hand. Right from her entrance, she does match Latimore's original vocal line but makes it something all her own. With her incisive start, McCrae offers surprise as the fundamental element in a cover and suggests a whole other way to approach the situation. McCrae's voice is extremely beautiful, resonant, with the slightest scrape along its round edges. Her faculty with using her voice to reveal something that was in the song all along is carried throughout her oeuvre—*and vice versa*, as her voice institutes in song things for others to live on. This is absolutely palpable in her groundbreaking 1972 version of "You Were Always on My Mind." McCrae's was the first release of that song that would later become a signature for others from Elvis to Willie Nelson. In "Let's Straighten It Out" McCrae has clearly studied and listened carefully to and with Latimore: when she begins her version, it puts the song and us in a whole different place. Find it here and go with her.[83] McCrae shows that she knew the song in advance of its writing. She even said as much with a tender, knowing laugh of delight after I suggested that her version was better than the original.

McCrae is one of the most powerful voices to emerge from Florida and is perhaps best known for her gorgeous 1975 single "Rockin' Chair," written by Clarence Reid and Willie Clarke. McCrae was born in Pensacola in 1943 to Minnie Lee Mosley Hawkins and George Washington Mosely.[84] Her mother was born in Thomasville in Southwest Georgia and was a touring jazz pianist. While Hawkins was on tour, she met her future husband, Mosely, while he was working as a porter on the railroad.[85] The couple settled in Pensacola in a wooden shotgun house on Yonge Street, and Mosley left a life of the road to sing and accompany gospel choirs in local churches, especially the House of Chapel Church. Young Gwen Mosley would watch her mother as she would play, first from a pew and eventually from inside the choir. This early conservatory provided by her mom was accompanied by other teachers and their recordings that caught her young ear at the time, including Sam Cooke, the Caravans, and especially Shirley Cesar.[86] Young Gwen would meet her eventual husband, George McCrae (who was originally from West Palm Beach), after he joined the US Navy and was stationed in Pensacola. They would become a major wife-and-husband musical duo and performed in clubs all over Florida, especially West Palm Beach, Pompano Beach, and Miami in the middle to late 1960s.[87] The couple was eventually introduced to Henry Stone (the recording impresario behind several of Miami's independent record labels) by Betty Wright (whom we will hear a lot from in chapter 4) in 1969.[88] What is important to reiterate here from the studios above and from Wright's personal introduction: these are just a few details from the ample connectivity between Floridian musicians, of tight collaboration between a close company. McCrae, Betty Wright, Latimore, Timmy Thomas, and Little Beaver would become an ensemble that played, accompanied, wrote, lived, and ate together often.[89] McCrae's prolific career would eventually move out from Miami-based labels to Atlantic Records, where she would release her extraordinary albums *Gwen McCrae* (1981) and *On My Way* (1982). Like many Black women vocalists from the United States, she remains an especially beloved performer in Europe, with its sustained fixation with the past and present of dance music. In the United Kingdom, for example, she is known as the "Queen of the Rare Groove."

In the summer of 2020, I asked Gwen McCrae to name her favorite collaborator of all time, and without hesitation she responded: "Latimore. *Latimore.*" Latimore twice. The first to set the record and the second to revel in the phenomenon. And just after this, McCrae also mentioned that she had a picture of Betty Wright (whom she called Sister, for their musical-spiritual connection was very close) right in her bedroom. This attachment to collaborators over the span of five decades gives us a different model of working from those who make the smash hit and then run. This long durée of conversation made between Latimore and McCrae, the forms it took and takes in and outside of song, refuses to stay put in the enclosed place fables of the recording studio. It thwarts the impulse for the glossy authoritative documentary. Instead, hearing Latimore and McCrae's different versions of a singular song, and all the versions between then and now in their contemporary repertoires, opens up what Deborah Vargas calls "a musical imaginary of what could be" because we know there will be more.[90] Or in Latimore's axiom, more, more, more. Theirs is a future-oriented practice rooted in a collaborative past. Their growing up together nurtures a "what could be" that is regularly made, picked up, and rearticulated across South Florida's musics across the genres and generations. The long view of the telling happens often in the song, not always in the narrative apparatuses constructed around a song.

V. As much as *The Florida Room* provides ample room for connection between artists who may have never technically shared the same space, there are nevertheless many others, like McCrae and Latimore, who were in direct conversation. To bring in one person involves the invitation of many others. I look back to who is already here in this chapter and what they make possible. They have given a set of historic structures with ingrained signs of migration. There is the assumption of aeration and heaviness together and not at all paradoxically. There are the adaptive and baroque arts of survival. Hurston's proposal, Curtis's assembly, and Latimore and McCrae's conversations are amplifications of how the musically conceptual can also be structural. I insist on all of this. I have not held back noise. Nor can I hold back the approaching noise that wants to be here too. To tend the ground of the finale performance I discuss below, there is a lot more to build out, and I, and everyone involved here, ask for your bearings. It involves walking a long stretch of shore with more company.

Felix Sama, one of South Florida's most influential DJs and musical deltas, was born in 1965 in Havana's Santos Suárez neighborhood, the birthplace of some of Cuba's musical greats such as Frank Emilio Flynn and Celia Cruz. Such does his mix artistry inform all his practices that during one phone interview, he subtly patched in his mother, Caridad Sama, to the call, mid-sentence and without my realizing, so that she could say more than he could. In Havana his mother was a secretary at the Department of Public Works, and his father, Marcos Sama, repaired and cleaned firearms. When I asked her if she had any musical background, Ms. Sama said that her mother was always, always dancing and that this was foundational in fostering her love of music. Of her musical attachments while in Cuba, Ms. Sama said she was especially fond of Chilean singer Lucho Gatica, affectionately known as the "King of the Bolero." I want to hold on to this bolero surround during Felix's infancy.[91] The family (immediate and extended) left Cuba in 1967 and went straight to Chicago, where Sama's uncle Tony already lived. Together they pursued the family dream of opening a TV repair store called the Sama Brothers, which they opened on the Southside. While there, Felix recalled listening to eight-track tapes of Barry White and Teddy Pendergrass in their family's Impala, music that had been introduced to them by his uncles and cousins and by the soundwaves of the Chicanas/os and African Americans who lived in the neighborhood.[92]

From these early backseat experiences in the Impala, and with his ear tilted to radio, Sama recalled that "I always attached myself to music." Note how Sama goes *to* music, and meets it there, rather than making it come to him. Sama's Chicago childhood was a happy one, and "because we were mixed, people wouldn't bother us much." Sama, who firmly recognizes his family's African, Chinese, and Spanish roots, was quick to note that he did not experience racism until he moved to Miami. The family had grown tired of Chicago's cold and its cost of living, and they wanted to join Sama's paternal grandmother already in Miami, so they left for south in 1976. They first lived in one of the houses that used to line the Okeechobee Canal in Miami Springs, but the cat-sized rats, so large they "would squiggle their way out of the traps," sent them in quick search for elsewhere. They moved to North Miami, right across the street from North Miami Senior High School, and this is where Sama first experienced racist violence. Young Sama had been walking down the street when a big truck carrying a Confederate flag tried to run him down, screaming vicious epithets his way. He ran for his life even as he was unable to comprehend that they were *actually* trying to run him over. This dual mode of staying alive while also expressing incredulity is something that can be heard across Sama's later work. At the new house in North Miami did you have a Florida room? I asked. Sama replied immediately. "Yes. It was kind of like the hangout spot where we would watch TV." Theirs was not a given form, however. It was once a carport that Felix, his brothers, and their father turned into a Florida room. They used a mix of construction elements (wood, cement blocks, laminate flooring) and installed a set of interior glass doors to separate it out from the rest of the house. The room was particularly prized because "if you were the first one there, it was like you owned it for the day." They turned their carport into a Florida room—a zoning unthinkable—in full view of North Miami.

Sama has two older brothers, José and Eduardo, and in the great sibling tradition of the musical hand-me-down would train his ear. They turned Sama on to Earth, Wind & Fire and the repertoire of *Saturday Night Fever*. These attachments were foundational and strong. The first single Sama recalls buying was Bed-Stuy's own Stephanie Mills's "I Never Knew Love Like This Before," with its sweet synth opening and vocal that helps us all to process a new sensation as the singer documents her own. Hold on also to this single as one of the adolescent building blocks for Sama's later work. The subsequent record he purchased for home was the Sugarhill Gang (from Englewood, New Jersey) and their "Rappers Delight," which helped Sama become a strong contender in playful competitions with friends involving who could memorize all the words. This single and many others were bought at Spec's Music on 163rd Street, where Sama would spend countless hours before being chased out at closing time. This alternative library was being constantly researched while Sama was being exposed to DJing at house parties. There he would observe closely how DJs would put their collections toward *making* the rooms. For this dream just out of reach, Sama worked as a stock clerk at Jafee's Printing Company and as a grocery bagger at Pantry Pride to save money to buy DJ equipment and records. He started with a mixer, a turntable, and a tape deck, all "pieced together Sanford and Son style." While describing the early dexterity required to edit between tape deck and turntable, Sama gave a theory of his developing aesthetic: working with what he had, however incomplete or broken.

Sama started DJing house parties as a student at North Miami High School. His sets included Evelyn "Champagne" King, Shalimar, and Howard Johnson, and this early career development was a magical time. Sama eventually started doing mobile DJ gigs for weddings and bar mitzvahs, where he learned about all kinds of music and how to tailor music to the different scenes, which meant learning a lot about Frank Sinatra and Motown. Such gigs gave him his "first footing with massive crowds," which later brought Sama, as an underage seventeen-year-old, to a standing gig at the Playboy Club near the Miami airport. Just by reading all these sentences, you may feel some effects of all this nightlife compressed in a short span of time. But there is more, more, more. *Then* Sama worked the cruiseship circuit to the Bahamas and other ship triangulations to Ocho Rios, Jamaica, making people move in his way as they crossed water. Let's review this already prolific career by the time Sama was barely twenty-one: from Santos Suárez to Chicago to the Okeechobee Canal, to North Miami house parties to everywhere Miami weddings and bar mitzvahs, to a "gentlemen's club" and aboard huge ships. All of this and there and them became chosen additions of migrations into his DJ sound.

Sama would come to define one of the most innovative eras of Miami radio after submitting a mix tape to Hot 105 FM. Station managers were so impressed that he was brought into a guest spot, which turned into permanent top billing from 1985 to 1990. The burgeoning celebrity mobile DJ circuit brought Sama out of the studio to gigging some of the city's hottest nightclubs and other vital musical laboratories, including the Hot Wheels Roller Rink (see figure 1.13). A change in programming brought Sama to Power 96 FM, then the broadcast place of intrepid, badass live mixes from 1990 to 2002 (see figure 1.14). To some listeners these sets emerged from the radio waves as if by magic, and because they happened in the live, a listener had to bring all faculties when trying to feel their construction in real time. These live sets could be heard again only if you have been armed with a tape recorder at the right place and right time. For Sama, these mixes were events of intense study and rehearsal. It was mixing, blending, and transitioning that required twenty-four-hour-type rehearsal.[93] Of all this preparation, Sama recalls, "I was enfermo." Home rehearsal was about learning transitions, how things did and didn't fit, or how he could

FIGURES 1.13 AND 1.14 Felix Sama, DJ radio personality. *Top:* Sama as headline DJ "mixing the jams!" on a promotional flyer for Hot Wheels Roller Rink, ca. 1988. *Bottom:* Sama mixing live at Power 96 FM, circa 1997. Photos courtesy of Felix Sama.

take things and build them to fit. Sama's gift for the transition and making patterns through editing made him the go-to person to for "mega mixes" (or mega mixxxes), a practice of compressing many things into a singular track. Sama has made expert mega mixes of genres (say songs across house, Freestyle, hip-hop, Latin) or has taken other people's repertoires, often per their request (e.g., Trinere, Luke, Poison Clan) and blended them into one danceable track. The mega mix is as much a structure that can hold an unimaginable many as it is a form that can transform an individual artist into the multitudes.

It is to one of Sama's mega mixes that I turn to, to turn up, back and forward, the past into the future and back again. It is the greatest possible tie-together and send-forth of all these proposals for the Florida room: Felix Sama's 1996 "Mega Mix" of DJ Uncle Al on the album *Liberty City* (see figure 1.15).[94] For many Miamians, Uncle Al involves a sacred gesture when invoked. Born in Liberty City in 1969, Albert Leroy Moss was one of the great innovative artisans of Miami music and, especially, its Bass, a rumbling lifeline for many (hear chapter 4). Moss was a beloved, bold, and beautiful activist with a robust and interlocking set of community practices. He made pirate radio-show broadcasts, gathered the young and the old for Sunday sundown gatherings on 71st Street and 15th Avenue in the mid-1990s, and started initiatives such as the annual "Peace in da Hood" celebrations, which gave people a safe place to go and dance.[95] In the words of his son Albert Leroy Jr., his father's events were all "about positivity and about bringing people together."[96] DJ Uncle Al was tragically murdered on September 10, 2001, and the immediacy of the loss—physical and spiritual—is still palpable. Miami lost one of its most luminous musical freedom fighters, and it is hard not to weep while dancing and listening to his records. But Uncle Al's music, even prior to his death, always made tears of joy and pain. I do not want Moss's death to signpost an end, for it is an active and urgent project by many—from his family to his fans—to keep him and his legacy alive and present. And so, with this longer initiative, I turn to the "Mega Mix" on his *Liberty City* and to how Felix Sama textures the dizzying, maximalist work of Moss and how he records their direct conversation. By going *there* and remaining in that hinge between primary and secondary mega-mix material, Sama models how we may tenderly pick up the fragments we are given and left to build the most coveted of hangout spots.

Uncle Al chose to incorporate Sama's "Mega Mix" on his original album rather than relegating it to a separate, follow-up release. Moss agreed to handing over his a capellas—or vocals without beats—to Sama, who was

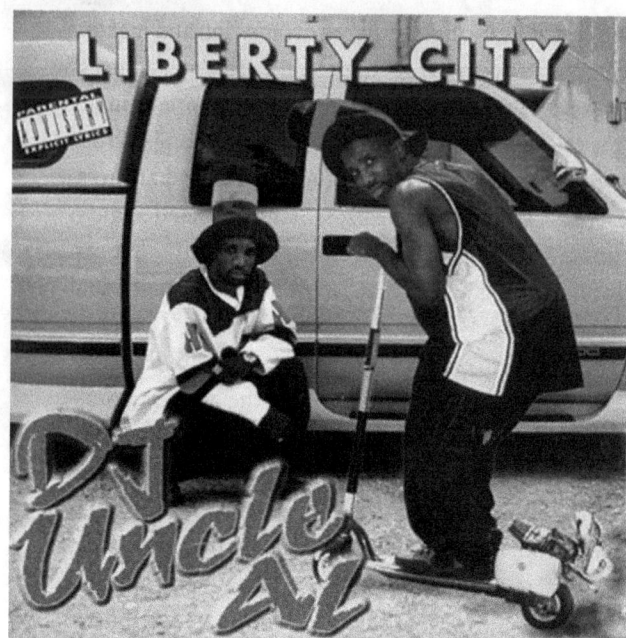

FIGURE 1.15 Cover of DJ Uncle Al's *Liberty City* (On Top Records, OT-9034, ca. 1996, compact disc). Collection of the author.

an artist he had long admired. As Sama tells it, "I really wanted to do something special," and when he said this, there was a Stephanie Mills sweetness in his tone. Moss's pirate-radio aesthetic, which very much extends from island living and wrecking practices, gave his vocals certain characteristics. Because his broadcasts—whether from a hijacked signal or from a live party—were always about bringing people together, they were very much in the spirit and timbre of open calls. Calls that could be heard outside and for several blocks away at least. Moss's calls were for all who heard him to participate in some way in a public seen and unseen, actual and felt. Take in all of DJ Uncle Al's different possible entry and exit points, their potential for adaptation, the myriad planar options, and most of all, how he urges all to stay with it: "Mix it up," "To the floor to the floor ya'll," "Keep dancing," "Shake it on," "Say what?," "Slip and slide," "To the ground." Moss repeats each phrase in quick succession, and the bass that grounds them gives plenty, if fast, opportunity to alter with the repetitions. Moss would often mark Miami history outright with his recurring yelling of "goombay," marking for real and for good the city's Bahamian foundations and ongoing parties. He would tuck in other funny phrases for breaking bread and gift giving too: "Chomp that chicken" and "Santa Claus coming."

Sama took all these vocals, samples of Moss's own signature songs, and created his own drum loops and patterns to make transitions, in-betweens, that did everything to honor all the who and where and when together.[97] It is a direct conversation between two DJs and the histories they carry. They were called by Moss and put together by Sama in a new way, and his mega mix is a bountiful addition and extension to many more. In the "Mega Mix" Sama and Moss make innumerable parties of past and present. And for now, and for here, there is no other way I can put it: it is *furious and joyful*. Sama's unrelenting mobile sound that takes up fragments borrowed from Uncle Al, Havana, Chicago's Southside, New York, and the various Miamis moves you around so many places in quick succession. And yet it happens in one structure, in one song, in one mega mix. It is beyond what could be dreamed possible about where you can be, all at once, in the company of everyone. *The Florida Room* aspires to resound all the fury and joy of this conversation, of those others who live and lived in the foregoing structures, and for all those to follow.

Chapter Two

MIAMI FROM THE SPOILS

There is an island off the Dinner Key Marina in Miami's historic Coconut Grove, an area that won early renown as the "most unproductive and isolated in the United States."[1] Dinner Key was originally an island, but the ocean floor was dredged to make its attachment to the mainland. The leftover dregs—all that matter from the seafloor—were thrust into landmasses around the marina. These "spoil islands" are but a few of the anonymous but locally nicknamed remains of early twentieth-century redesigns of the Earth. Usually made from dredged channels, spoil islands can be found all up and down the East Coast of the United States, especially around desirable ports of entry and exit. For architectural scholar Charlie Hailey, the spoils are "places for seeing past and future, even if their marginality makes for an unlikely location to perceive mainland histories."[2] To perceive Miami's past and future from this dislodged earth is an unlikely embarkment, but as the following pages reveal, a necessary one to bring together the rooted, displaced, and all combinations of sediment brought there. Spoils are generally found just offshore, and their risk to the city's narrative limits allows for bands of water to add rich delay in perception. As manufactured places that thrive despite being founded by throwaway parts, spoils offer just a bit of estranged distance from familiar stories about place. Hailey says that spoils "put you in places you normally wouldn't—and probably shouldn't be. Their insular status presents burden and opportunity and mixes ambiguity with ambition . . . these islands constituted topographic blind spots, forming a part of the visual field but frequently overlooked in their double marginality as island and waste. . . . They are in the public eye, but they also linger unseen."[3]

In 2004 there was a small flurry of reportage from a spoil island by Dinner Key that gave account of a Cuban man named José Montaner, who, along with his dog, Papo, made a home for himself there. He built a house out of driftwood and with a donated generator powered up its sole lightbulb and TV set. Because spoils tend to filter much of the discard from the mainland, Montaner would begin and end his days cleaning up: "The island was empty and dirty when I found it. It needs me and I need it." Beyond keeping it tidy, Montaner had a strong urge to adorn the spoil, and he decorated it with the flotsam that filtered into the mangroves. His cultivations abounded. He was able to coax a pile of coconuts to sprout. Other parts of his landscape design included a garden of flip-flops, chancletas, mismatched rights and lefts that bore traces of seaside leisure and seacenter drownings. He adorned trees with CDs and stuffed animals, raised chickens, and built an accessible dock so that students from the Shake-A-Leg sailing school for people with disabilities, just offshore, could come visit.[4] Montaner was born in the coastal city of Caibarién, Cuba, was eventually jailed for stealing milk, and then in 1968 sailed to Key West, then onto Miami, and onward still to New York. While in New York, Montaner worked as a janitor and salt spreader for the city before all that freeze made him flee back down south to Miami. "I couldn't stand the inhuman frozen conditions," he said.[5] He injured himself soon after return, was considered unemployable, became homeless, and lived in abandoned buildings before making a home on the spoil island. It made him better. He brewed Cuban coffee every sunrise on a propane burner. He would take roots from the spoil's mangrove takeover and ferment them into a nightly tonic to ease his chronic back pain and insomnia. As steward of these dregs, Montaner insisted that "I belong here in the water and I'm not going anywhere."[6]

Montaner, like so many of Miami's covert community advocates and archivists, urges us to resist the nihilistic, catchall labels for eccentric phenomena such as "Because Florida" and "Because Miami." By taking his spoil island practice seriously—a practice that tends to sites of discard and destruction with rehabilitative care and creative renewal—we can honor and listen to all the washed-up stories he gingerly picks up in objects thrown away, stolen, given, lost. And we learn how we may pick up stories too. Montaner's activity isn't collection and its calcification; it is not the box cake mix of irony, eros, and disregard burdened upon tropical souvenirs. It instead reveals established sustainable practices developed by many with living relationships to the shore and to the marsh, and a special fluency with how to take in disparate objects all at once. This dexterity finds the beauty and utility of an ever-unknown given that is nonetheless constant. One can expect the tides but not what they bring. Montaner's story also thwarts the meth-y, meme-ish peaks and crashes that foreclose analytic space and time for the careful, aesthetic decisions made by human beings. In Miami these decisions are everywhere, in the anonymous altar at the foot of a ceiba tree, in the tear of a subwoofer made to give sound a strange air. Montaner, in a place of past and future, salvages the throwaway, turns it into ornament, makes medicine of it. He made this made-up island at the limens of the real and not a resource for others to visit. And through all of this, Montaner inspires a different kind of writing about place, one that doesn't merely account for shifting ground but does away with familiar ideas about ground altogether. Such an invitation tends an open place for anything or anyone's imprint, of sharing new ways to document migration patterns on displaced sand and soil, of circulating a list of survival skills, of making aesthetics a part of public health. From the spoil, Montaner gets us to move in a parallel way to the given and, perhaps most crucially, shows how making home doesn't mean taking possession. His model from the spoil is a design for the record, as object and verb and account.

Others saw in Montaner a perfect mix of all that is undesirable to Miami's established and distressing yearn to be modern at any cost. As a Black, homeless immigrant who dared to make clean—and, more upsetting to his critics, make pretty—something that he didn't own outright, Montaner raised the suspicions of developers and their defenders, who have long had an alarming foothold in the Grove area. *New York Times* reporter Abby Goodnough quoted Stuart Sorg, of the Miami Waterfront Advisory Board, who saw Montaner as an eyesore. Sorg asserted that "we've got to go through that island and disassemble everything. . . . This city has become too sophisticated, too cosmopolitan for that type of thing." This line of argument has been deployed over centuries in some form all over Florida, and certainly since the conquest of the new world turned to nation building. But for the specifics of Florida, especially Miami, the appeal for its sophistication, its progressive newness, always with affected pizzazz toward market potential, tries hard to conceal the fact that the bulk of it was built upon seized swamp, limestone, and scrub. The desire for proximity to waterfront in Miami has long determined the topographic bands of wealth that decrease as one moves inland. That is until recently. Given the destruction of the natural barriers to flooding by developers and rising seas of climate change, Miami's inland—where displaced working-class people of color have been sent for decades—is now squarely in Sauron's eye.[7] Note how quickly it is to be carried off by the despair of Florida's brazen unfairness. This is why Montaner is this chapter's sentinel, for he guards over what so many have done in the midst of everything being taken away. To cast off his story as one of charming idiosyncrasy betrays the hard work of his and other's living practices. From the spoil, it is possible to learn a few protocols for taking in what the tides bring. From the shore, we look and listen closer to those lingering unseen and unheard.

II. "To draw a pen picture of the City of Miami today . . . is beyond descriptive power of even the most talented writer." What a pass we were given long ago by Ethan Blackman in his fascinating 1921 text *Miami and Dade County, Florida: Its Settlement, Progress and Achievement*, said to be the first published history of the area (figure 2.1).[8] This Methodist organizer and Civil War veteran from North Pitcher, New York, attempted to press pause on the disorienting blur of the city's founding. And yet it is beyond description. If the city is beyond apprehending it to writing, we need to ask: What is he actually doing? And more importantly: How to interpret all the voluminous matter that eludes familiar tales such as these? Blackman's book is not a stand-alone object. As one moves through the text, it is possible to trace out a few tendencies in the larger narrative making of Miami. The book's very title is hard evidence of words making up Miami and fast. Its achievement is a fait accompli affirmed a mere twenty-five years after its official founding. His astonishment is a crucial element in the genre of the success story that has long governed Miami's marketing strategy. Blackman hopes to maintain the place's strangeness while at the same time bolster its nonthreatening atmosphere for unbridled development. An object like Blackman's text is not an albatross to be carried lightly, nor is it one to overmine the city's founding. It is the kind of surface history one must again and again face, if not exactly recognize, in Floridian letters. And yet like these surface histories, *Miami and Dade County* is the kind of text that, despite itself, leaves all kinds of interesting dregs behind for stewardship. Its throwaway parts—castoffs from its smooth narrative exterior—compel the building of a makeshift shelter and, what's more, the impetus to make it pretty. While Blackman so badly wants the power of words to convey Miami's specialness—words he can't seem to muster—I use them to briefly describe what accounts such as his authorize, and then head offshore to delve at length into music that offers a whole other way to take in Miami's terrifying past and innovative beauty all at once.

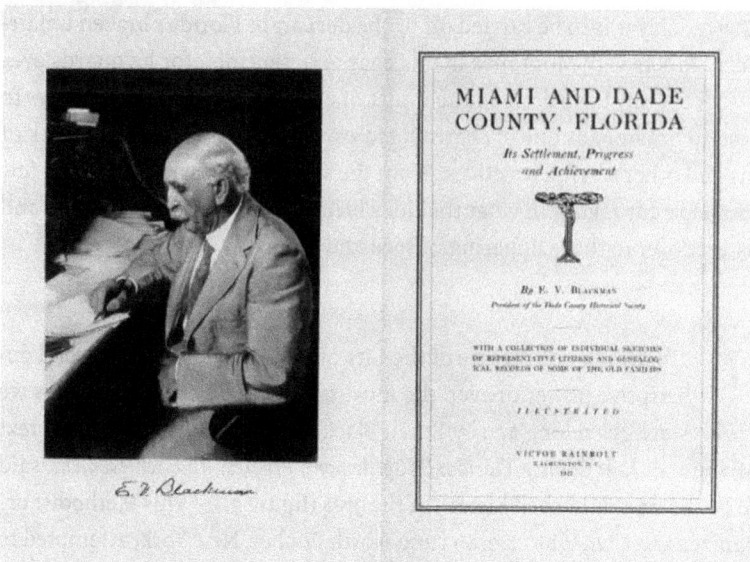

FIGURE 2.1 E. V. Blackman, *Miami and Dade County, Florida: Its Settlement, Progress and Achievement* (1921). Library of Congress, Americana Collection.

Blackman's book does not begin at the conquest or with the arrival of the first settlers. And from its outset, it is clear that nonpossessive figures such as Montaner will not be part of the story. Its introductory section, titled "Dade County," begins in 1808, when Spain gave a hundred acres of its stolen Floridian possession to John Egan. Blackman tells us that the property, situated on the Miami River, was handed down through the family to William English, who brought a large number of enslaved people to sow and then farm this land with tobacco, cotton, and indigo. English died without immediate heirs, and after many claims made to it over a few years, the land was eventually deeded to Julia T. Tuttle. Such quick exchange and, notably, quick *narration of exchange* of land ownership (a few paragraphs) is part of Blackman's method to get to the more "salient points" of the area's history.[9] Blackman then describes a subsequent land grant (this time given by the United States) to the scientist Henry Perrine, who wanted a territory on which to conduct experiments with imported tropical plants and trees.[10] These horticultural interests stemmed from Perrine's travels to Cuba and the Yucatán. After Spain's introduction of the orange to Florida, Perrine is among the most impactful of those who imported invasive species to the area. Perrine wanted to duplicate the tropics in South Florida to create new agricultural markets—and to add a kind of outside reference to the land. There was something about the exceptional Floridian landscape that gave Perrine a strong need to remake it in the partial image of another. Not exactly for an escapist image of tropical paradise, but to envision how a horticultural do-over could make the area profitable. Such a plan involved an aggressive method of land modification, one that would impose a chosen, imported otherness over its given, native otherness.

Perrine's two-step ideological and logistical plan first required the discursive devaluation and actual destruction of the native to make room for a curated foreignness. Perrine, a tropic-hopping tourist, hoped to cultivate his curiosity and curiosities in this different place that happened to match the weather patterns of his previous travels. Blackman cites an 1838 act of Congress—passed during the US war against the Seminoles and their allies—which entitled Perrine to six square miles on lower Biscayne Bay:[11] "Whereas, if the enterprise should be successful it will render valuable our hitherto worthless soils by covering a dense population of small cultivators and family manufacturers, and will promote the peace, prosperity and permanency of the Union. . . ."[12] "Hitherto worthless soils" is discursive primer for land sequestration and manipulation, and for the subsequent displacement of anyone who happens to live on it. For the US legislative body, Florida as testing ground of agriculture, the seized land that could provide it, what it could be disciplined to produce, and its pending success, held actual and symbolic stakes for the union. Perrine was killed by Mikasuki Seminoles on August 7, 1840, in Indian Key before he could carry out his designs.[13] As the scientist behind such place-identified fruits of South Florida such as the key lime and the mango (which Perrine brought from Mexico),[14] he is made a tragic figure in much of the literature about early South Florida. Perrine is cast as a part of the heroic sacrifice made by the city's early settlers, and on paper his mission and demise were part of a larger tragedy regarding the agriculture that almost was but wasn't. His victory, we now know, was merely delayed.

What was it that Chakaika (cakâykico:bî), the leader of the group of warriors who killed Perrine in the attack at Indian Key, was trying to protect from further harm?[15] What may he have been trying to mobilize at this moment in the Second Seminole War?[16] I wonder if in addition to acquiring war provisions and to preserve their very lives, Perrine's horticultural experiments were perceived as equally clear and considerable threats to not only the land but to a whole way of life as well. After inserting Perrine as a central character in the city's plotline, Blackman spends another few paragraphs writing about the topographic dimensions of early Dade County and a few more that detail the white "pioneers" he credits for its development. He makes no mention at all of the indigenous lands, or the exploited labor used to clear and build the area, although he unwittingly included them, uncredited, in the photographs that show the building of such structures as the Royal Palm Hotel. In the last page of this introductory history section, Blackman ends with a paragraph titled "The Seminole Indians":

> No history of the early settlement of Dade County would be complete without mention of the Seminole Indians. When Florida became a part of the United States the Indians were a menace to the peaceful development of the country. These troubles culminated in the Indian War, which cost 1,500 lives, twenty million of dollars and eight years of time. It ended in 1842 by the banishment of the hostile red men into the fastness of the Everglades. . . . The Seminole is a familiar figure in Miami and Dade County. Where their crude and gaudy dress attracts the attention of the stranger . . . the Seminole is healthy, industrious in his own way, moral and just. Devoted to tribal customs, he is usually kind to his women and children and reverences the Great Spirit.[17]

Much like Perrine's experiments on land, Blackman's endeavor thrives in the established pattern of devaluation of the native, to then pick and choose what's prized among the detritus. For all the pages Blackman devoted to Miami-Dade's founding, indigenous peoples and their lands that were being shuffled right under their feet were not mentioned until this paragraph. The lines stun for their quickness of contradiction: menacing, hostile, wasteful, and at the same time familiar, gaudy, and moral. Blackman seems to have no trouble describing an undifferentiated *Seminole* (at once a nonspecific term used by settlers to denote all the native populations in Florida, a term of identification adopted by some, a name imposed by the federal government onto others). What the sign conceals is the difficult and dynamic histories that rumble inside of it.[18] Here, the Seminoles are made nonthreatening, even charming, through their segmentation. For certain narrations of the city, these histories and people may be an inconvenient "need to mention" but are replied upon to add something to the region's souvenir luster. Because Blackman's text is essentially an advertisement for developers, he encourages their further displacement. The Seminoles, pushed to the "fastness" of the Everglades, represent a transfer of dregs to dregs. Yet as Patricia R. Wickman notes—through Mikasuki elders Frank J. Billie, Henry John Billie, James E. Billie, Mary G. Frances Johns, Alan Jumper, and

Pete Osceola Sr.—"their ancestors had been migrating southward toward the lower reaches of the peninsula for all time because their medicine people always had told them that *ichî bolán*, literally 'the nose of the deer,' or the pointed tip of the southeastern peninsula, was the place where they would ultimately find refuge and peace."[19] For Blackman and many others, this foresight and pull is misread solely as reactive movement, and they are left somewhere in the limens of war criminals and nascent touristic curiosities. Blackman's paragraph was written just seven years before the completed construction of the Tamiami Trail, a main road artery that would go out of its way to disturb how people long made home in the Everglades. The undifferentiated Seminoles that Blackman puts on display here, along with all their ornaments, suggest the difficult and performative and strategic work of the i:laposhni:cha thli: who were in the midst of creating an industry to profit from settlers' fascination.[20] Soon, but not soon enough, the robust legacy of these unnamed but resounding presences will surge through these pages.

In his subsequent pages about Miami, Blackman went to tawdry extremity. He calls the city a "lusty infant," one that was "born in a day," and makes recourse to the empirical to assert its worth, over and over again. Such recourse reveals a writerly tic that continues to govern so many descriptions of the city today. Of the Dade County Public School Board, for example, Blackman reveals that in twenty-five short years (from 1896 to 1921), its holdings grew from zero to "the magnificent sum of $1,334,121.96."[21] I'm caught by the ninety-six cents that Blackman makes sure to include here. It betrays a hidden complex that emerges when trying to make a sale that you need but can't quite get behind. A refusal to round up or down as punctuation point. As a kind of analog to this ninety-six cents, it was Blackman who originally coined the moniker "Magic City" for Miami in the *The Florida East Coast Homeseeker*, a magazine fully dedicated to the Florida East Coast Railroad from 1899 to 1914 in order to get northerners to buy, occupy, and, in so many cases, make agronomic experiments on its land (figure 2.2).[22] The magazine was a precursor to the ones in the seat backs next to the airsickness bags, which try to lure travelers to actual places and offer instant contracts for more credit and more perfume.

"Magic," as it emerges in Miami's nickname, meant and still means "as if by magic."[23] It was a way to say presto for the area's rapid population growth and the infrastructure built for and as a result of it. It was a way to name the arriving populations that counted to city planners and to expunge the existing ones that didn't. "Magic City" adds just the right allure

FIGURE 2.2 *The Florida East Coast Homeseeker*, featuring "Miami—Florida's 'Magic City,'" February 1908.

and slightly Orientalist appeal to adventurist buyers looking at South Florida in the early decades of the twentieth century. Shining outward and, just as forcefully, inward right into its own eyes, "Magic City" and its amnesiac glare does a lot of work to blind historical accounts of the people who built it, and of those who taught the city's early settlers how to manage living there—at the same time they had to survive these newcomers' project to wear them down and out.[24] Harder still for some historians to imagine is how Miami's builders, and the communities that supported them, were hard at work innovating new aesthetic forms and new architectures for music, dance, art. The "Magic City" moniker is an analog to Perrine's imposed and alluring fruit, and what their sweetness and exoticness concealed. Everything was made to look natural and given, made as if waiting to be taken for enjoyment and discovery. There is no denying it: "Magic City" is a catchall that persists and endures. "Magic City," now interchangeable with "Global City," continues to power this willful forgetfulness. Both serve as engines, as people and place removers that make okay and inevitable what it took, and took over, to make the city that way. But is it always, to turn one of its implied terms against it, successful?

To work with the suggestive gaps of Blackman's text, the violences of their exclusion and inclusion, the neurotic complex of his ninety-six cents, and especially his "Magic City" is to stand akimbo on the detritus in plain view of mainland history. Rather than giving up in the face of narratives such as Blackman's, perhaps there is much more to be found in, under, around them (despite his progressive intentions) beyond more exploitation and touristic commodification. This is a muscle one learns to use while thinking about Florida and thinking-in-Florida, especially if you came of age there. It is a necessary skill developed by some, over many decades, who were forced to make economy of their own display. There are many ways to anticipate, intervene in, and muddy rapid transactions that wrap material and spiritual land grabs in sunshiny gimmicks. There are many instances in the larger Montaner mode, *buoyant and grounded*, that sing: "I belong in the water, and I'm not going anywhere." There are many models that cannot be explained via a reactive resisting *to*—which suggests that violence is a condition required for creativity. There are many who have made pen pictures of the city of Miami *within* a collective's descriptive power. The musicians in the coming pages are but a few of the many who have told us how.

III. For many Floridian schoolchildren, a necessary part of citizen formation has historically meant living in the promotional with a kind of banal ease, of carrying a sense of promotion as all bound up with a sense of your place. "The Orange Blossom Song," for example, was often taught at the elementary level, at least until the late 1980s.[25] Local allegiance is a sung advertisement for the North to find the citrus, a product, we recall, brought by the Spaniards during the conquest. The song sticks hard to internal repertoire and edges out so many other moments to the great unremembered. My friend Liz will still sing it in the afterhours. There are some sophisticated mechanics at work here in being a living part of the state's trade from a young age, something that's shared in a way between Miami and all the islands, spoil and actual, that lie south and east of it. However, the way this catechismal imperative is handed down doesn't always align with progressive narratives of the New South or specific national resistances made in the postcolonies. There is a kind of living with and as trade that sometimes compels a willing participation in and as touristic spectacle for an outsider unfamiliar with the particularities of the city. When on the outside, it is sometimes easier to shorthand one's Miaminess through its centuries-old auto-exoticism. The story that Miami tells about itself in all of its varied matter, whether postcards, commercials, billboards, place-based jingles, international banks, or schoolbooks, carries a barrage of signals that try hard to tell its residents: this is you. Or: this should be you. Always available, colorful, happy; up for party time, sex, whatever; successful, with just a hint of eccentricity and difference. It is a bootstraps theory made over in strappy sandals. Across media, the aesthetics about these signals are quite varied, but they somehow bear intrinsic consistency over time. From the colorized promotional images of Blackman's era to the ways it is splayed across new music videos, Miami has been long made to mean a visual too-much. Yet for so many residents, their insides don't exactly match up with these broadcast outsides.

When confronted with the outsides of the sheet music for a song called "On Miami Shore (Golden Sands of Miami)," a waltz composed in 1919 by Hungarian composer Victor Jacobi (1883–1921) and with lyrics by William LeBaron, it would thus be too easy to cast off its aural insides because it traffics so clearly in the Floridian promotional (figure 2.3).[26] The viewer looks out from a voyeuristic position to an empty beach full of lusty possibility. A few unobtrusive palms grace the dunes; the moon is fixed in perfect position at the very stage it is at its most fleeting. Written at the time of Blackman's historical effort, it was recorded by multiple groups, eight by my count between 1919 and 1920 alone.[27] Surely, we could easily say, this is an object thrust from the city's deep commercialism.[28] But what happens if we actually listen to the song?[29] What happens when the ear dares to reach through the scratches of the 78, not in an exercise of making quaint attachment to it, not to turn something old into ironic fodder, but to listen to its real-time experiment? The version I work with is by the renowned Austrian violinist Fritz Kreisler, whose celebrated repertoire included Brahms and Mendelssohn, typically the songs that brazenly cited Europe's others, whether the Hungarian dance or the Danza Española. It is, to my ear, Kreisler's work with Chopin's mazurkas that feel especially present in his rendition of "On Miami Shore."[30] Kreisler had collaborated with Jacobi, the song's composer, on *Apple Blossoms*, a comic operetta that premiered on the Broadway stage also in 1919.[31] Kreisler's phrasing of Jacobi's song—and really, it is a very pretty song—give us a set of lovely ascensions, slightly modified from one phrase to the next, that gently make their way back to the waltzic ground played by the rest of the collective. It is a "valse moderato," making a softly

FIGURE 2.3 Viktor Jacobi and William LeBaron, "On Miami Shore (Golden Sands of Miami): waltz song" (1919). *Vocal Popular Sheet Music Collection*, score 1111.

moderate versus strong oom-pah. The playing instructions suggest that dancers should not be made unwilling captives to its time.

LeBaron's lyrics do well to work within the ongoing fantasy of Miami when he sets the following scenario and feelings to Jacobi's music:

> Down on the shore of Miami
> Lit by the moon above
> Kissed by the waves that are sighing
> Wonderful stories of love
> How can a fellow resist them?
> Often I tried in vain
> There is allure in Miami
> A pow'r that I can't explain
> On the golden sands of old Miami
> There I always find a girl whom I adore
> Ev'ry year it seems to happen o'er and o'er
> On the golden sands
> Where love commands Miami shore.[32]

Again we learn of a place that always leaves open the possibility of amorous encounters, a place whose nature is there to help along some guy's story, and a place that, once again, resists explanation or description. Still, a question persists: What is Jacobi's song doing other than the familiar channels laid out by its visual and lyrical presentations? Victor Jacobi was born in Budapest and died at the young age of thirty-eight soon after arriving in New York City. As a renowned figure in a group of Hungarian composers who wrote for European stages in the late nineteenth century, Jacobi was best known for his smash operetta *Szibill* (*Sybil*), one of the most successful musicals in Viennese-Budapest operetta.[33] After a brief stop in London, he moved to New York around 1917, which brought on his death (caused, some said, by a broken heart after the commercial failure of *The Love Letter*). After Jacobi's death, his music was featured in an operetta called *Miámi*, which was set in Florida and premiered in Budapest in 1925 to lackluster success. Kurt Gänzl reports that aficionados and former fans shunned this phase of Jacobi's later work, which they felt had been watered down in his move from Budapest to America.[34] So not only Jacobi's going abroad, but in particular, his going to Miami (which we can't actually verify)—*even if it was just a musical visitation*—did much to tarnish the legacy of one of Hungary's great composers.[35] In the pathos of this story, we relisten anew to "On Miami Shore" during Blackman's Miami, and as postmortem feature in *Miámi*, bearing an Ashkenazi melancholy, its exilic feeling set down in Jacobi's unsettled time. Imagine its composer, and the melody he needed in the move from Budapest to London to New York to the beyond, while the whole world was at unprecedented war.

"On Miami Shore" offers other sensations with which to gauge how Miami may have functioned in the global imaginary in the first decades of the twentieth century.[36] Beyond its use as lure for more development and displacement, inside of Jacobi's composition we hear something different. It is a real and imagined place of relief that one so badly wants while on the road, capacious enough to carry other kinds of traditions, in this case musical ones from the "dregs" of Eastern Europe, who were then facing unprecedented forms of cruelty. The song is a stage for a mournful story with a dulcet ending, any and all mournful stories and dulcet endings that need a place to rest and record. Jacobi thus beautifully creates more conditions with which to keep imagining the Miami, any Miami that resides beneath the surface. As a catchphrase, "Magic City" may have had an intended traveler in mind, one who would follow through its unspoken contract of tandem enjoyment and construction. The lyrical narrator of "On Miami Shore" cannot resist the allure of the place. We sense he will settle there for good in order to make his desire for surprise encounter permanent. However, the music that lingers on its insides sounds like it has had enough of surprise and wants the privilege of constancy. Its melodic flights return to a place, even as the base note changes.

IV. The nonintended "Magic City" is a bustling place to live. As a theme imposed and inherited, it is a thrill to listen to just how many have anticipated and thwarted its calculated designs over time. Tuning in now to one of these alternate renderings, take in a composer and her song that work in parallel with the given. In 1965 Elena Casals composed "Magic City," a tribute to Miami that took up the city's nickname and revels in parts of that other place beside it, if not of it. Born in Pinar del Río, Cuba, in 1927, Casals was an up-and-coming bolero songwriter and poet with a robust career in Cuba (figure 2.4).[37] After she married, Casals left the island to accompany her husband, a North American geologist, to Venezuela, where she would become pregnant (not by her husband, but by a dashing Hungarian fortune seeker who would meet her during the Wednesday matinees at the only movie theater in town), and from where she wrote her "Noches de Maracaibo." Casals later came to live on a dairy farm in Gainesville, and just after divorcing her husband, arrived in Miami flat broke in 1958 with her two young sons.[38] Moving into a housing project in Liberty City, Casals continued her compositional practices on a broken-down and out-of-tune Wurlitzer piano (figure 2.5).[39] She entered one song, "Magic City," into a competition launched to find Miami's new theme song, sponsored by then-mayor Robert King High.[40] Casals won the contest. And whereas there was no money, there was recognition, although we have to imagine what the song sounded like, as there are no recordings that exist of it in the then-time of its composition. We hear it in unfindable promotional materials, and it may still live in the mouth memory of some schoolchildren who were made to sing it in assemblies for local pride, even if they were living in conditions of destitution, like the composer herself.[41]

There is an extant recording of it from 2012 and sung by Grisel Sánchez, an esteemed musician from Miami who has long taught at Miami Dade Community College (now Miami Dade College). The lyrics tell us the following:

There is no place in all the world as beautiful and blue
Magic City is the name I'm calling you
(Oye)

FIGURE 2.4 Elena Casals, Pinar del Río, Cuba, 1945 (age eighteen).

FIGURE 2.5 Elena Casals at the piano, Miami, ca. 1965. Courtesy of Desmond Child.

> I want to show
> My thanks to you
> To you Miami
> For giving warmth and all the love I came to see
> I'll tell the world this is the place
> Where people are happy
> If I depart, deep in my heart you'll always be
>
> The weather's nice
> A paradise
> This is Miami
> All year around the sun will shine over the sea
> And the next year you'll see me here
> There is a thing I would like to make clear
> There's only friends there are no strangers in Miami (2x).
> The Magic City of the World.

The song bears a demonstration of what Miami helps to front, conceal, and/or enjoy in difficult times. Lyrically, it could easily circulate among touristic commodities, but this facile reading falls apart when we consider its writing by a nonlandowning woman newly arrived to these shores. One wonders how the composer may have made this song to make a home and to tell herself and others the necessary optimistic fabrications needed to stay alive while there. The song is along the lines of needing rest and sweet familiarity heard in Jacobi's "On Miami Shore." What more does this song provide for Casals, her kids, and all the kids who weren't her kids? This tight circle of a song is a good time in a short space. The lyrics help the listener trot along with the montuno with the heart tilted upward. The song oxygenates alienation as a way of saying: let's feel good for a minute, especially because we don't. There are a few things that may not have been in the original composition, but the contemporary recording tells us that Casals made ample and implied room for them. Take Sánchez's "Oye," that great Cuban ear-opener that asserts, with finality, what in Casals's time was just beginning to whisper: "Magic City" as a majority-immigrant city. There are congas present in the recording, which meant that they were in the bones of the composition. As much as this room leaving innovates a Latinate sense for the later Magic City music to follow, it leans on other traditions of swing and swagger.[42] The song is an anticipated, feminist undoing of Paul Anka's later "My Way," one that, musically and otherwise, puts others first.

Casals's "Magic City" doesn't exactly conceal the compositional heaviness she explored and helped originate in Cuban idioms such as the bolero. Casals was a part of (and eventually displaced from) the time and place of mid-century Cuban musicking. At that time the island was in the thick surge of filin (feeling), a movement in Cuban music deeply involved with American jazz, especially inspired by its vocalists. Imagine, for example, picking up what Sarah Vaughan was doing with her phrasings and then transposing them into other Cuban instrumental lexicons. Among many other things, filin took up the bolero genre and made it roomy for experimental work. You can hear Casals being influenced by (and her contributions to) these decades of profound musical play. Casals learned to play piano at her grandparents' house in Pinar del Río by overhearing an aunt play classical repertoire. Casals took up the guitar, likely part of her troubadourian command of melody to accompany the fullness of piano.[43] She was primed to become part of a musical dynasty, especially in her move to La Habana, which would later involve the world-renowned Olga Guillot, "The Queen of Bolero," becoming her sister-in-law. You can find three of Casals's boleros that were recorded in Miami in the early 1960s by Cuban singer Roberto Ledesma. "Muchísimo" (A Whole Lot), "Triste" (Sad), and "Que seas feliz con tu dinero" (May you be happy with your money) are titles that say everything about what boleros do in content and form. These songs are a perfect trinity that gestures toward bolero's held losses, both embittered and bittersweet, the testimonies its narrators so badly want and need to give, and fantasies of revenge fulfilled and not.[44] Boleros, and Casals's boleros in particular, feel formally written for singers. They are compositions to be sung. Their compact, seemingly simplistic lyrics are really showcases for voice, crafted in such a way to allow a vocalist to interpret the hell out of them, in all their highs and lows. In Casals's "Muchísimo," take in how much its one-word title works itself into the opening line, "Muchísimo, te extrañaré muchísimo, y lloraré muchísmio si tú te vas (A whole lot / I miss you a whole lot / and I will cry a whole lot if you leave)." It is rendered long, drawn out, and slow, and the singer is given the opportunity—right there in the opening line—to give three different senses of missing/being/loving too much. Casals's "Muchísimo" is among those that merit the superlative "bolerazo." Such a distinction adds emphatic emphasis to a song's boleroness when it feels particularly heavy, or when just after listening to it, such an honorific can't help but be immediately given. *Bolerazo*.

Picture Casals after her arrival in Miami, broke, and in the bolero style, a single mom raising two sons in Liberty City.[45] One of her sons, formerly John Charles Barrett (born 1953), a precocious musician tutored by his mother in the everyday of her practice, reached adolescence with an acute dissatisfaction with his zoned school. He eventually lied about his address and would take three buses to Nautilus Junior High in Miami Beach (figure 2.6). Barrett later moved on to Miami Beach High School, where among other things, he befriended a young Mickey Rourke, who defended him from the school bully. On the lawn of Beach High, Barrett befriended a girl named Deborah Walstein, and together they agreed to form a musical duo called NIGHTCHILD. Wanting a stage name that had something of the uniqueness of Elton John's, Barrett became the name and persona Desmond Child.[46] Desmond Child, son of Elena Casals, would become one of the most prolific and successful songwriters in contemporary popular music. The author of many greatest hits, Child is the kind of songwriter who is *always* on the radio somewhere, anywhere.[47] Child, the brilliant gay Cuban Miami misfit, is the author of not only colossal Latinate hits like Ricky Martin's "Livin' la Vida Loca" and "She Bangs" (co-written with Draco Rosa) but has also penned many songs across generic lines (figure 2.7). Child wrote other missilic hits with and for artists as seemingly divergent as KISS, Bon Jovi,

FIGURE 2.6 Desmond Child and Elena Casals at the Miami Zoo in Crandon Park, 1966. Courtesy of Desmond Child.

FIGURE 2.7 Desmond Child in Desmond Child & Rouge. Photo by Ciro Barbaro. Courtesy of Desmond Child.

Aerosmith, Barbra Streisand, Garth Brooks, Katy Perry, Michael Bolton, Joan Jett, the Scorpions, Alice Cooper, and Cher.

Of his childhood Child recalls, "My mother was a songwriter *and so there was always a song being written*. I didn't know people didn't write songs. I thought that's how human beings expressed themselves."[48] Note how his description is in the passive voice, deferring the subject, arguing in some ways for a subjectless songwriting. How did Casals give her son, in Winnicott's lovely phrase, the "world in small doses"? The pleasure and difficulty of being the child of a musician is listening constantly to the parent writing out loud (through instrument, through voice) in phrasing that's not language but something parallel to it. One has to imagine the yearning felt in this parallel language, especially by those whose life responsibilities don't afford them unbounded time or studio space for creative inspiration. It is part of why music, especially in Cuba and the Caribbean and Miami, is so dynastically based. Because it has to be made at all times, in front of everyone. And why its more marginal entourages are so important. It is why rumba, and its drums, and the intergenerational rehearsal space it is made of offer the time and place to think about time and place in ways parallel to language. Songwriting and the constant, unrelenting refinement it demands make conservatory discipline of experimentation and faltering. The tireless work—snuck in those exhausted pauses between shifts—manages to make a concrete something else for giving away.

What did Desmond Child inherit as he listened to his mom work out on the piano songs like "Magic City"? What did his ear catch as she tried to write a home for herself and her kids without taking possession of it? In this dislodged sand and soil, there is Child's "Magic City" surround. South Florida of the late 1960s was, among other things, a place for rock-music festivals—what Child called the "Woodstocky ones"—where Jimi Hendrix famously performed in the 1968 Miami Pop Festival (an experience that was the inspiration behind his "Rainy Day, Dream Away"). He also sang along with Janis Joplin, who played on the University of Miami campus in 1969. From the audience of these humid rock laboratories, Child would reflect to himself: "We're so poor . . . but you know what? I'm going to be a rock star."[49] This early grounding in late-sixties rock was but one part of his Miamian music education. While attending Miami Beach High and working as a pool boy at the Eden Roc Hotel, his weekend snowbird friend Lisa Wexler, Jerry Wexler's daughter, introduced him to her dad's productions for Atlantic Records: Otis Redding, Aretha Franklin, and, especially formative for Child, Laura Nyro.[50] After he dropped out of school in eleventh

FIGURES 2.8 AND 2.9 *Left*: Promotional poster for Rouge Live at the Yellow Brick Road. Illustration by Chris Pettigrew. *Right*: Desmond Child & Rouge (Capitol Records, ST 11908, vinyl). Collection of the author.

grade, NIGHTCHILD tried hard to make it in New York, only to come back to Miami to disband. Later, on the campus of Miami Dade Community College, Child teamed up with Maria Vidal and Diana Grasselli to form Desmond Child & Rouge. With his Cuban and Italian American gang, Child then moved back to New York City to attend NYU, where they recruited the key talent of Myriam Valle. To get a sense of Desmond Child & Rouge in sound and spectacle, take in the promotional flyer announcing their live set at New York's the Yellow Brick Road (with bonus WBAI tie-in). It is a resolute mix of sublevel cabaret with DIY punk aesthetics, and the band promises-as-sendoff, "P.S. We'll put a little color on your cheeks!" (figure 2.8). It is an endearing and astonishing trace of formerly Miami kids making strange new sounds in America's metropolis. You may or may not recall Desmond Child & Rouge's Billboard Top 40 hit "Our Love Is Insane" (figure 2.9). This song is a thumping shoreline that gives its voices so many chances to swell and soak notes with the intensity of affection that makes lovers do crazy things. In Rouge's work, you can hear Child's early experimentation with rock sounds in the milieu of dance music, a setting within a setting, that would resound throughout his later catalog.

You can feel this setting within a setting, a gritty disco, in Child and Paul Stanley's 1979 collaboration "I Was Made for Lovin' You," <u>a song</u> that became a monster hit for KISS.⁵¹ It was also a song whose royalties enabled Child to pay off his mother's debts and make a comfortable home for her. A song made for housing her. The hangry experience of 1970s New York, and his schooling with Casals in a hangry Miami, established for Child the infrastructure for his future songwriting career. For Child, New York became the compositional hut where his songwriting came from hard city living and loving, the travails of working people trying to survive, and what could be made and done in a state of being always "halfway there." It was a place to be partially employed through dock and/or sex work, to be all torn up in terms of not knowing what and where your place is. With all this, Child helped to tend an open place for anything or anyone's imprint, to document shared migration patterns, to circulate a list of survival skills. As one among many concrete examples, refer to Child's 1986 collaboration with Jon Bon Jovi and Richie Sambora, "Livin' on a Prayer," which was recorded by Bon Jovi and became the unofficial state song and, one could argue, governing aesthetic for New Jersey.

One can expect the tides but not what they bring. Here are a few items of washed-in wonder before continuing: the woman who wrote the theme song for Miami made the man who wrote the theme song for New Jersey. To reckon with Casals's aesthetic play in Cuban filin, and its setting within a setting in Miami, is to cherish her actual, material trace in one of the most circulated pop-rock anthems of all time. It is to live in the beauty of a confirmed hunch and the pearl of unexpected surprise. These kinds of past-due recognitions always make abundant connections to others, their supplements to musical story lines always open playrooms. As just one form of proof, in the midst of the dizzying knots of this research thread I happened to meet a man named Frank Ferrer at the bag next to me in a kickboxing class in January 2018. In the space of a warm-up, I learned quickly (one always learns quickly) that he was Cuban and a drummer, actually, the drummer for Guns N' Roses. Because of Cuban agility in medias res, I told him I was in the middle of writing this whole thing on Desmond Child. Ferrer quickly interrupted me to say that what called him to rock and roll was seeing KISS perform in Madison Square Garden in 1977 and that he remembered Desmond Child & Rouge opening for them. We both discovered much later—after a funny swirl of back-and-forth texts between Ferrer and Paul Stanley, Child, and myself—that they did not actually open for KISS. It is likely that Ferrer must have seen Desmond Child & Rouge playing at clubs such as CBGBs and Trax. The actual when and where is secondary really. The important thing here is that KISS and Desmond Child & Rouge forged a singular memory in Ferrer's brain, making a match of them as powerhouse equals of rock and roll. What needs to be repeated but doesn't need arguing: when we move with musicians, their songs, and all that's involved in them, the listener is given deeply moving material assistance in learning the what, where, and who they hold inside of them. This beautiful bit of unimaginable context to "Magic City" happened upon on a chilly Saturday morning, helps reiterate to nascent archivists and critics the importance of still talking to people. When you least expect it, there will be a thunderous connection to your musicking.

V. The crossings of all of the people and places in the foregoing make some things apparent in the mangrovian tangle of some thing, some activity we might call rock and roll. If part of the privilege of maturity is letting go of story lines, to proceed with rock and roll not as a solidified, exclusionary genre category but as a capacious and aspirational sense of sound rebellion would open it up to a more historically accurate sense of the foundational personnel inside of it. Having moved inside and outside a few Magic City recordings, and flowing with the drifts made in song, there emerges a way of working that refuses to settle certain bodies and their sounds into a familiar chronological template. To backtrack/fronttrack: this chapter began from the spoil of Dinner Key Marina in 2004, spaceship-jumped a century back, made a brief rest stop in Budapest, involved Miami's unexpected arrivals of Havana's mid-century, live-wired to punk New York of the 1970s, and relished a research wind rush in 2018 New Jersey. To return to Montaner's spoil mode, and his own parallel with the given, assumes all extant models and prior innovativeness. To honor South Florida's peopled antecedents as enduring and present currents, rather than presumably extinct forces in inter-American place fables, may be uniquely encouraged in and with music. Music as portal for noisy return of the repressed *and* conduit for the new wave future was innovated well in advance by a musical group named Tiger Tiger. The group was helmed by two brothers, Stephen and Lee Tiger, beloved sons of the Miccosukee Tribe of Indians of Florida, and progenies, innovators, and conduits of South Florida's rock-and-roll sound rebellions.

Stephen Tiger once described his music as holding "the quietness of the 'glades, along with the heaviness of the weather, lightning and thunderstorms, [and bringing] that side of our heritage into a pop-rock context for all peoples."[52] Such quietness and heaviness put into notes is a transfer made possible by the Tiger brothers' deep reserve of and for their history, and it can be felt across their oeuvre even when a song is authored by another. Their version of Patti Smith and Bruce Springsteen's 1978 "Because the Night," for example, appears as the first track of their 1980 album *Eye of the Tiger* (figures 2.10, 2.11, and 2.12).[53] It takes just a few seconds too long to start, a withholding not to be confused with a production mistake. Such slightly delayed beginning recalls something of the *has it started?* effect of Bob Marley's "Natural Mystic." The introductory piano of the original has been extended slightly; it is an incoming rain with piccolo addition. Stephen Tiger enters to pronounce its intimate opening stanza with breathy "Take me now, baby, here as I am," and before you have the chance to get settled, you are interrupted by his sudden, tenacious, growling: "come on now try and understand the way I feel when I'm in your hand." The song highlights Stephen Tiger's vocal furiousness; his ups and downs are somewhere between contralto and countertenor, with a melodic command found in country music. When meeting Smith and Springsteen's book, Tiger Tiger carries the unintended of the original. It asserts the difficulty of how recognition must appeal to another's understanding. It demands another kind of attention in your narration. It bears the full blood-and-guts weight of the past, not only of a story of individualistic desire but also a collective love that reaches toward the intergalactic. Heard in "Because the Night" are Stephen Tiger's boyhood dreams of a place at rock and roll's table and the raucous place preset for him by his warrior predecessors. Of his nascent teenage training (the master class of looking up to slightly older cousins) Tiger recalled, "We wanted to grow our hair long and play in a band. It was very important to us."[54] An aesthetic cultivation of Tiger's insides to meet his outsides stood in open rebellion to the assimilatory haircuts forced upon him and his forebears. Stephen Tiger's hair is something other than just hair.

As more evidence of their legit countercultural track record, the cover of *Eye of the Tiger* was designed by Shusei Nagaoka, the legendary graphic artist behind much cover art of the seventies and eighties, including Earth, Wind & Fire's Egyptological *Helios* and Jefferson Starship's *Spitfire*.[55] The cover places us with a view from the wetlands at bird's or treetop's eye. The sunrise is not at all an affected rendering of tropical fantasy, but a true representation of the 6 a.m. hour in the wetlands. And then we have the pyramid, a sign parallel to other lived antiquities, both Mesopotamian and Egyptian, that argues always for the stunning ability of human beings to build amazing things. The back cover puts us in the wake of a spaceship well on its way

FIGURES 2.10, 2.11, AND 2.12 *Above:* Sleeve of *Eye of the Tiger*. Stephen Tiger is third from the left. *Below left:* Front of the album Tiger, Tiger, *Eye of the Tiger* (Clouds, 1980, vinyl). *Below right:* Back of the album Tiger, Tiger, *Eye of the Tiger* (Clouds, 1980, vinyl). Collection of the author.

to the celestial white tiger, toward the constellation that shares the band's name. The album is a critical hallucinogenic within and without, and there's no other way to put this, but it makes a person feel special when holding it. Yet Tiger Tiger eludes the collector. The eBay seller sent me my copy of *Eye of the Tiger* sandwiched, for protection, between two empty and defunct album covers. Packed inside of Doris Day *Sings Her Great Movie Hits* and Bert Kaempfert's *Strangers in the Night*, both defaced with big black Xs and the context "Packing Material," it is stirring to try and describe how Tiger Tiger, as recorded object, arrived. And the "Taste My Love" bargain 45 I ordered arrived in kitchen Saran wrap.

Protected by waste, though priced far, far below other rock collectibles, the packaging of *Eye of the Tiger* and "Taste My Love" finds correspondence to how Native America is made to circulate in the telling of South Florida. Rendered as a slightly precious though cheaply obtained item, circulated in provisional wrapping, disposable but protected, the record is somewhere between keepsake and nuisance. It is made to bear both an archaeological burden and what José Esteban Muñoz calls a "burden of liveness."[56] Out from the refuse we are given an amped-up "aesthetics of survivance," what Gerald Vizenor theorizes as "an active sense of presence over absence, deracination, and oblivion; survivance is the continuance of stories, not a mere reaction, however pertinent. Survivance is greater than the right of a survivable name."[57] Tunneling back to Blackman's text and one of its more telling spots of his and the city's perpetual undoing is to listen to the anticipatory feedback by the undifferentiated "Seminole" he likely did not mean to mic.

To begin with Tiger Tiger *from* their music enables a swerve away from the contextual protocols always burdened upon Indigenous peoples. To begin with what they played, in their then-and-there and our here-and-now, offers room to wonder about their active aesthetic roots. This wonder refuses the violent tendency in some scholarship to immediately sequester them to the anthropologic. Even in the midst of a cover (or stuck between two covers), Tiger Tiger reveals how their aesthetic traditions gird, in an underground, undersea way, South Florida. Tiger Tiger's music is an opportunity to intuit the material, genealogical contributions—creative through and through—that led up to their sound. Stephen and Lee Tiger were the sons of Buffalo Tiger or Heenehatche (Bird Clan), the first chairman of the Miccosukee, who was instrumental in gaining the tribe's federal recognition in 1962. Listening with Tiger Tiger requires some deeply felt time with their father, through which we not only get to hear some of their musical antecedents but also what led up to the foundation of the Miccosukee Tribe of Indians of Florida.

The Miccosukee are a group of i:laposhni:cha thli: who sought out a political identity on different terms from those offered them. In the early 1930s there were three known councils that were chosen to represent the various groups among the Seminoles. One group (which would eventually become the Miccosukee) was known as the Trail Seminoles and had long resisted reservation living and preferred to reside in makeshift camps in the Everglades and along the Tamiami Trail. Buffalo Tiger, who could read and write, was selected as this council's secretary and interpreter.[58] Consensus among the different groups of Seminoles became increasingly difficult to build, especially during the "termination era" of American Indian policy in the early 1950s.[59] Questions of how, and vitally to the resolutely antigovernment Trail Seminoles *if*, to negotiate land and peace treaties with the United States emphasized cleavages in the identities of the groups. Invasive settler practices such as dynamiting, drilling, draining, and fencing land in the Everglades made it especially difficult for the nonreservation Seminoles to preserve their independence given the nearly impossible recourse to justice and redress.[60] Refusing to share in the compromises made by the other councils, specifically around the exchange of land for money and relocation to reservations, Trail Seminoles moved to separate into their own tribe. In 1952 they adopted the name Miccosukee because it was the name (and spelling) of the eighteenth-century town in northern Florida their families had founded.

Buffalo Tiger was among those representatives who took their fight to Congress with demands for the land, not solely for the sake of title, but to petition for exclusivity of hunting, fishing, and frogging rights, and the cutting of cypress for the building of chickees and canoes.[61] These legislative details hold a world of preserving a way of life and livelihood. All of this activity was instituted by the Miccosukee in spite of the loud and large backdrop of the federal draconian plan to terminate services and sovereign status for nations and tribes around the country at mid-century. Seeking internationalist support, to advertise a firm sense of the autonomy of the Miccosukee, and to reassert their "unconquered" status (having never made formal peace with the United States or any other nation), Buffalo Tiger and a group of representatives brought their Buckskin Declaration to France, England, and Spain to seek out support in their demands for land.[62] In the same year, Tiger and the Miccosukee representatives went to Cuba as invited guests of Fidel Castro during the inaugural 26th of July celebrations in 1959.[63] There they found the kind of recognition they failed to gain elsewhere. The budding relationship with revolutionary Cuba may have been the tipping point for the United States to note and deescalate quickly the

Miccosukees' case. This kind of tireless creative performance is found throughout Tiger's chairmanship of the Miccosukee Tribe from its official recognition in 1962 until 1986. It was one early sign that moved Harry A. Kersey Jr. to later argue that Buffalo Tiger was "one of the most innovative tribal leaders of the twentieth century."[64]

Before Buffalo Tiger became the great leader known and beloved and contested by many, before he became known as the father to rock stars Stephen and Lee Tiger, he was a young Seminole boy raised in plain view as an exhibition in "Musa Isle Seminole Indian Village." Musa Isle was one of Miami's first tourist attractions, on the corner of N.W. 27th Avenue and N.W. 16th Street, close to downtown on the Miami River.[65] This attraction was one among an increasing many where the i:laposhni:cha thli: would present both wares and themselves as spectacle during the tourist season. Historian Patsy West's work on the i:laposhni:cha thli: strategic development of what she calls the "tourist attraction economy" is a treatise on Floridian living-in-the-promotional. In addition to a life of study of Seminole/Miccosukee history, West conducted oral histories with those who once worked in or had family members who worked in these attractions from their early heyday. Because of the infamous draining of and imposed violence on the Everglades—the formerly inland sea was suffocated by settler designs for its agricultural profitability—many i:laposhni:cha thli: ways of living were disrupted, and as a result, they once again made ingenious plans for survival. And so they went to Musa Isle seasonally to live, sell crafts and handiwork, and cohabitate with native and imported wildlife. Tiger suggests something of the banal transaction behind the work: "The attitude my family had was go in there maybe a couple of months and come home. Get those dollars and come home with materials and food." In Musa Isle the visitor was promised "specimens of wild life," a "large curio shop," and "Seminole Indians at Home" (figure 2.13). Alligator wrestling and performances of everyday tasks were for onsite enjoyment while coontie bread and patchwork could be bought and taken home.[66]

As one player in the larger company of i:laposhni:cha thli: who performed in and as tourist commodities in Musa Isle, Buffalo Tiger would execute his woodworking skills in front of visitors. Here are some fragments of an emerging artist, practices that cannot and should not be minimized, even though they were taken of him while on display. Figure 2.14 shows a portrait of Tiger as a young artist, painting a drum at Musa Isle and turning momentarily to face the camera. Note the delicate but deliberate designs of his drum skin, the adaptable sense of scale it took to make the abstract figures

FIGURE 2.13 Buffalo Tiger, "In the Trading Post of the Village You Will See the Most Interesting and Comprehensive Collection of Indian Curios and Handiwork in the Country." Undated postcard, #34. Collection of the author.

FIGURE 2.14 Buffalo Tiger as a young boy. Courtesy National Archives, photo no. 75-N-SEM-16.

FIGURE 2.15 Fifteen children (mostly Bird Clan) pose with Musa Isle's popular "alligator" photo prop in 1932, Miami. The first chairman of the Miccosukee Tribe of Indians (organized in 1961) was Buffalo Tiger, the second tallest. Postcard 883, Seminole/Miccosukee Archive.

FIGURE 2.16 Buffalo Tiger and Bird Clan family members exhibiting their crafts at Musa Isle, Miami, 1940s. Color photo by H. W. Hannau. Postcard 1022, Seminole/Miccosukee Archive.

for rain clouds, and the brush control behind the curlicued words "Musa Isle" and "Miami, Fla." Buffalo Tiger became especially known for making these "pan Indian" souvenir drums for purchase—drums he learned to make from Blue Bird (John Carillo), who spent some winters at Musa Isle.

Imagine Buffalo Tiger's coming of age as strategic auto-spectacle between two picture postcards (see figures 2.15 and 2.16), one as a very young child and the other standing in profile behind his drum handiwork. In both we're given a fully self-possessed posturing for a settler's lens. These documents of a childhood and adolescence do not appear only in photos in family scrapbooks but also in an unimaginable number of unseen and unknown travel diaries. They are proof of a stranger's having been down there. And yet there is so much withheld by the people in the photographs. For example, in figure 2.16, no one looks straight at the camera. Also unavailable are the hours of play before, during, and after the children are assembled in figure 2.15. I want to honor the ongoing withholding and unavailability as these images are circulated here. What do these performances demand even as they cause discomfort? How do they continue to disorder settler desire? And look again at Tiger painting a drum (figure 2.13) in a colorized postcard that brightens colors to the point of rendering the subject hard to recognize. Such postcard enhancement was meant to vivify the cheapest of souvenirs and added even more otherworldliness to the photographed location. Of Musa Isle, the postcard promises "Here, Truly, One May Procure a Real Florida Gift or Souvenir."

Yet and always, Tiger and his work demands that we reach through what the colors say and don't say, the effect they give and don't give, to see the detailed brushwork he uses to paint a headdress, a sign of the native that he borrows from an elsewhere he hasn't been. His other works are arranged, in curated repose, around him as he works. Tiger's work at Musa Isle was part of a family business, a nascent economy for native peoples to retain autonomy from the federal government and resist a sedentary life on the reservation. This enduring insistence for independence and privacy, learned at a very early age and throughout his developmental years, prepared Tiger as an elder statesman whose lifelong demand of the settler was for his tribe to be left alone. In full and fully conscious view of the promotional, Buffalo Tiger withheld, in reserve, the grit and spirit of perseverance of those whom have taken up, promoted, and disidentified all at once with being a heritage site.

Lee Tiger recounts his first experience with music when he was six or seven and his family still lived on Musa Isle: "It was there we became acquainted with the sounds of guitars coming from our cousin's *chickee*

FIGURE 2.17 Buffalo Tiger lecturing from his airboat to Florida Humanities Council event attendees on the Everglades and its environmental destruction, 1993. Photo by Patsy West. Mikasuki Collection, 93.56.6.

(house). It sounded so natural, and we had never heard anything like it, so we came closer. . . . We were amazed by how these guitars all looked, all polished up and well taken care of. . . ." This early visual introduction to an instrument planted the seeds for future rock-and-roll fantasies. At another pivotal moment, Lee Tiger recalled a pile of donations that were sent to "Indian" families for the holidays. Among the gifts, the Tiger brothers found two plastic guitars in boxes, and to their astonishment "they could actually be tuned. Even though they were not Gibson guitars, we were introduced to the world of music."[67] This musical origin story, revealing something of a spoils practice in their sensing beauty in the castoff, happened while the boys were part of the touristic spectacle. Note the complexity of experience that shores up in Musa Isle and the strategic practices of making do during brutal dispossession. To fully dismiss the work in these places as pure exploitation, however, is a common and condescending dismissal by liberal fantasies of benevolence in the 1930s and onward that takes furious hold in contemporary gaming debates. What of the legacies of the players who lived inside? Although their residence at Musa Isle was out of material necessity, original aesthetic practices were forged behind the scenes of commercial performance. Lee Tiger later recalled of his father's chairmanship, "My father's first accomplishment was putting an end to what I call 'living on display' at Musa Isle Indian Village on the Miami River."[68] As some of the last players on display, the Tiger brothers would eventually take forward the resolutely adaptive legacies of Miccosukee entrepreneurship and especially its relationship to performance. Musa Isle closed in the 1960s, but it is only one example of the i:laposhni:cha thli:'s strategic and performative relationship in tourism's trade. Buffalo Tiger's closing of the site allowed experiments with other models of visitation, of which his sons would be helpful architects. As chairman, Buffalo Tiger additionally founded the tribe's own school, where instruction and sustenance in Miccosukee traditions were central. At the same time, he founded an airboat tour business to show outsiders the beauty of the Everglades (figure 2.17). He ran Buffalo Tiger's Airboat Tours into his ninth decade of life before moving on in 2015.[69]

To take in Buffalo Tiger's work as a form of songwriting, and to imagine what is inside and in excess of his practice that his sons inherited, is to enliven what is meant by musical tradition. In their interview with West, we learn that Lee was thirteen and Stephen was fourteen in 1963, when the Tiger brothers formed their first band, called the Renegades, a name and frame that reveals a strong and sophisticated disidentificatory practice in their adolescence. After Stephen left for boarding school in Oklahoma, Lee remained in Miami playing gigs around town with the school's Agricultural Department Band.[70] After being reunited, they formed a band in 1966 called Sun Country, which put the Tiger brothers on the rock-and-roll circuit that flowed through Miami in the massive festival shows that were so influential on Desmond Child (in fact, Child was in the audience when they played in the Miami Pop Festival in 1968). Sun Country shared bills with Led Zeppelin, Jimi Hendrix, and Procol Harum, and backed eminent musicians such as Chuck Berry and Bo Diddley. The Tiger brothers eventually trod that then-common itinerary of moving to Woodstock, New York, and eventually to New York City. A folkway, you may recall, later walked by Desmond Child. After recording an album with RCA, a brief stint playing in the Los Angeles club scene, and with the encouragement of their father, the Tiger brothers returned to South Florida, where they committed themselves and their work to developing and promoting Miccosukee outreach programs.[71]

The songs in this period of Tiger Tiger set Miccosukee-focused lyrics in that interim sound that emerged between the late 1960s and early 1970s rock. Anthemic Indian Pride lyrics were adorned with the strummed residues of sock hops, and their rebellious sound marked by metallic feedback. As they played their songs in South Florida nightclubs, their commitment to the tribe became their central priority as artists. Embarking on a tour equal parts rock and education, Tiger Tiger hoped to show outsiders the Miccosukee and their way of life and to promote tourism for their enduring autonomous project. The Tiger brothers seized opportunities that were happening in parallel with Miami—for example, their exploitation of the city's "See It Like a Native" slogan, to which they appended actual natives. This brilliant hijack diverted thousands of city visitors to the events they organized such as the Miccosukee Music Festival in 1980, which featured Cree rock heroine Buffy Sainte-Marie. In the midst of all this activity, Tiger Tiger recorded *Eye of the Tiger* and in the years that followed worked tirelessly to bring in much-needed income in those difficult, hungry years before gaming would come to dominate their economy. Their work was practical and immediately useful. They would use the profits from their music festivals to buy playground equipment and offer summer programs at the Miccosukee Tribal School.[72]

In 1974 Tiger Tiger recorded a song written by their father called "My Heart Is with Nature." According to Lee Tiger, it is a documentary put to music, a story "of his life growing up as a child born in 1920, watching all the changes of the earth, the problems of cultures colliding, and the differences between the Indian and non-Indian. He watched as Tamiami Trail was put through, and the Everglades became threatened by big developers that wanted to dry up the wetlands to make land deals."[73] The song begins with wind, some bells, a guitar playing with mild distortion. It is sung in repetitive relentless drone. Its observations are put in phrases like language instruction. We are put in the narrator's scene in the present, its tense a real-time description of the surround:

> Inside the stream I see fish dancing
> Look up I see the colors of nature
> I see as far as I can see
> At night the streams are running against the wind
> I see in water moon and stars are dancing
> With the stream
> I can see the trees blowing in the wind
> Dancing with the streams the moon and stars above

Winds against my face, whistles past my ears
At this time I realize I'm a part of nature

Look up it is gray I could not see colors
Of the trees
It seems as though I'm surrounded by gray
The fish that danced before me are hidden
By clouded water
Nature I once loved has been wounded
There are no more fish dancing in the streams
Brightness of the colors are no longer there
No longer is the moon stars and water clear
Once I learn that there was another life but I still love the life I once
    lived so I keep hanging on hanging on hanging on hanging on
    hanging on hanging on hanging on hanging on

Hanging on no less than eight times over, this collaboration between the brothers and their father documents resilience several ways and several generations over in one song space.

VI.

This mode of unconquered past within the present invites a coda to Montaner's spoil island. I began writing about him when he appeared to the news in 2004, and some sixteen years later I went back through the periodical chain to see if anyone knew what happened to him. Calls went unanswered, and without having access to a boat, I could only squint from the shore. Few knew who or what I was talking about. I turned back to see what else I could find in the extant paper trail following Montaner's eventual story. This time, and unbelievably for the first time, I turned to see what I could dig up in the Spanish-language press. In an article written by Helena Poleo for *El Nuevo Herald* on May 4, 2004, Montaner was now firmly known as Robinson Crusoe and had been evicted from the spoil island. We learned that a houseboat donated to him by the Children's Environmental Group of Coconut Grove was to become his new permanent home. During its repair, and with the helping hands of the Shake-A-Leg Foundation, Montaner had been staying aboard a donated sailboat on Kennedy Pier. For some, his was an aqueous homelessness: squatting on water, an eyesore in a new location. Homeless Services and Parks and Recreation officials were called in to proceed with his total eviction. As one official stated, "We could not let the situation continue. The fact is that it was on City property and we did not allow the homeless to sleep in the parks without our consent." As he was being evicted, Montaner complained of severe chest pains, so he was brought to Jackson Memorial Hospital. City officials were adamant about admitting Montaner to a homeless shelter, which he had refused because he did not want to be separated from his dog, Papo. Poleo quoted the founder of the Children's Environmental Group, a man named Guillermo García Rodilles, who stated on his behalf, "He's a man of the sea." The article abruptly ends with Montaner in critical condition in Jackson Memorial Hospital. Poleo concludes her piece with a statement by Rodilles, who promised that as soon as Montaner recovered, "I want him to come to my house so he won't be persecuted anymore."[74] Guillermo García Rodilles, Guillermo García Rodilles. The name kept washing out my ears, touching on some vague memory. I wondered if the name was misspelled and the man in question could be Guillermo García Rodiles, none other than the famous conga player for the band Chicago who had a special presence on Chicago VII, which of course is their most experimental album. Yes, it is all too much. Searching for Rodiles to affirm my hunch, I found his name in the white pages (how do we always find them in the white pages?). I called him up; I asked him about his music. I eventually asked him if he was the same Guillermo García in the story on Montaner: "Yep, that was me." And do you have any idea what happened to Montaner, I asked? "He's still there."[75]

Chapter Three

DRUMS TAKE TIME

....

To prime the percussive work in these pages, we will first hear the philosopher Sylvia Wynter describe a childhood experience in her grandparents' home in the Jamaican countryside. It was her special away place from Kingston. In a seated interview with David Scott, Wynter explains the following practice-based theory she learned from her grandmother:

> So if I went down to the country, with let us say, eight dresses, by the time I came back, I came back with two. My grandmother would have given the other six to the group of poorer children whom she had informally adopted. I remember we all slept together, stacked horizontally on a large four-poster bed. Even today, the memory of that gives me a sense of grounding in an existential sense of justice, not as grim retribution but as shared happiness.[1]

Note the mechanics of redistribution here, so established in Wynter's mind that they bolster her inventiveness in the interview format. The given-away dresses shorthand the grandmother's prophetic sense of measurement for her collective's various paths of future need. The dresses were not exactly taken but extended from young Sylvia, who then got the chance to become a part, to become learned, by an ongoing slumber party of measured survival. The four-poster bed, recalled to cramp and expand a sense of scale, precludes any stable position, and her grandmother's shrewd know-how makes it okay, indeed ordinary, for things to be taken away and given. This grandmother's playroom offers lessons for arrangement. It is a game with numbers that teaches the children of back then (and all us now) to make place with and for the other, and to make radiant, full togetherness while making do. It is not the brooding resentment of sacrifice.[2]

Wynter's detail of her grandmother's practice is a portal into musicianship. From the grandmother's vista—a point of view we'll want to always aspire to—the children allow for her to be in multiple places and times at once. They all bear a past and present that can be either recalled or imagined. And although she might know where they came from, she can't know where they are going. How did the grandmother take in what young Sylvia brought with her when she came to visit? How did she send her home with what she needed, nothing more or nothing less? What is made recognizable and repeated, different and idiosyncratic, between visits? Wynter is a link between her grandmother and her Kingston home and reports on the happening extensions of both. The children in the grandmother's surround, given and taken in, have legs and limbs that may or may not look like her own but nevertheless bear resemblance. Watching children grow—whether their development is underfoot or in the distance—is a way to take time. It is also a way of being in time that affirms all we can and can't be a part of. From the vantage point of a child, the four-poster bed presents the discomfort that sometimes comes with being taught, the skillful negotiations of sharing everything, and the required, subtle readjustment of hands and feet and elbows that happens even in sleep. It is being alone in the presence of everyone. It is collectively landing on the one led by a skilled another.

What might be richly educational and fun if we take all of this—the prescient sense of human needs, the negotiations of cramped space, the multiple times and measurements involved, and Wynter's grandmother's arrangement of it all—as a theory of polyrhythm? "Polyrhythm" is often made an abstract or lazy shorthand to denote multiple rhythms in shared time. When paired with the catch-all "complex," there is irresponsible dismissal of intensely trained and sophisticated decisions. All of the involved knowledges developed by Wynter's grandmother, and how she orchestrates them in and for love, stun for their intricate rigor. Opening up the flippant obscurism of "complex" to get at the real-time work of polyrhythmic performance, Kofi Agawu writes that "the plurality enshrined in polyrhythmic playing (or singing) is *a disciplined plurality*. Maintaining the integrity of one's part while at the same time ensuring the coordination of the ensemble as a whole is an impressive ability that has been cultivated over several generations. . . . The manifest many-in-oneness is invariably constrained by a central point of reference, one that is always felt but not necessarily sounded."[3] The dresses and the four-poster bed are both measures for disciplined plurality (established but not always sounded by the grandmother), and while there is a little room for errancy, there is no room for selfish dilettantism. Through all this we might begin to approach a sensibility and practice called island care, and its highly skilled faculty with time and reallocation.

How might this establishing theory of polyrhythm help us to take in music, and especially the drummers and drums of this chapter, as a permanent activation of company? How to experience music as a willing and banal redistribution of possessions, actual and immaterial? Performance can allow for a giving away and, after the giving, experiences of shared happiness. Wynter's grandmother helps us to live in a visionary sense of measure and to study rhythms as plans for the future needs of others. We learn that music might recognize our being *from* somewhere without knowing where we'll end up. And what's more, we might depend on music as that which watches us grow, whether we get to be with it live or recorded, underfoot or in the distance. Wynter's grandmother offers some theoretical (and technical!) tools that a listener can bring with her to understand time and then make it different, to hear the sophisticated procedures through which rhythms have been handed down, taken in, stretched, experimented with. What Wynter helps us to do is to open up our hearing of traditions to include that grandmother, and all the other formative figures (with or without musical instruments), who train the apprentice. We get to bring in all the genealogical forces that make music sound the way it does. Wynter's telling in the interview—her writing about performance as she performs—offers a model for description as a doing. The search for models of how to write about music is often frustrated by the presumed need for its explicit musical content. Wynter is one among a bountiful many who shows us that writing about music is everywhere, even those places where it seems that no notes are sounded. Musicians, especially those who have zero interest in critical silos, cue listeners to bring all content and everything they have to what they hear. This is their assignment to us.

To begin and then to extend a grandmotherly theory such as this with some reflective work on percussion is far from radical. The call to make communion between them is already in the demands of their traditions. It often goes unheard. The conventions of "music journalism" might find the circular+linear quality of the stories I tell as examples of playing something incorrectly, of including too many and not the right kind of details. Its outposts in magazines such as *Modern Drummer*, or in the larger scatterings of music reviews assembled under deadline, nevertheless provide an important service. They leave behind kernels the writer didn't or couldn't play with, usually because of lack of time and/or imagination. Their dismissals are abandoned playgrounds. The more musicologically inclined texts about drums and drumming in particular, those that give the charts and expect your fluency, again provide a really crucial service for scholars. The better versions show readers, in painstaking detail, the decisions and executions and material traditions of music making. But how do musicians invite other intuited philosophies about their practices?

This is the work being asked of the listener, the listener who does not expect music to merely *serve*, the listener who assumes effort as part of the experience. What is it that the nonspecialist, the unskilled, feels in a drummer's work, and what may they bring to it? For those who might have trouble locating the one on some chart, but easily grab and hold it with their body, there are other chances, other visions, of what it might mean to be in step with what drummers are doing. Critical literature on drummers is striking for its predominantly male-driven decisions of agreement and disagreement. But not always! María del Carmen Mestas, who wrote one of the most powerful and moving books on rumba, *Pasión de rumbero*, opens her study with a memory of her childhood in La Habana's Atarés neighborhood: "Caminaba dentro de la rumba, la percibía, pero no era capaz de distinguir de qué se trataba . . ." [I walked inside the rumba, I perceived it, but I was not able to distinguish what it was about . . .].[4] For the investigator, what might be important about that kind of entry, of choosing to walk inside something and being open to who and what interrupts that walk as a condition of its unending tutelage? No longer must we feel captive to the bemusement of the flaneur. Mestas's required-reading model encourages other preparations, intuitive fact-finding, and play with interviews when trying to get at how it is that drummers make things move. Extending her walking analytic to drumming opens up other and otherworldly theories of rhythm, of touching downs, and what its practices require.

So begins my walking inside music made by Dafnis Prieto, Obed Calvaire, and Yosvany Terry, three percussive artists, educators, and philosophers who make Florida room gatherings of polyrhythmic theory, history, and place. The steps I take to study their works are deliberate and cautious, as if finding my way through marsh, at once trying to feel how the ground will give or resist my capabilities. The social worlds they have made in their recordings, live performances, interviews, teachings, and compositions carry stunning connectivity. These musicians have crossed paths many times, having been in the same rooms and bands, and continue to follow similar itineraries. They have shared teachers and classrooms. They share a few other striking similarities: the combination of the aleatory and the grounded to describe their work, a deep specificity about their direct and indirect elders, and the happening upon chance but magical objects for their training. But they are also something all to themselves, and to think of them together means to also consider them apart. To not force them under the sign of cohort is to write about them in the spirit of Agawu's disciplined plurality. The biographical details I fold into these pages are an attempt to arrange their dynamic works and all the people they involve in a four-poster bed mode, so as to intimate some of the structural negotiations involved when writing about music.

II. The luminous drummer Dafnis Prieto often gestures toward his relationship to the book *Stick Control for the Snare Drummer*, a technical manual written to train hands and time published by Boston-born George Lawrence Stone in 1935. As a child in 1984 Santa Clara, Cuba, Prieto's early attachment to the book was nurtured by the fact of it being the only one around. It was a chance and opportune object. At ten years old, Prieto adjusted, or better put, *expanded* Stone's specific lessons for the snare to involve his entire drum set. This misuse was not prescribed by the author but nevertheless invented by a reader who did not know English. Prieto bypassed Stone's prefatory "hieroglyphics," moved straight to the notes, and began a lifelong training with exercises that would soak into bone and muscle.[5] Prieto's intimate familiarity with Stone's techniques gave him early and extended play with composition. Such discoveries were an "immense joy" for Prieto, and for his drumming they offered *"a structural awakening."*[6] This accumulation of forms, of another's rhythmic language, of other ways of moving and feeling time, gave Prieto foils with which he could play against Cuban rhythms such as the clave and cáscara. After a few years of his involvement with the text, Prieto discovered the first, skipped-over pages that tried to tell him what to do: "I am thankful for the lapse, which forced me to rely on intuition and imagination, making virtue of my ignorance about these specific instructions."[7]

What might be richly educational and fun about making virtue of one's ignorance about specific instructions? What is made possible by a lapse between an intuitive practice and a given directive? *Lapse*, from the Latin *lapsus*, meaning slip or fall, is a place of error where memory falters and rectitude crumbles.[8] Prieto reveals it as a thriving zone even and especially as it is based in blunder. Playing something wrong is not an impediment; it creates conditions for a flourishing.[9] So many texts end up in places they are not supposed to be, or in places that were not imagined as part of their intended audience, and they aren't always sent or received intact. For Prieto, the lapse established a way of being with the drums specifically, and living more generally.[10] It may be hard to imagine a ten-year-old child making practices so uniquely their own, but the brief lapse prompted by Stone's book was robust enough to stay with Prieto to the present day.[11] This lapse leaves behind a set of implicit and turbulent questions that involve music and place, text and instrument, and technique and time. While specific to Prieto, it is a playroom to imagine how a place, person, and chance object might converge to give shape to new forms.

Note in the above how Prieto offers theories about reading, formal adaptation, and accommodation of the surround. His thoughts on technique offer instructions for taking in the unfamiliar; they slow down the interval between being given an assignment and responding to it. As he offers these suggestive starting points for thinking and listening, Prieto also manages to tell a story: the recalled needs of childhood, the subject that plays within given constraints, and the imaginative thereafter of an early plot twist. The example of Prieto further expands those to whom we may turn as guides when approaching a book, a song, or a philosophical question, and not just those that make an available match of context or geography. To take in a musician's counsel such as the one Prieto offers here is to recognize both the learned practices that go into their work and the insightful possibilities they lend to our own, regardless of our place or instrument. Prieto's unique sense of how to make time anew teaches us how a found object and chance experience can offer opportunities for a structural awakening, and how they can provide—despite their intended use—foils to be written and read and listened against. The example of Stone's *Stick Control*, a text that happened to be there, expands how books can be picked up. They can be objects that we inadvertently misuse or bring our own readings to out of necessity.

Structural awakenings often occur without our knowledge; they are fostered in the element of surprise. In the first few weeks of the quarantine of 2020, Prieto posted a video on his Instagram account that extended his lifelong training in making beauty of scarcity (figure 3.1). The video was on offer for those who had nowhere to go and, beyond the confines, modeled the hope and desire to make time different. If there is no way to speed up or slow down a given condition, what then? Prieto made the video, on inspired whim, during his early-morning dog walk around his neighborhood in Hollywood, Florida.[12] The video was self-recorded from a bottom-up angle and frames Prieto's sunglassed face against a dawn sky. A mature

FIGURE 3.1 Dafnis Prieto under a flamboyant in Hollywood, Florida. Still from @dafnisprieto's Instagram video, posted March 30, 2020.

flamboyant (flame tree, *delonix regia*, native to Madagascar) makes a wild, meandering crown around his head as he stages his mobile lesson.[13] Prieto gives his followers a thirty-six-second master class in the impossible:

> Hello everyone, I just want to share this example from the book that just came out: *Rhythmic Synchronicity*. This is from the third level already. A little bit advanced. But I just want to share it with you. So this is a five in triplets, subdivided as 2/3, against the clave in 6/8. All right? 1–2–3–4. Chan chan chan chan chica can chican chan chan can can cachi cachi chan cachi chan cachi chan cach chan cachi cach chan chan.[14]

The video ends with Prieto's Buddha smile. As a teaser for his *Rhythmic Synchronicity*, the second of two self-published books, Prieto shows how its reading can be taken outdoors, practiced while out on a walk, and its ready expansion from the drums to other surfaces, bodies, and minds. It is a dream problem set for drummers, seasoned and nascent. For nondrummers, he refutes any sense of shame around technical limits. It is a lesson and salve for social isolation. While Prieto's numbers and the codes might be hieroglyphics, they still help to make something beyond being an exercise we are not ready for. Prieto encourages his public to begin from the place of "a little bit advanced"; they can drop themselves right in. This is an invitation to begin from the rim and settle there; it is not a demand to sink or swim. What might be okay about not necessarily knowing what a "five in triplets, subdivided as 2/3, against the clave in 6/8" is? There is a recognition that whatever it is, however a few sets of passing seconds are divided up—and how it is all supposed to work *against the clave*, the innate intuited pulse of Cuban music—it is really hard. Instead of simply abandoning this performance to the experts, find another way in, unearth a practice. Try and transcribe the sounds that Prieto makes with his voice, and one thing is made immediately clear: there are years of monastic dedication involved when trying to mark these passing seconds. Drummed play with time is still measured.

And if that sounded like an imposed platitude, figure 3.2 shows the exercise as it is written in Prieto's book: "One way I like to picture this exercise is by using 'dots and lines' as symbols for the numbers.... I've found that arranging the patterns this way (in four consecutive columns) helps me visualize the organization of these patterns and feel the intricate rhythmic interaction more easily." Here we get to witness the making of yet another system, one that works as interchangeable notation with the daylight walk under the flamboyant. Through the upper-line clave and its submarine subindented Morse code, it is clear that there is an intensely organized structure to both systems. Together they form polysemous notation. Visualizing in order to feel, whether through dots and lines and/or walking dogs at dawn, Prieto encourages a using of everything, every possible tool to be in another time while grounded in a given one.

A key phrase that emerges and repeats throughout Prieto's texts, personal conversations, and interviews is levitation or levitación or levitado. It is an aesthetic quality and an aspirational experience that he builds into his compositions and practice. Levitation is not exactly an ascent, but a floating above. There is a supernatural quality to it. It is a word used to name the in-between of life and death, as when the spirit hovers over the body to decide its next move. It can describe the lift of an overly somber mood. Levitate finds further etymological company in pain reduction and bread making. These just-above, otherworldly, medicinal, and fermenting qualities are sensed in both examples, with the deliberate movement into the flamboyant treetops and the clave that hovers. Prieto told me that when he was little, he dreamed constantly about flying. He recounts the persistent repetitiveness of the dream as one of ordinary planar transition: "I was walking and would just jump into the air and start flying on top of the city . . . that feeling is still inside of me."[15] To be in and slightly above Santa

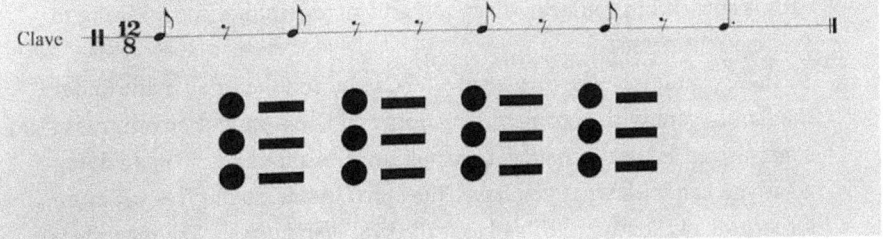

FIGURE 3.2 Dafnis Prieto, "Exercise example 164," in *Rhythmic Synchronicity* (Dafnison Music, 2020), 47.

Clara, Cuba, is a quality that Prieto has palpably taken to other lived and living locations, both geographic and musical.

Back to the Instagram post and Prieto's tender query: "All right?" The question is itself a lapse between instruction and performance, a check-in that expects both slippage and faulty memory. It gives the listener a rest to let the direction settle while also tending a cue to begin play. It asks: Are you ready for what is required? It also asks: Are you okay to continue? Whatever your answer, Prieto will continue for us, and his drum-sung chan chica ca-chis can be things to follow, copy, rearrange, or transpose to a wider set of instruments. Many of us will never get there, but that is not to say we can't go there. In place of the frustration felt from not being able to do what Prieto does, there is an opportunity for wonder: there are people in the world who can do a kind of work in and with time, and they give us a chance to be there with them. As Agawu beautifully puts it, "The time of music is its own time. Musical time is not—or not necessarily—a microcosm of ordinary time; it is not a domestication or translation of some other temporal realm."[16] This time apart is a place that musicians give us even if we might not have the technical lexicon to describe how they do it. As this video suggests, even during times of pandemic, Dafnis Prieto wants to show us how he does it.[17] His pedagogical style suggests that there is propriety involved in order to play. His is a kind of porous classroom that includes and extends out from the seminars he offers at the University of Miami, the workshops on display in the seven stunning albums he has made as leader, the more than fifty others that he's lent his work to as a player, the repurposed winnings of his MacArthur "genius grant," and the innumerable live shows he's played at all over the world. In his bios and interviews, Prieto refers to himself as a drummer/composer/educator, in that order. The fullness with which he oxygenates each is something you hear, discretely and all together, while listening to Prieto on the drums.

These examples—the misuse of *Stick Control* and the video made under the flamboyant with accompanying dots and lines—might be otherwise summarized as the disciplined misapplication of a found form *and* a doing what you can with what you have. The spirit inside them gives yet more structural awakening to this place called *The Florida Room*. The meandering quality and geographic specificity of both stories, in form and content, and the open, ample accommodation for what and who and where are all already here. They are not precisely locatable but fully involve Cuba, West Africa, Florida, and even Boston. When closely engaging musicians, there are many chances to recognize the gems, both bright and rough, that are tucked into their biographies. In addition to this recognition, however, there is something else happening and that *happens* in music all the time. Studious involvement with a musician's work can magically color everything else. It can touch dream organization, word choice, and the shape of sentences, even alter the sound of your internal reading voice. Their noise beautifully and thankfully dulls your own. It can turn you to archival places you normally wouldn't visit. This is not something we can immediately "get" by fact of our enjoyment of music. Possession has no place here. Nor can it be explained by some overidentification or even disidentification with some musician or music, but by something that sidesteps identification altogether. What I'm after in this musical study is to reveal the generous transfer of skill to the unskilled, from the musician to the listener, and all the people and places they bring with them; and a mode of reception, by that listener, who not only wants but also *needs* music as a place to live.

The best drumming tells us that there is room for everything in a definite structure. For what it holds, for what it does for the rest, for giving the water and making the waves, drumming is a hard-earned and miracle-making practice. Prieto's drumming occurs as a problem solving in real time, though not the kind that calls for a fix and resolution. Rather, it is the met challenge of transitions that link seconds, those great puzzles and points in time that ask for involvement and, eventually, a shape. In his transitionary practice, making all time an in-between, Prieto will throw a baroque webbing into the air while also allowing for something or someone else to adjust its provisional scaffolding. And if and when you get to see it unfold in the live, it is mystical and devastating. The marrow of the sacred. Watch Prieto, and you may see a many-armed Durga, and you may feel as if you are standing in a hurricane, on the edge of the eye's sun and blue and its most furious gray. Armando Suárez-Cobián once turned to me midshow to say: "es una locomotora." He is a locomotive. And he was right, if we can imagine a locomotive also moving in spiral. The circular and the linear, together. This sense of charge or charging is made by Prieto's possession, a resourcefulness that can only happen from practicing so much and so hard that it hurts. And only then can it try and heal. That certain show, performed in La Habana's La Fábrica de Arte Cubano in January of 2019, was Prieto's first performance as leader, with him playing his own music, on the island in more than twenty years.

The larger, longer drama of return often overdetermines the movements of Cubans when they come home to the island, even for those who spent most of their lives outside. For his concert at La Fábrica, Prieto did a preshow interview with the radio personality Juanito Camacho who made much about the firstness of Prieto's performance. Prieto was quick and careful to respond that he comes to the island all the time but that his trips there have been more about rest and seeing family rather than for professional work. To turn La Habana into a place of rest—rest, in a musical sense, a necessary pause, not the rest of leisure—that involves catching up with home was a lapse he built into the performance, one that importantly delineated what he was willing to do and give that night. Prieto's response slayed any sense of opportunism that many make out of such a voyage, disordered its easy marketability, and refused the prodigal narrative. Prieto's navigation of the desire for the drama of his return was embedded in his set that evening. He remained firmly in the spirit of "a little bit advanced" that is his oeuvre. The song that prompted Suárez-Cobián's locomotor description was from Prieto's 2015 *Triangles and Circles* album, a track called "Blah Blah." More shapes, more hieroglyphics. The recorded version of the song asks, over and over, "All right?" It then gives you an intermittent series of bust-a-move parts to release all that pent-up rightness and readiness. In the live version that night, and with his sextet, Prieto said: I will give you this and nothing more. But the giving was *full*, and it was complete, ending once and for all the uncertainty around whether withholding is a form of giving. That night Prieto gave us what we needed before we knew we needed it, and the correct dosage too. He also additionally gave what we might not have been able to bear. He was maniacal, dexterous, hilarious, subtle, a surge. With music the writer has to deserve the use of adjectives and metaphors, but with Prieto there's no way to not use them because they are true, and they are asked for in abundance. This is one of the ways Prieto gives the unskilled a practice. His facilitation of, but pressure on, any writerly protocol inspires you to play it wrong with curiosity and discipline.

Saleem Reshamwala (KidEthnic) made a short documentary of Prieto's return and performance at La Fábrica and the premiere of his big band at Teatro La Mella. Titled "Regresar: Back to Cuba" (2019), the short selects a set of encounters to show Prieto while on the road, in rehearsal, in concert. In a required viewing moment the camera follows Prieto as he visits his high school alma mater, the renowned La ENA (National Art Schools), which he attended from 1989 to 1993. Overwhelmed by his younger selves and his return to the school after almost thirty years, he said, "I almost started crying." In a master class to the teenage artists, Prieto stated:

> I don't actually think about genres when I do music. I'm not interested in all that. I'm not interested. Or rather, I accept the quality of genre, but as a creative musician I'm not interested. Genres were created by human beings like you and me, eh? They don't grow on trees, genres. They are neither avocados nor mangos. They were created by people like you and me. What interests me is the music that I hear in my ears and that I feel. I don't think in genre.[18]

Note the nod to structure (acceptance) and the quick step away from it (noninterest). Also note the flora, the banal hanging fruit, that he mentions as an everyday undoing of the imposition of Wordsworth's daffodils.[19] By insisting on genre's human component, Prieto denaturalizes it and exposes it as a decision that holds an ongoing set of agreements and disagreements. He accepts "the quality of genre" but is not interested in being faithful to any of its (falsely) perceived limitations that can and do produce real-world constraint (and usually not the good kind) on the musician. As a suggestive bonus, he also rejects the identitarian matchup between genre and person, whether imposed from within or without, that especially falls upon musicians from island elsewheres. To the students, Prieto offers the potential of what is possible in music when you are not interested in entering genre's argument in the first place, to instead move toward the lapse. How Prieto's loosening of genre, and giving the permission to not be beholden to it, will rebel-root in the future practices of these young conservatory musicians is impossible to know. Perhaps it is just the affirmation they needed to hear that willful experimentation is a healthy part of music, or maybe it created some relief, or suspicion, or a mix of both. It is all seedlings for later fight and flight. Prieto's counsel has dubbed effect, at once offering advice to young artists and, in the additional context of the documentary being taken of him, loosening the stultifying grip of the genre of Cuban return narratives. Prieto talks about this particular trip with partial astonishment about the press and the big deal made of his trip but always redirects the topic to the music, what it took and what it takes.[20] This is sensible in the documentary through which he accepts its momentousness, but it also makes the viewer and listener return to the everyday rehearsal it required. Prieto's dexterity across the media and his expansion of given exercises reveal how his axiom to "not think in genre" threads across his practices.

To return to Wynter's Jamaican countryside aesthetic philosophy while listening to a drummer such as Dafnis Prieto is not to impose or flatten the experience of her grandmother with another's. And yet, there is a bountiful linkage to Prieto's family origins in the Escambray Mountains, his upbringing outside of capital, and outside the capital of La Habana. There is also the undertheorized gem that Wynter was actually born in Cuba.[21] It may have the effect of learning more about the peopling of rhythm, those figures and methods that drummers may learn from, that again, might not be formal music teachers. To reconnect back to Prieto's misuse of Stone's exercises for snare, I ignore any prescriptive hieroglyphics and expand Wynter's biographic detail as performance theory. I would like to keep Wynter and her grandmother—and their coterminous practice-based theory—along for a hearing of Prieto's song "Thoughts." Recorded with his Si O Si Quartet (Yes or Yes!) at the Jazz Standard in New York in 2009, the song features Prieto on drums, Peter Apfelbaum on tenor and alto saxophone, Manuel Valera on piano, and Charles Flores on bass. Like other Prieto compositions, it begins with the drums, not so much in the way we're used to hearing them prepare the group for playing, but to institute the melodic figure for the song. The wading in is gentle; it is not the thrusty drumsticked "1–2–3–4" of rock preparation. In "Thoughts" the figure set up for the song's and the after-song's ongoing repetition is a tapping that is somewhere between toddling and faltering, stepping away and homecoming, respiration and arrhythmia. The taps are made with soft mallets, and sound as if they were made by what my daughter Manuela once called touch buds to mean fingertips. As much as Prieto's touch buds establish a language from the outset of "Thoughts," a language that somehow feels as if it is already inside the listener, there is a kind of melancholy throughout the piece as Prieto becomes hard to locate. At once profoundly present and ephemeral, the listener is constantly brought home with the orienting thrummed figure, but that constant return asks that you find your way, without him, through mist. The rest of the quartet plays another melodic line above his thrum; "it is levitating on top of the sequence,"

FIGURE 3.3 Dafnis Prieto in his home studio, July 2019. Photo courtesy of the author.

as Prieto put it. These lines form two different but noncontradictory times in this singular song.[22] "It is kind of a rubato," Prieto said of their playing in a different time from his figure. It is a theft or a sequestering or a safekeeping of another space inside the composition, away from him, away from us. Prieto's "disciplined plurality" happens within his singular body while at the same time making it work together with the ensemble. "Thoughts" is a teacherly song, yet it feels older than Prieto for its aspirational sound as if walking in the too-big shoes of Wynter's grandmother.

After many years of studying Prieto's music both recorded and in the live, I had the beautiful opportunity of interviewing him at his home in July of 2019 and to see the studio, his Florida komponierhauschen, where he creates, records, prepares classes, and distributes his rebel ecology of records, books, and online instructional videos (figure 3.3). The counterpoint of his domestic studio to the (mostly) New York venues I have seen him play in felt like the repeated figure heard but all grown up in "Thoughts." During the conversation's wind-down, Prieto invited me to share a Cuban coffee on his screened-in patio. In the sliding-door threshold between house and patio, Prieto slipped on his chancletas for the transition from smooth

FIGURE 3.4 Photo of Obed Calvaire at Jazz Club Moods in Zürich, November 21, 2017. Photo by Urs Leuenberger.

to pebbled tile. The flip-flop transition is a gesture so ordinary, but for this displaced daughter of the south who lives in the north, it evoked such immense tenderness for its identifiably Cuban and Floridian propriety. This slipping on is part of the everyday marking out of another time and space that weather almost always permits. With the café and with the chancletas, Prieto deployed two elegant cues in the cultural repertoire to hasten the interview's denouement and to generously extend yet another space for his company. I read this subtle alterity as a late-afternoon ethos for *The Florida Room*: make a subtle move to the patio and bring all you have to entertaining so that the transition from one place and person to the next, from one social setting to another, may be as smooth as slipping into flip-flops and asking how many sugars.

The Miami-born and -raised drummer Obed Calvaire saw Dafnis Prieto play live for the first time at the Jazz Gallery in 2002, when he was playing with a group led by Yosvany Terry (figure 3.4).[23] These were weekly performances under the heading "Jazz Cubano," a historic series curated by Terry between 2002 and 2003 that is often regarded as a vital and primary artery for the introduction of contemporary Cuban and Latin jazz musicians to *and* reactivation of Cuban jazz in New

York City.²⁴ As he watched and listened to Prieto, Calvaire recalled: "It just sounded like three different drummers at once. I was like: *What is going on? What is happening?* After the hundredth time he saw my face, I had the courage to ask, 'Mr. Prieto, I'd love to take a lesson with you.' And he was kind enough to come all the way up to Manhattan School of Music and give me a free lesson . . . And *just the other day*, I pulled out that lesson."²⁵

For many, pulling out a dusty syllabus or some assignment two decades after the fact is usually a nostalgic exercise involving some recollected fondness about a former teacher. But in Calvaire's case, the lesson was something he returns to for learning anew. What was the lesson? Calvaire responded, "How to improvise or comp over cáscara or clave. . . . How to do certain things without affecting the groove. He gave me a few tools that I will use the rest of my life."²⁶ This cumulative instance of structural awakening in Calvaire has a durational quality: it was tended in live performance, adapted to a freely given lesson, and transformed into a take-home assignment (an instructional book!) that kept giving more than two decades later. The lesson given to Calvaire, the then up-and-coming drummer just seven years younger than Prieto, is one of the striking but not at all surprising coincidences that overlap in *The Florida Room*. Not only for the fact of their actual crossing but also for the ways a pedagogical text rustles up crossings between other times and places. In this case, it is Prieto's own lessons for stick control that have given Calvaire other rhythmic languages to bring into conversation with his own.

I wasn't sure how to make a transition between Prieto and Calvaire until I remembered that experience on Prieto's patio, a lesson that said: just invite movement between their work for the larger project of social living. When Calvaire surprised me with this casually mentioned anecdote, it produced the thunderbolt that affirms the hunch of one's assembly. A casual pickup of these pages might hope to find some corrective work on Cuban/Haitian relations, which have been especially fraught in Miami, or comparative work between two worlds that often aren't put into comparison, especially in the diaspora, even if music has been made and happening between them for ages. With this actual storied link between the drummers, and their Floridian, Cuban, Haitian, and New York rhythmic and geographic connectivities, the surprising inevitable that drew me to them *together* was something of the discipline of their drumming while managing to keep room open for play. Strict and roomy. As is already perceptible but soon to be verifiable, both drummers are also deeply entranced by flight and are firmly united in and by the sensation of joy. Aleatory and blissful. These are shared aesthetics that get at something inside but also press beyond their specific Miami/Haiti/Cuba/New York contexts. It is my hope that their biographies and works and, most of all, *styles* may offer another place in scholarship—which would usually hesitate to connect them or, worse, force some cross-cultural "encounter"—in place of staid arguments about geopolitics. And although their work is very different (you might say that Prieto's style is slightly more Vulcan than Calvaire's), their studiousness, and the places and people that aided the studiousness, are a blessed and bountiful hinge. Calvaire is also a musician I have been listening to and seeing live for many years, and the quarantine's grounding of musicians pushed me to finally reach out to interview him.[27] As we recall well, no one could be in session or out on the road. On a sunny Wednesday afternoon, Calvaire did not sit *for* but *gave* the interview over the phone while standing, bouncing, and beautifully fussing with his four-month-old son, Cazzian, who was bound to his body in a BabyBjörn, facing outward "so he can see everything." Even in the juggle happening within and withon his own body, Calvaire good-humoredly prefaced the interview by saying: "One thing we do have now is time."

Calvaire, now one of the most innovative and in-demand drummers, was born in Miami's Jackson Memorial Hospital on December 12, 1981. His arrival came soon after his parents left Port-au-Prince.[28] Although his parents are foremost on his mind when he talks about music, Calvaire's sense of them before they were his parents is a bit of an enigma because, as he put it, "Haitian families barely speak about their pasts." His mom, Gerda Meley Calvaire, was born in Port-au-Prince, with matrilineal roots in Baradé, a coastal town known as Haiti's Venice because of the canal artery that runs through it and for its strong Rara traditions.[29] His mother has long worked as a nurse, first at Hialeah Hospital for thirteen years, and for the last seventeen years and counting at Jackson Memorial. When Calvaire briefly mentioned her recovery after her possible coronavirus infection, he waved away sympathy and said simply: "My mom is tough." His father, Fritz Calvaire, though born in Aux Cayes, was orphaned and informally adopted by family friends in Port-au-Prince when he was eight years old.[30] Obed's parents met at a church there and remain devoted Christians. His father is a merchant by trade and a well-known gospel singer who was called by music when he heard the band La Petite Trompette play in church.[31] Fritz Calvaire's practice was very much inspired and influenced by the Cap-Haïtien singer Roger Colas, one of Haiti's legendary and much-beloved vocalists.[32] There is a rare but still findable CD of Fritz Calvaire, a gathering of his greatest hits, and the technical influence of Colas is palpable: he carries a similar flutter around his vocal edges. Listening to the elder Calvaire reveals a tight musicianship, but this is not the rote carrying out of hymns. Just under the surface is a very controlled play with genre that puts his music firmly on the swinging side of Caribbean gospel. Stylistically, it bears a strong resemblance to La Canzone Napoletana in structure, chosen decor, and, most of all, for the ways it fills the air on Sundays.[33] In addition to being a treasured and well-known performer, Calvaire has been a vital programming conduit for the gathering and augmentation of the Haitian and Caribbean gospel music scene in and around Miami.[34] Much of Calvaire family life revolved around the Hillside Church of God, a cornerstone place of worship and community in Miami's Little Haiti. As a living extension of the church, Obed Calvaire's home was brimming with gospel music. Brass-heavy bands such as Symphonie Angelique were played constantly, and secular music was discouraged. The sounds accompanied and soothed the family when they first lived in friends' efficiencies around Little Haiti until they later managed to save up enough money to buy a home of their own. The efficiency—another form of Florida room—remains and has always been an important, generative site in Floridian aesthetics.

Attending his father's rehearsals was an ordinary part of Calvaire's life from as far back as he can remember. When he was three years old, a close family friend (and honorary godfather) named Peter Honorat noticed that little Obed went straight for the sticks and started "messing around" on the drums. One of the most astonishing and consistent plot twists found in so many musician biographies is the presence of that one person, whether family or a neighbor or friend, whose early observations would firmly declare the child's future in music. The prophetic outsider who pays close attention to the playful musical experimentation of a child can be considered among their first teachers. Although Calvaire does not have any memory of this or the few years just after this, he does remember in crystalline detail his call to music and when he learned he would do nothing else. Sitting on his family's couch when he was about ten years old, Calvaire was listening to something (he can't remember what) and vividly recalls that he started banging along on the cushions. It was at this precise moment Calvaire "just had this emotion of joy, there was just *so much joy* . . . this is something I have to do." The sofa cushions continued to work as his first drum kit, and he would practice on them for hours. He would drive his mother crazy for his percussive use of all surfaces and all objects as vessels, from her pots and pans to collectible pottery. He would even take to the air and beat out phrases on oxygen. A story that seems designed for *The Florida Room* is when Calvaire recalled practicing on the sofa and just there, on one of the armrests (his ride symbol), was one of his mother's prized framed pictures. The picture was of a beach scene that offered an optional switch for strategic backlighting. As Calvaire recalled, "It was one of those picture frames of a beach, but when you lit it up, the lighting made it seem like the water was waving. It had *waves*." After he knocked over and broke this cherished decor, he found trouble like no other.

Young Calvaire would watch his father and band from the church sidelines and constantly beg the drummer to let him play at every opportunity he could. He eventually began backing his father and became a permanent fixture in Hillside's musical lineup. Of his father, Calvaire says with reverent tone: "I would not be the musician I am today if it were not for my dad. He instilled a level of perfection . . . there was zero room for error. Zero." A prime example of this is when young Obed was about twelve years old and decided to test out a drum lick that he had heard and coveted in a 1997 popular gospel album that Kirk Franklin made with God's Property. Just after dropping the lick in the midst of praise and worship, Calvaire quickly realized: "What a mistake!" His father immediately stopped everything and kicked him off the drums. The punishment was perhaps less about disciplining his son's desire to be an adventurous drummer and more to do with trying to school a potentially selfish tendency of playing something that didn't belong. Young Calvaire was forced to walk away in front of a congregation of almost a thousand people to make way for the next drummer. As Calvaire recounted this story to me with humor and tenderness, baby Cazzian's singsong picked up in tone and volume as if to emphasize the drama (and catechismal function) of the story. At the time of this happening, Calvaire had been attending Thomas Jefferson Middle School under the tutelage of Melton Mustafa Jr., who was/is the school's director of the jazz band and wind ensemble. Mustafa is the son of Melton Mustafa Sr., who was one of the great trumpet players to play with Count Basie and a beloved teacher and architect of the famous bountiful musical worlds of FAMU (Florida Agricultural and Mechanical University). All right?

Melton Mustafa Jr. strongly encouraged Calvaire to audition for Miami's New World School of the Arts, the public performing-arts high school that pulls children across the city into a tidal pool of inter-American aesthetic experimentation. There are few connections that can be made between children in Havana and Miami (especially in the 1980s and 1990s); however, there is a link that can be made between Prieto's and Calvaire's high schools because both are public conservatory environments that emphasize academic as well as artistic training. Both continue to be playrooms for misfit kids. In their best versions, both ENA and New World students are recruited (with very demanding audition processes) and accepted from different neighborhoods and backgrounds. New World sent an assembly to Calvaire's middle school, without which he would not have known that it existed. Upon gaining acceptance into the school, Calvaire was overjoyed. When he arrived at the campus in downtown Miami, Calvaire said, "I remember walking into New World, and it was so healthy and warm. . . . I can't find any more amazing adjectives to use to describe the feeling when you got there."[35] The bountiful high school learning lab for Calvaire was not only pivotal in terms of his musical and academic training but also for the expansiveness of its social worlds. For Calvaire, this meant being exposed to secular music he was unfamiliar with. When he was a freshman, his classmate E. J. Strickland (also a very important drummer in New York City) would make him compilations of artists such as John Coltrane, Miles Davis, Jeff "Tain" Watts, and "a pile of different records he put into one tape for me." This compression of unfamiliar artists in a singular object was hugely instructive for Calvaire, who at this point was mostly fluent in the rhythms familiar to gospel music. Along with this incredible introduction by Strickland to the jazz cadence, Calvaire also reflects fondly on other extracurricular musical learning that happened to and from his commute to New World. For example, Calvaire would listen exclusively to the Spanish-language station Sol 95 because there were "just so many different kinds of rhythms." These emphatically pronounced details of Calvaire's autobiography strongly challenge the segregated narratives of influence that persist not only in Miami history but greater musical history as well. This movement across influences accentuates Prieto's not "thinking in genre" as a not being in genre.

As a high school student, Calvaire would gig with local South Florida musical luminaries such as Ruby Baker and would play countless weddings, bat mitzvahs, corporate events, and well-known clubs such as O'Hara's, and others around Palm Beach and Jupiter. Calvaire worked with other South Florida R&B top 40 bands such as Instant Attraction and eventually toured with Melton Mustafa Jr. These lucrative gigs made a huge difference in Calvaire's life, especially as they enabled him to earn a living. However, the late nights presented particular challenges while he was in high school. Although he would always arrive to school on time even after playing gigs that lasted until 1 a.m., he would fall asleep the minute he sat down in his first-period classroom. After his mom restricted his gigging to the weekends, Calvaire would also continue to play for his and other churches around South Florida. I pause here to honor all of this professional activity in the life of a fifteen-year-old. Of his work in churches, Calvaire would find ways "here and there" to play within the structure of the music he was given but would otherwise stay in line with what was expected: "It was what the music required." This flexible set of practices learned at home and school and refined on Floridian roads instituted the efficient but stylistically adventurous spirit that Calvaire is known for. Far from seeing these early constraints as hindrances, Calvaire found in them vitalizing places for erudition: "I was always put in a situation where certain times you would be able to do certain things and certain times not. . . . Playing for top 40 bands was an amazing lesson because half of the time there's people dancing. So in order to keep Grandma tapping her feet, you need to keep a certain groove."[36] Note the instant reach to the grandmotherly example here. Of all the faces in the crowds Calvaire could have made present in the anecdote, it was not only a grandma, but what's more, a grandma who needed to be kept happy in that unique way of dance opportunity. Generic flexibility is also a generational one, and here Calvaire presents us with another reimagining of Wynter's grandmother's theory. How does the younger create and make polyrhythm with and for the elder? How does her body want and need to move, especially in a world that expects its stationary decay? When considering the myriad demographics involved in the gigs he played, how did these grandmothers nevertheless bear resemblance even as they were born worlds apart? There is beautiful propriety in all this. A deep consideration of others, especially elders, that says: this is not about me. It is a golden rule mode of playing that shares happiness. On his cue, his version of a patio invitation, it is also what turns these pages to deep consideration of Calvaire's immediate elders.

If his performance at the Zadymka (Lotos) Festival in 2017 is any indication, Calvaire can even keep grandma, and anyone else really, tapping their feet from the mountains of wintery Poland. At the festival, Clavaire played in a trio with British-born double bassist and Miles Davis alum Dave Holland and Chicago–South Carolina and Red Rodney alum, the tenor saxophonist Chris Potter. I invite you to their performance of the song "Good Hope," a song that later made it onto the album *Good Hope*, featuring Holland, Potter, and Zakir Hussain, who made the rhythm with the tabla in 2019.[37] In the live version with Calvaire in the trio, Potter's composition is swung along by Calvaire, and while he appears as a singular drummer, he resounds in three different temporal registers. He sounds ahead of, side by side with, and behind the others all at once; it is a kind of turn taking in tandem. His playing leaves a dual-sided wake that gives the song and its two other participants constant befores and afters to play in. We hear Calvaire use his stunning agility to maintain lines that feel straightforward but then give over to some perfectly angled-in samba toques. When a furrow is opened for Calvaire's solo, we don't hear him take it outright; we hear him wade out of the main song while holding on to and extending his attachment to it. He begins his solo with figures that recall both Holland's and Potter's. It is not an act of imitation but a transposition of them into another language. At a certain point that you can and can't feel coming, Calvaire brings in a submerged idiom all his that bursts through their surface, introduces other places and other times, and is "a little bit advanced." The audience tries but can't pull off that clumsy out-of-time clap-along that happens especially in concerts featuring drummers of color. Calvaire only barely withholds that from them before opening the shore for Potter and Holland to reenter. It is a generous and spacious portal for return. Holland extends an impressed smile. You want and need to get up from your chair but don't. Your feet are surely tapping, but you stay put until the song is done.

There are a few extant mini-documentaries to be found on Calvaire—for example, shorts of a few minutes in length that promote the work of the SF Jazz Collective (of which he is a member) or as featured on stick-supplier Vic Firth's YouTube channel.[38] The philosophical pearls he lends to them are like adjacent versions of Prieto's books and Instagram posts. In these documentaries and in the interviews I've conducted with him, Calvaire always begins with his birthplace of "Miami, Florida" said in the traditional way, reminding all who hear him of the city's important past and present. This is one played style of where he is from; it is his version of some documentary not yet made called *Retounen*. Along with his mere pronouncement of his natal city, there are other kinds of subtle documentary practices that Calvaire makes across his repertoire. His solo up there in mountainous Poland is one compressed but full-length autobiographic document. To walk inside of it is to take in microclimates and larger weather patterns, from the ancestral Baradé to the efficiency in Little Haiti to the West Village, to a prime-time stage at the Zadymka Festival. The solo-as-autobiography is partial and full, temporary and staying. It is not some direct expression that marks all the places he's from or has been, nor does it permit an arrogant listener's attempt to chart everyone and everywhere in the solo's danceable strangeness. It is all his and all him. "I was in the zone," he said.[39] It is a solo of one, but he is far from alone. For residents both fleeting and permanent of Florida rooms everywhere, there is something about this adored native son's movement in place and sound that is also made ours. Calvaire's shared movements resound intense pride *because* of the local—that is, how quick we are to say of his accomplishment: he's from Miami. Calvaire's work, his audible walk with everyone and everywhere he has been, and *his extensions of the local* say that he and we are all from the places implied by "Miami" too. By this vital encouragement, "He's from Miami" means Miami is from Port-au-Prince. None of these places are stable, especially when set to drums. For Calvaire, being from a place can also be measured as a sense of time. As an example, his joy in playing with the SF Jazz Collective is partly because all of the musicians know the one or know how to be in the one. As Calvaire admiringly states, "Everyone is going to be 'there,' and so I have nothing to worry about in terms of being able to express myself."[40]

When I asked if there is a Miaminess to his playing, if there is a Miami feel to it, Calvaire responds, "I'm sure I would be a different drummer if I lived in Dallas." This of-course response is an argument that there is no way not to sound or not to bear sound from where one is from. But for Calvaire there is a specificity to it; there is a choice to be and bear where one is from. Where he is from is a place of the many:

> It's not just about Miami; there are a lot of different drummers from Miami that stick to one thing. I would say my past from Haiti, and then my falling into this deep, deep love with Afro-Cuban music when I was really, really young allowed me to understand that language musically speaking. And also playing in gospel and funk bands. I got a taste of so many different styles of music, but playing it with people who grew up playing that music their whole lives. *So it's almost like I lived in four different countries, and was born in four different countries, and was able to speak those languages too.*[41]

I didn't want to ask him to clarify which countries because I knew what he meant, but I also didn't want to know exactly where he meant. To be open to more than one thing and, more importantly, to incorporate it and try it out against all fear of consequence—whether it is the tantalizing lick in Kirk Franklin, the cowbell comedic bit in "Good Hope," the saplings of *Stick Control for Snare*, or Sylvia Wynter's performance theory—is all rooted in what I have elsewhere called a Miami interdisciplinarity.[42] Calvaire's refinement of the practice in his statement and in his actual playing shows the discipline and willingness to fail that's required of it. Because it was not about just deciding to play different styles, but learning it alongside those for whom they were first languages. These early experiences in deep apprenticeship with other senses of sound and time offered a unique fluency. Calvaire's wonderful and inexorable quadrilingual immersion program based outside of all the master's languages, forged in love and insurgency, is felt throughout his oeuvre. Listening in to his work on Yosvany Terry's 2012 *Today's Opinion*, Calvaire's playing makes the local and the everywhere converge. He drums alongside Pedrito Martínez (born 1973), who is one of the world's most important sources of knowledge in Cuban rhythmic lexicons, both sacred and secular. Of working with Pedrito, Calvaire said, "It's so easy in the sense that his language is so deep, there's so much depth to what he's doing, playing along with him is basically staying out of the way. . . . I just keep my ears open, and I'm pretty much coloring in what he's already doing."[43]

Staying out of the way is not self-effacing; it is a confident steadying of the whole. It is often "what the music requires," making something other than the egoistic self the guide. It is a sometimes-spiritual recourse. And when you hear Calvaire play with this ethos on the first track of Terry's *Today's Opinion*'s "Summer Relief," you get to live in the song's radiant halo for almost nine minutes. This song brings us relief in all senses of the word as an object, deliverance, alleviation, a giving up and over. It begins with an Abakuá invocation—the Abakuá being all-male mutual-aid societies with roots in the Cross River region in southeastern Nigeria that helped to make Cuba's anticolonial swing around the early nineteenth century. In addition to Calvaire and Martínez, Terry assembled some more of the Cuban greats such as pianist (and frequent Prieto collaborator) Osmany Paredes and bassist Yunior Terry. Added to this collective is another player who offers more Miamian contours to the sound: the Cuban-Ecuadorian trumpet player (and New World alum) Mike Rodriguez. Calvaire and Rodriguez's performances first enact a matter of policy: everything they do explains why we need arts education funding in our public schools. And then there's all the other stuff they do: Rodriguez's trumpet and Calvaire's back line are sinews that are pleasurable and difficult to attach to in this unsettled but still moving structure. The trumpet's unexpected and unsettling trill elevates the instrument and you to some kind of elsewhere. But his playing hurts too. Because of the pitches it dares to move into, it treads in a place in the scale that you didn't think possible, and for that reason feels hard. Perhaps part of its difficulty is that it marks the search for some way to blow something out. Calvaire's drums add something else, a Little Haiti and Melton Mustafa something else to the Cuban majority, in a way that is both set in and apart from it. It is all very beautiful. In the penultimate section of the song, it is Calvaire's drums that transition everywhere and everyone into relief from the preceding incredible tensions of the song. He holds tightly and throws into relief the four different countries involved in him and in the performance.

Though he isn't explicit about it, Calvaire's deep love for Afro-Cuban music may have been nurtured as early as the Cuban-influenced brass sections played on records at home of the Symphonie Angelique, or the generic promiscuity of Roger Colas's voice, which bears deep influence on his father's own. He will indicate some Miami-based teachers who came to him by way of the radio, the live, and the classrooms at New World. He specifically names a few drummers who officially bumped up the various levels of his practice: the first was Ignacio Berroa, the second was Dafnis Prieto, and the third ("the deepest one") was José Luis Quintana, also known as "Changuito," perhaps the most important timbalero and drummer of the past few centuries. Quintana's pioneering work with songo for Cuban supergroup Los Van Van continues to dizzy people who want to make time different the world over, be they drummer or dancer.[44] Dafnis Prieto even dedicates a whole section of A World of Rhythmic Possibilities to the great Changuito, who he declares "A MASTER DRUMMER both musically and technically—and I must write that in capital letters. His deep knowledge and understanding of the Cuban rhythmic tradition and his intense creativity are worthy of great admiration and respect."[45] From the book form, Prieto manages the fist-pound on the table to reiterate the physical and intellectual gravitas of percussion's beloved godfather. As Calvaire describes his study with and from Changuito, "It wasn't about facility . . . it was about a certain vocabulary; it was so deep, almost like the doctoral courses you take." My inclusion of Changuito here is not merely to pile on names, to overwhelm those unfamiliar or even familiar readers, but to mark guiding posts. Changuito is a most vitalizing homework, an assignment for the reader to keep returning to, to prepare you for listening to Prieto and Calvaire, and everything else really. As Calvaire perfectly put it, Changuito is "where it started." He did not say it was Changuito "who started it"; he does not reduce his practices to an individuated body even as he honors it, but opens it up to a *where*. Among many of Changuito's superlative nicknames is "El Misterioso" (the mysterious one). Many ride in his deeply grounded sound but are unable to predict his fills that come seemingly out of nowhere (everywhere).

Calvaire's work and the stories that he tells constantly point to a specific peopling and expansive placing of drumming. They are the teachers of the four countries, and although they carry their own hard-earned techniques, Calvaire does not sort them out by place. They are brought to the scene of his playing as vocabularies from some prior conversation. This is part of what Changuito extends to all, and if you can, find his instructional book *Changuito: A Master's Approach to Timbales*, where the examples recorded in the accompanying CD leave in the rooster crows and the Havana traffic, the country and the metropole all present.[46] The learning lapses any drummer may encounter with Changuito and his deep vocabularies are as embodied as they are temporal. In his book, there is subtle instruction of learning to walk from a toddle, of how to incorporate in order to try out. The section titled "How to Practice this Book" has a special subheading on "Feel." Changuito states:

> When encountering patterns which require your learning new independent movements, pay attention to how your body feels. Are you relaxed during these patterns and exercises? Are you playing slow enough to where you are performing in a calm manner? Or are you tense? Perhaps performing a bit too fast? By paying attention to signs of tension in your body, you can better tune in to the exercises which may need more work and/or more time. Don't neglect the tension in your shoulders when trying to play mambo bell and clave, nor the stiff feeling in your forearms when practicing the chacha bell pattern. These signs can actually assist you in the learning process![47]

These lessons can equally apply when writing about Prieto and Calvaire and Terry (who is holding all this together from the greenroom). The growing pains of trying to write about the drums involve constant fledgling tension with and then a relaxing into new challenges, be they technical, contextual, geographical, linguistic. Always invitations to more work and more time, these tensions of inexperience are there to help you write alongside music. But I am coming to know, slowly, that it is in the music itself that relief may and must be found.

Writing about music offers an important unavailability to the writer. There is something always withheld from her: the music is still required for a sense of fullness, health, history. This is not a ranking of one practice over the other, or an ordering of one before another, but of making something in the lapse together, the lapse between music and the writing about it that does not seek to replace or replicate the experience of listening. Critique can only be supplemental; it cannot be felt alone in isolation. I need music as the place to live that I cannot possibly write. And so, if there is anything at all that is "a little bit advanced" about these pages, it is their relentless invitation to listen to all of these songs and their mangrovian appendices. The prior knowledges here, deep in these musics, cannot be neglected. Nor can the feel of the writer or the drummer. How does it feel when it feels right? I asked Calvaire. He first quieted Cazzian and then took some time to respond: "How do you explain to someone what skydiving feels like? . . . Certain things, you can't really, there's no explaining, you'd have to actually experience it . . . *you could maybe get close*. . . ." "You could maybe get close" encapsulates all the more powerfully this welcoming and, in some ways, homecoming of indirect experience; "to maybe get close" suggests always the possibility and the impossibility of approximation. The writer can never exactly meet or even catch up to the drummer (this is, importantly, withheld). The world that can happen in the maybe is plentiful enough.

But really, how does it feel? Calvaire pushes himself to answer: "The closest thing I can come up with off the top of my head is like flying . . . like when I see an eagle soaring through the air, just floating, it doesn't matter wherever the wind takes him, he's not flapping his wings, he's just pretty much still, but you can still see him gliding to the left to the right, it is wherever the wind decides to take that eagle . . . because when you're in that zone you're not in control." How might this loaned sense of gliding maybe get listeners closer to what's involved in the fluency in the vocabularies of the four countries? Though still preserving the mystery of which four, to take the countries of Haiti and Cuba and the multiple vocabularies (and countries) held within them, and their ongoing dispersal, is to think them *together*. All the learned spaces, the miraculous crossings, impossible survival, and grandmothers who brought these musicians and their traditions together gave them the currents in which to glide. There is historical accuracy of the airwaves involved here, and there are constant verifiable hunches of their connectivity. These connectivities happen in Agawu's words, now a necessary refrain: "The time of music is its own time" (158). This time, music's own time, can be shared across different songs made centuries and miles and waters apart. Haiti begets Cuba begets Miami begets Haiti begets Cuba. Island begets island begets "island" begets island begets island. Inside of the other, because of the other. This is not a hopping type movement, but a learning from and dependence upon all those others who allow your lift and shift in a special kind of safety. To Prieto's levitating practice is the addendum of Calvaire's gliding, a trusted place of being slightly above ground, a place for apprentices and teachers, uniquely made possible in dream or drum life.

IV. The aleatory as painted by Prieto and Calvaire happens in close parallel to the grounds, aqueous and otherwise, of Cuba, the peninsular bottom of Florida, and Haiti. Flight and flying are central to new world Afro-diasporic history and aesthetics, as fugitivity actual and spiritual, in robust lifesaving folklore, and as is the case in the four countries, perpetual outings to el monte.[48] Prieto and Calvaire's flight in parallel happens as they hover over and then make contact with their drums. The practice enables a mixing of air and land and water, and the inherited or invented time figures offer visitation to places one might not have been before. For touring musicians, the visitations can eventually become actual, as when we see Obed Calvaire in Cuba, having touched down in Havana for the 2018 Jazz Plaza festival with the Yosvany Terry Quintet. Fragments of the experience were documented in a short 2020 film directed by Fabien Pisani, "Return to Havana," which follows Terry and the quintet on much of the same itinerary made by Prieto the year after. In the film we accompany Terry to his parents' Marianao home and get to be in the audience for the performance at La Fábrica. Although Terry's return tour was one year before Prieto's, the documentary about it came out two years after. Here is another palpable repeated figure of the common and communal itineraries, and the asynchronous crossings of this inter-island cohort, that helps us to hear them all together, even if not at the same time. They bring their various schools with them, too, invariably making palimpsestic institute wherever they are, as student or teacher. We follow Terry as he takes New World School of the Arts alums Calvaire and Mike Rodriguez to teach young students at Havana's ENA. How beautiful to see another version of that school, *our school that's from Miami*, in another place and time. The sameness about them, especially the familiar languid limbs of the students, is stunning.

The documentary eventually takes us outside of the city as Terry took the quintet to Jovellanos, a town in the Matanzas province known for its fierce preservation and continuation of Afro-diasporic musical traditions both sacred and secular. The quintet takes it in, joins the bembé. There is a lot of smiling and concentrated brows. Calvaire is working something out with others on some tambores arará with a borrowed set of drumsticks made from guava tree branches. Recall that it was the Thursday night "Jazz

Cubano" at the Jazz Gallery in New York where Calvaire first became involved with both Terry and Prieto, and where Terry and Prieto played together. From avid audience member to a central part of Terry's quintet not a decade later, and then still another decade to this first trip to Cuba. Seeing Calvaire play on the drums in Jovellanos is like witnessing a homecoming on an unfamiliar and common ground. We hear the common ground of Cuban and Haitian musical traditions after having been reintroduced in the New York extension. These places share the techniques of music making given the historically forced movements of the people and plantations between the two islands, and have long exchanged secret unrelenting practices over the centuries. The sharing is as historical as it is conceptual. As Terry said of their collaboration, "Obed has a lot of information we share even if we were born apart, that only one that was raised in the Caribbean has (because at this point Miami is part of the Caribbean), that goes back to the Caribbean, back to Africa, that goes back many generations that he can tap into and access when necessary. And this type of information I don't have to explain to him, you know?"[49]

The radiant Yosvany Terry, born in Camagüey, Cuba, in 1971, is a composer and musician and professor who plays the saxophone and the chekeré (figures 3.5 and 3.6). For him the instruments are not oppositional traditions, merely different languages, and his work on both is magisterial.[50] Though not a "drummer" in the conventional sense of the kit, Terry is a deep initiate in the drummer's language that keeps the ensemble together. He understands this language as the ability to change the mood and to also know that "what you will change will affect everything."[51] With Terry this technique applies as much to the instruments he plays and the compositions he writes as it does to his distinctive faculty with gathering company and collaborators in music. His timepiece, the chekeré, is a percussive instrument that can either be played alone (an instrument that holds the many in the one) or keep time for the band. It is a gourd wrapped in a loose net of beads, and its construction allows for additional challenges for time, play, flight. The player must anticipate in prescient flashes when to turn or tap the gourd so that the beaded net strikes in the desired time. There is the time of the gesture but also a set of evolving plans for its aftereffects. There are doubled, four-continents kind of times and textural considerations as one plays.

Terry was born into one of Cuba's great musical dynasties. He is one of three sons of the eminent Eladio "Don Pancho" Terry Gonzalez, known as one of the great masters of the chekeré tradition from the Lucumís (Yoruba) in Cuba, and who was responsible for introducing the instrument

FIGURE 3.5 Yosvany Terry and Yunior Terry with the Ancestral Memories Project at the Side Door Jazz Club, Old Lyme, Connecticut, June 2018. Photo by Nicola Dracoulis.

FIGURE 3.6 Yosvany Terry with the chekeré at the Duc des Lombards (Paris), January 15, 2020. Photo by Emilie Aujé.

to charanga dance bands and orchestras.[52] Without the boomscrape hiss achiquiraca of the chekeré sound, charanga would have less of its danceable charge. Its earthiness makes the genre's progressive movement feel grounded in the Earth rather than lording over it. This instrumental introduction was extremely significant, as it would be later when the younger Terry would insist on it for the New York jazz scene. For Yosvany, the chekeré "has this magic thing that is able to fill empty spaces but at the same time gives it color you cannot get with other instruments . . . and at the same time connects everything more direct with Africa."[53] It is a time/space portal as much as an instrument.

Instruments, far from naturally given or empty vessels, are the result of active and urgent decisions by people to carry on. Don Pancho learned the practice from his uncle, Dionisio Guzmán Gonzalez ("Tanguito"), one of the most important priests of Eleguá (the sentinel orisha of entrances and all roads) in Camagüey. When Yosvany and his brothers, Yoel and Yunior, were little, Don Pancho handed the practice down by having them first play with beans in plastic bottles.[54] And when their hands could handle it, Don Pancho started them on the gourd without the net. This was so they could learn how to tap and slap and turn the primary drum aspect of the instrument—to acquire a training in a certain set of times—before adding the additional layers of the net's other introduced times. They had to learn to drum it first before introducing the delay. Here again we see a nascent musician, this time a young Terry, toddle toward an object to play, toward the call and his calling to a life in music. *At the same time* of this early chekeré training, Don Pancho also taught his sons the violin (he was an accomplished classical violinist). Part of what is crucial to mention about Yosvany Terry's upbringing, music, and legacy (although one finds this often in Cuban musical families) is the beautiful ordinariness with which he was brought up in multiple traditions and the tranquil way he moves between them. One of the magical things about seeing Terry play in the live is his supple, no-big-deal movement between playing his saxophone, putting it down, and picking up the chekeré and back again. The transitions alone are a master class in live adaptation. Both instruments are handled with a similar tenderness, yet there is something slightly more automatic with the saxophone, and slightly more ginger and careful when picking up the chekeré. The sense you get is the chekeré is a being. The hold is a cradle. The choreography involved throughout is silken, light, without burden. Watching Terry play, you wonder why then, why at that point was that instrumental move required or desired? What are the internal secrets of those transitions?

Terry's music is testimony to those grounds that prepared and nurtured his polymathic musicality; it is a sensibility nurtured in sound but expanded into a general theory of living. As Terry once put it, "Music was in my house since before I was born. Being born was more like a recognition of where we were. An awakening to the things around."⁵⁵ This birth notion does not assume any blank slate, but rather that his material body is a continuation in a much longer conversation he was already made a part of long before conception. To imagine being born as a recognition and an awakening is to come into the Earth assuming the plans of elders, to recognize the instructive paths they left open. To be born as a vital and meaningful part of something, of an already in-place band. Part of the larger band he was born into was rooted in the Haitian community in Camagüey. Terry's grandmother Basilia León Charles was born in Cuba to Haitian parents by accident. Her parents were living in Cuba and ready to board a boat to return to Haiti, but when there was an unexpected delay, her mom went into labor, so they remained. With transplanted roots from Aken and Zanglé, Haiti, León Charles grew up to become the lead singer of vodou ceremonies in Camagüey. And this is how Terry's mom, Lydia Cabrera León, considers her first language Kreyol. The Haitian community in Camagüey (especially in the neighborhood La Guernica) was an incredible nursery for Terry's sensibilities, musical and otherwise. In a practical sense, Terry was younger than five and already practicing for ceremonies on pots and pans in his aunt's backyard. He recalls fondly: "We had a band."⁵⁶ Terry, his ancestors, and his ongoing family ask us—*in music*—to consider this training, secular and sacred, all at once across idioms, religiosities, codes, fluencies, and frequencies from infancy as we listen. You can hear Yosvany Terry set back and forward the time, in the time of music, with his chekeré in "Ojun Degara," a song on his 2014 album *New Throned King*. The pebbled contours of the net as they move with and around the gourd are a pot stirring, another suggestion of the circular and linear happening together. The chekeré's circularity suggests a story that can't be told directly, and its linearity insists that doesn't mean there is not *not* a story here that involves both elders and youngers. After his chekeré sets the figure to ready the scene, the other band members enter in a cloudburst to take up, in an oblique but swinging way, what was readied by Terry. Notable in many of his songs, but extra delightful on this track, is his brother Yunior on the bass, pulling down for the larger get-down of everyone and every place involved in here. The song is something you wish you could name high modernity while evacuating the violent attachments to the phrase. The song is, as Terry said about his musical ethos, "a past that is both present and future at the same time."[57]

Wherever the Terry family lived, whether in Camagüey or years later, in La Habana, Cuba's most important musicians would constantly pass through their home for hospitality, for catching up, for music. Terry especially honors the part of his childhood in Florida (a municipality in Camagüey province and irresistible sister-city for this book), an influential carnival town and stopover for bands that would travel from Oriente (the eastern part of the island) to play in the capital, La Habana. Part of Florida's situatedness as a musical crossroads had to do with its train station, an important east-to-west depot. For Terry, the town was an open junction for music and his house "a musical embassy." During these years magnificent bands such as Orquesta Aragón, Orquesta Ritmo Oriental, Los Van Van, and Miguelito Cuní y Felix Chappotín would all pass through his house. It is impossible to imagine all of the detailed schooling that Terry and his brothers picked up in all this musical opportune. What I would like to link up to this depot, this crossroads of so much, are Terry's deep social practices—putting together seemingly different sounds, his world-making curatorial work of the "Jazz Cubano" at the Jazz Gallery series, and forming bands and live shows for all of us here. Terry is a musician's musician, deeply respected for his technique and musicianship. He is also one of those generous, gravitational figures who bring all kinds of people and places together. The six degrees of Yosvany Terry is not a game but the marking of actual genealogies that trace connectivity in the New York, Cuban, and inter-American musical scenes and publics. These social practices are as rooted in this coming of age in an actual crossroads in addition to a spiritual one (recall Eleguá of the family's chekeré traditions). Relisten to "Summer Relief" played in the above, consider the biographical details involved in its players, all of the travel this song allows for listeners, and it is possible to feel Terry's social practices in a singular song: "Many-in-oneness."[58]

Being ready for anything and anyone, whether on a set schedule or arriving unannounced, Florida, the surround of Camagüey, and his grandparents' Haiti gave Terry this early theory-based practice: "When you're moving into many different spaces without questioning them, when you live also within different worlds, that requires a different access of your consciousness, and you never question that either, and when you've heard music and elements of those spaces then combine at the same time, you believe that's how it should be. You actually strive for developing that abstract space that you create in which all of the other belongs."⁵⁹ "All of the other belongs" does everything to gather Terry's myriad practices across instruments, traditions, and collaboration with others. You feel it in every composition, live show, recording, conversation. It is as present across the bands he forms from his quintet to Afro-Cuban Roots to the Bohemian Trio. "All of the other belongs" is not a happy narrative of resolute multiculturalism, nor does it cater to the fantasies of "World Music," or encounter generally speaking. It is a difficult place that asks for constant transformation and development. For a skilled initiate such as Terry, and the rites that he was fluent in before being born, the spatial and temporal striving finds beautiful echo from Wynter's grandmother's theory: "a sense of grounding in an existential sense of justice, not as grim retribution but as shared happiness." It is not as if anyone can just enter what Terry proposes here. There is careful preparedness, an offering of time signatures, an invitation to dance, all facilitated by those who both chose and were forced to make flight and join with strangers and corners to combine sounds together. "Erzulie," a track from Terry's album *Ancestral Memories* with French pianist Baptiste Trotignon, is another of his exuberant, almost eight-minute compositions, a length that is just enough and too much time for the LP, and a form that Terry consistently shows gorgeous faculty with. The song is named after the family of loa associated with water and femininity in vodou. It begins with a drummed entry by Jeff "Tain" Watts, a deliberate if unsteady walk into the waters. Watts's adjustments open space for Trotignon and Terry's gentle entrances until something else is required. Terry's sax changes the urgency of the piece, and when his brother Yunior enters on the bass, the song gets caught up and then swims through swirls and currents. All of the other belongs, but in composition and play it is far from sloppy incorporation. It is an alchemical place, a little bit advanced. On this song Terry's chekeré might be materially absent, but its sense of time—the drummer's language that affects everything—is palpably present in the ways it does and doesn't tell an ancestral story.

Terry's familial lessons and structure provide the grounds of his practices. To slow down his movement after leaving Camagüey for school in La Habana is to show how well prepared he was for his coming of age to extend these natal practices to others. It is also to show the strands of the involved tangle of these musicians and these musics assembled here. I resist any "full-circle" model, as do the artists themselves, given their relentless dedication to work with many unexpected people and places. This is also to say, with concentrated emphasis, the foregoing includes just a few fragments from very full, detailed lives that are impossible to get at in a few pages, as if pages could even come close to the idiom required to connote them. Their songs, their playing, are what suggests this fullness, as Prieto and Calvaire's solos suggest, as Terry's compositions and chekeré allude. This is all an assignment to listen to and follow their work and their future development. And again, while they share similar itineraries, they do not always reside in the same places at the same time. But they make temporary place here in *The Florida Room* because they have, together and apart, offered structural awakenings for what being "there" means and what a "disciplined plurality" might feel like when writing about music. And what it might feel like to *maybe* get close to gathering together many in "the time of music."[60] To transition out from this chapter by underscoring their points of contact made in shared schools, ancestral ties, and the asynchronous tutelage by the same teachers, hopes to make a new band for aleatory and grounded critique.

Here is a very spare and partial version of how Prieto and Terry came to meet at school. When Terry left Camagüey to study in La Habana, he first attended the other music conservatory, Amadeo Roldán, because there was not yet a bed available for him at La ENA. After one semester at Roldán, Terry enrolled in La ENA, where he eventually met Dafnis Prieto, slightly younger but already in residence there.[61] They soon bonded over their musical tastes, such as Jan Garber and Egberto Gismonti, and played together in a band formed by fellow student Carlos Masa, a Chilean pianist whose family spent their exile in La Habana.[62] With Masa they experienced touring life, especially in Europe, where they were introduced to important Cuban musicians in the abroad such as Paris-based Alfredo Rodríguez.[63] It is also where Terry made the acquaintance of Steve Coleman, who was among the early voices telling him to move to New York.[64] In 1997 Terry and Prieto decided to form their own group in La Habana called Columna B, inviting Roberto Carcasses and Descemer Bueno to join. Descemer Bueno, you may instantly recall, is the author of the 2014 megahit "Bailando," performed with Enrique Iglesias and Gente de Zona, and a big part of what we might call a new Cuban groundswell in US Latin music.[65] Columna B was a historic band that played in and around La Habana, toured Europe, and eventually made important contact with Bob Murphy, one of the founders of the Stanford Jazz Workshop, a bountiful link that brought these young musicians to the historic Cuban music presence in the Bay Area. From there, eventual pathways to New York, to the Jazz Gallery, to playing in front of a young Calvaire in the audience. A beautiful abundance of solo-led and sidemen projects and, alongside these, some small comfort in an only slightly steadier gig called academia. Prieto moved to South Florida to become a professor at the University of Miami. Terry, while based in New York, became a professor at Harvard University in Cambridge.

How I happened to come under the training of all the teachers of these and other schools: I first met Yosvany Terry in 2006 at Rose's in Brooklyn at a party involving some Cubans and other friends. At one point the Orquesta Maravillas de Florida's "Búscame el abanico" came to play off the CD that I had burned for the occasion. And I just happened to be dancing with Terry, who subtly mentioned, "This is my dad's song." From there, it was *from there* dancing to and with, Terry eventually extended introduction to his Havana, and his music grounded a willingness to push my ear harder through active attendance at his concerts and interaction with his recordings. A first book about the elders involved directly or implicitly in this orbit. Then the next level: Prieto in the live, always all around the same time, with a particular dizzying and affecting memory of a concert where they both shared the stage in Madison Square Park in 2013. The third and in some ways deepest level: hearing Calvaire on Terry's *Today's Opinion*. A later invitation to Terry and Calvaire to Princeton to play in 2013, where I got to bring them food backstage and find out the New World School of the Arts connection between myself and Calvaire and Mike Rodriguez. We made that shared unspoken Miami language in a place that tries hard but fails to make folks forget their shared unspoken languages. A long interim to get ready for them all. Then everything picked up quickly on some unexpected cue. That 2019 trip to La Habana to see Prieto's Fábrica concert finally gave me the courage to request an interview through the unofficial mayor of all metropoles, Armando Suárez-Cobían (of "una locomotora" fame). Prieto's patio (!). Terry gave me Calvaire's email address at the beginning of the quarantine. His friendship was a diplomatic passport to Calvaire, but I was also blessed with a shared allegiance to our Miami high school, which was "so healthy and warm." That place, that school from Miami, facilitated a sense of trust and a different starting place for the interview format. And finally a crossroads figure to help me walk between schools. From the dream Caribbean theory institute founded and refined by Sylvia Wynter, rooted in the choreography of her grandmother's home and four-poster bed, her early career training in playwriting and dance, and her walk within and between another set of overlapping islands, comes a joyful announcement for and shared happiness with all who passed through this depot.

Chapter Four

BASS IS THE PLACE

....

The tourist industries of the Caribbean want you to come. All they require is your decision and your capital. Miami is often the departure point to allow for some climatic adjustment before moving farther south. There have been a lot of convincing objects made to get you there: first-person accounts, postcards, package deals, and commercials from at least the mid-nineteenth century to the present. The advertised enticements haven't changed. They promise happy locals, exclusive beaches, native artifacts, widely available sex, real estate, debauchery, and—somehow—"family fun." The 1951 brochure shown in figure 4.1 reveals some itineraries, routes built within centuries-old trade in people and sugar that would eventually pave the way for the all-inclusive above. The conversion of the colonies as sites of absentee extraction into live amusement, and the movements between them into leisurely joyrides, are on display here. The fonts themselves perform the desired fantasies (before visitation) for each location: a cosmopolitan brothel in Havana, a colonially policed Nassau, some cane and drum exotica in the West Indies, and the native woven handicraft that is Mexico.

There were so many possible combinations made possible by the Midway Travel Service, yet the brochure's selling point is that the consumer could pursue their own curatorial choices. Add in the additional options of Jamaica, Haiti, Puerto Rico, and the Virgin Islands as featured on the back flap, and the buyer's options were endless. US citizens did not need visas to enter any of these places, so it was a matter, once again, of deciding to go and to pay. Pick and choose, mix and match, combine at your convenience. The brochure makes them and there all slightly interchangeable, with a few unthreatening but charming differences. Finger trace the

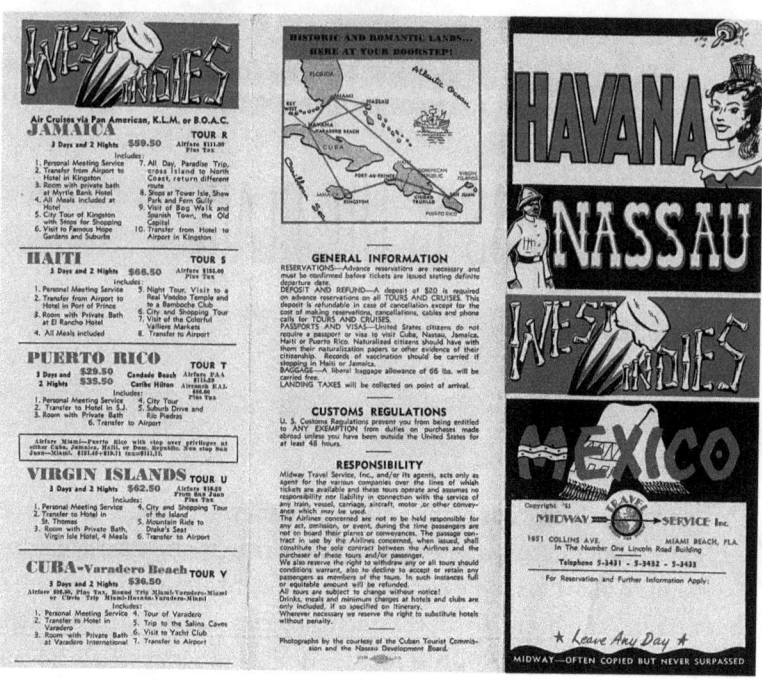

FIGURE 4.1 Midway Travel Service Brochure, ca. 1951. Courtesy of Special Collections, University of Miami Libraries, Coral Gables, Florida.

line on the small map on offer here, however, and the strange geometry may offer other kinds of trips. Make a tranced entry straight through the highly commodified realm and toward the ghosts involved in objects such as these. They are portals to imagine those for whom movement might have meant displacement and work, and all that they picked up en route and upon arrival. This is part of the assignment that Buffalo Tiger well prepared us for in chapter 2. These lines may appear to enforce the lane staying required by colonial mandate, but they intimate many important infractions. There are things hidden, stashed away, and played with beyond the touristic imaginary, even and especially for those who are often made to be at the service of it. This activity is not interested in putting all its energy in resistance *to* this imaginary however. There is a lot of something else going on beneath these lines, inside and extended from these well-worn routes that have created a lot of pain and pleasure. All along these itineraries of past and present, there are other formations of geographic thought and aesthetic experiments that have been made by the people working in, and in spite of, its service economies.[1]

FIGURE 4.2 The Eloise Trio, *Come to the Caribbean and Meet the Exciting Eloise Trio* (Decca, 1962). Collection of the author.

The music industries of the Caribbean want you to come. All they require is purchasing an album. It would seem that a lot of music of the Caribbean wants you to come too. The packaging of recordings suggests or outright endorses it. And yet there is often an internal acknowledgment in music that knows you won't stay away but nonetheless sounds a guarded assuredness that it will not be taken away. The best parts of that acknowledgment and assuredness are the deliberate decisions that so many musicians make as to the who and what they want to make place for in their own terms and times. While there may be fierce protection of the local, there can be a capacious sense of how to adapt and incorporate the outside. Much of this involves tremendous faculty with what Suzanne Césaire called "the great camouflage."[2] Take another kind of brochure, this time the cover of the great Bahamian musician Eloise Lewis's 1962 *Come to the Caribbean* (figure 4.2).

The trio looks down on the viewer from a sand dune, a raised natural barrier that protects the land from sea surges and teems with important fauna and flora. As borders to the instantaneous grasp of the shoreline, they are often considered eyesores for the beachfront-owning types. They are difficult to cross: scrapes and bites are usually involved. Lewis moves to the dune's summit and steadily holds the guitar, poised to play. Her fellow

BASS IS THE PLACE 119

members angle out her directional. Bert poses his maracas and Bucky steadies the double bass while balancing in dry sand. They also make their bodies fit into the frame. They are all dressed in folkloric signs of the Bahamas' Out Islands—sartorial marks of the island rural as also seen in Puerto Rico, Jamaica, and Cuba—to suggest that they may even be there waiting to play for you at the airport. But even in the visual assembly that might make this a typical touristic lure, so much is withheld. The horizon and the water are hidden. The trio must be passed before access is given to either. The dunes are places of shoreline heat, usually crossed over before the water's relief. The tourist will want to walk on an adjacent pathway made for their beach access, also refused here. This album, in its visual nonpromise, keeps you, the tourist purchaser, in your place. Those who are viscerally familiar with the important protocols of these dunes know that this album will offer a different experience than some smooth ride to go there. These listeners, typically unseen or undesired by market demographics, were likely a part of the after-hours, off-strip formation of the sounds held within. This album cover is an open wink to them.

The title song, "Come to the Caribbean," is a fascinating piece of Gulf Stream psychedelia—a new world countercultural anthem—that offers you a trip. Perhaps the journey is not the one you might have signed on for.[3] The song is, for some, a noninvitation inside a glossy envelope. It prohibits all curatorial choices for island hopping, and it makes unpredictable assemblies to stall your departure. The song revokes your decision to just go. What Lewis performs in and as this song is more transformative than this, however. She thwarts the reflexive analytic that would make *resistance to* bad things the only aural point. Instead, she makes something new from the dune. "Come to the Care-ra-be-un," Lewis decidedly whispers; it is both a seduction and a troop rousing. Her bandmates join her in the preparations, and they all keep asking or, rather, daring you to come. It is a disorienting order of rapid strums, maracas, double bass, a goombay drum, her characteristic yipping and laughing at some things that aren't funny. All this gives ground for her sung melody that haunts any desire to go there. Here are some lyrics:

> Come to the Caribbean
> The magic moment is calling you
> When the gray sea turns to green
> I'll be your slave if you'll be my island king
> Come to the Caribbean Come to the Caribbean

> Come to the Caribbean Come to the Caribbean
> Come Come Come Come Come Come Come Come Come Come Come
> Come to the Caribbean Come to the Caribbean.

Before there's any possible handle of this contorted brochure, she presses some vocal scat and scrape firmly into this song. Lewis withholds words to better tell you about an actual rather than fantasy Caribbean and, in the meantime, also manages to tell you about yourself. Everyone is implicated here. Lewis's yelps, her anachronistic vocals, her slides and stops, her samples from elsewhere are more than a refusal of the touristic. You can't just come. Like this, this way, she sings. To realize this irreverence, she experiments with the capability of voice and time, even as she is packaged for consumption.

The Bahamian Lewis was born in 1935 in Jacksonville, Florida, in the northeastern tip of the state. Jacksonville is also the birthplace of James Weldon Johnson, whose mother was from Nassau, the legacy of a common movement pattern for Bahamians in the early twentieth century. Unlike Johnson, Lewis left Florida as a young girl and was raised in Nassau. Her family made a reverse migration from peninsula to periphery, and you can hear something of this in her modulation of her Bahamian and northern Florida accenting of words.[4] As one of the most prominent, if mercurial, figures in Bahamian music, Lewis was the first Bahamian to record for the UK Decca label.[5] Her music is commonly understood in the "goombay" genre, whose loose parameters (always true of genre) included rules *and* infringements. *Goombay* is also the word for a goat-skin–stretched drum, but, as a music market lure, it is meant to include everything that captured the attention of brochured itineraries in 1951. Part of the function of goombay was to name the comingling of genres from other island locations, such as merengue, son, and bolero, which, given all the unsanctioned ocean crossings of the arts, were well established in Bahamian musical practices anyway. Goombay was also used to differentiate itself from and compete with an increasingly undifferentiated calypso. It is an aesthetically discerning mash-up that could supposedly deliver (or not!) the Bahamas to the ear.[6] In "Come to the Caribbean" you hear the song as a holding place for all of goombay's currents, especially rumba, junkanoo, and rake-and-scrape. You hear her vocal nod to "Summertime" and the living is uneasy, and there's even that place in France, which is really "The Streets of Cairo, or the Poor Little Country Maid." The whole mass of song is, to reactivate the words of Dafnis Prieto, "a little bit advanced," and it disappoints all expectations for instantaneous comprehension.

As a vigorous part of a larger aesthetic legacy, Lewis and her galvanizing irreverence asks for formal recognition in other performances. This quality as incorporated into *The Florida Room* has, like all the book's other incorporations, a historical basis. Lewis's migration between Florida and Nassau recalls and recognizes Bahamian women's migration to and from Florida since at least the mid-nineteenth century. In Miami, for example, part of its early history that sets it apart from other cities is that immigrant populations constituted its early majority and, according to some statistics, were 60 percent women. This is a result of the service-economy jobs in the year-round tourist and pioneering sectors, where their labor and expertise were what made South Florida livable for white, northern settlers. This is a different population than that for seasonal agricultural sectors, which required temporary men's labor. Many women immigrants established early roots in the city, and others, even while they laid down roots, also moved between the larger wage-work service economies of the Gulf Stream company town.[7] These foundations, and other forms of work done while also making home, are what I hear in the aesthetic experimentations to come in this chapter. Around the Straits of Florida, Bahamians had much experience and know-how with wrecking—that is, salvaging ships and their bounties that didn't come to dock on the American mainland.[8] Many ships from the old world met their fate in the shallows of the area. They thought they could get closer to land, but eco-intermediaries thwarted this desire by throwing a reef or viscous sand in the way. As Craton and Saunders helpfully illustrate, "'Wrecking,' indeed, became the perennial favorite activity of Bahamian mariners, in pursuit of which they were prepared to sail close to either side of the narrow line between legitimate and illegal."[9]

Imagine what these great ships looked like as they keeled over and stuck out of the shallow waters like tilted monuments. Masculinist images of sailors and narratives of shipwreckage have been deployed in many places of Afro-diasporic studies. In other critical sectors, pirates are usually defined as roguish British male expats, made to figure as proto-renegades that are at the heart of the Anglo entrepreneurial spirit.[10] Through Lewis's music and Bahamian women pioneers, I want to think very carefully about the different labors of what it might mean to salvage ships. What must it have been like to approach that wreckage and leave oneself open to all the strange, glittery, morbid discoveries to be found there? To extract them piecemeal and make use of them? Which begs the question: Who was making use of them, putting all those things together, after they were brought back to the shore? Black women, as Toni Morrison beautifully put it, "had to deal with post-modern problems in the nineteenth century and earlier."[11] I hear these procedures of creative salvage in Lewis's composition and vocal performance—which is a fascinating apprehension and reconstruction of sounds as they move through the Gulf Stream. Much of Florida Strait architecture allotted special spaces on the roofs of where people lived so they could see the ships in those last naive moments before running aground. This view from the shore and the wisdom of the treacherous passage just beyond it, offer yet another space to imagine historical activities of counterconquest and how they came to sound thereafter.

Another brochure: this time in the form of an advertisement in the *Miami Times*, the Black-owned and -operated newspaper founded by Bahamian Henry Ethelbert Sigismund Reeves in 1923.[12] As a chronicle of Black communities in and around the city, this paper has been a crucial channel, assembly, and conduit for social life amid the racist terror and constraint of South Florida. It held and holds news both local and national unreported in the white press, featured society pages, cultural reports and reviews, graduation and employment updates from hometown children, and advertising space for Black-owned businesses. As an early material link between Miami and the Bahamas, the *Times* featured a column with "Notes" or "News from" or "In and Around the Bahamas" with intimate detail: who became a lawyer, who became a teacher, who was sick, who passed away. Some of the stunning mosaics made of advertisements and local stories in the *Times* are a dizzying composite of life and living in Black Miami. They offer a staggering range of documented experiences—its myriad difficulties and dynamic pleasures—regardless of the political leanings of the paper.[13] Take one page, alive with activity, from April 11, 1964 (see figure 4.3).

In the figure you see the tightness of community involvement on display. It reports on the Jackson Toddle Inn School taking a field trip to the Crandon Park Zoo, two gun-carrying women in violent altercation at a laundromat, student artwork from Northwestern Senior High (Liberty City) and Floral Heights Elementary School (Brownsville) in a renovated Roosevelt Savings and Loan. The *Miami Times* was and remains committed to events and places big and small: how to participate in local institutions from Black

Garth Reeves, left, and Jack Orr, two organizers of the Roosevelt Savings and Loan Association, look on as personnel and Wells Fargo guards complete the movement of over $2,800,000.00 in cash and assets into the new facility located at 6015 NW 7th Ave. Roosevelt unveiled into its beautiful new quarters next door on Monday morning. The fast growing Savings and Loan boasts one of the most beautiful institutions of its kind in the country.

The public is invited to view two art displays now in the windows of Roosevelt. They are by students of Northwestern Senior High and Floral Heights Elementary School.

Western Style...
Women Stage Gunfight At Laundromat

A woman was wounded in the head Monday afternoon during a gun battle with another woman at an automatic laundry.

Alma Marie Williams, 29, of 2071 NW 69th St., was in serious condition after surgery at Jackson Hospital.

Metro Homicide Sgt. John McKay gave this account:

Mrs. Williams drove to the laundry at NW 27th Ave. and 58th St. where Jean Tyson, 22, of 5250 NW 20th Ave. was doing her laundry with her sister.

Mrs. Williams, who had argued with Miss Tyson several days ago, pulled out a .22 caliber revolver and said, "I'm gonna kill you."

Miss Tyson then pulled a .32 lay on the front seat and pulled the back of the seat over her.

Mrs. Williams fired into the car twice, but both shots missed.

Miss Tyson then pulled a .32 caliber revolver from under the car's seat and fired once. She hit Mrs. Williams in the head.

Both women were charged with aggravated assault. Mrs. Tyson was held at county jail.

Jackson Toddle Inn School

The pupils, teachers and a number of parents enjoyed a fascinating sightseeing tour, and visit to Crandon Park Zoo Friday, March 27 which proved quite educational.

We are now looking forward to our May Queen contest which will terminate Friday, May 1.

Pictures and names of contestants will appear in next week's issue.

Watch for the Big
COSTUME BALL
Miami Beach Auditorium
Get your costumes ready

J. A. Summons
REAL ESTATE
INVESTMENT
APPRAISALS
NE 4-6875
1899 N.W. 53rd St.
Miami 42, Fla.

THE MIAMI TIMES — MIAMI, FLA.
SATURDAY, APRIL 11, 1964 PAGE 5

Complaints Made On Business School

Several complaints have been brought to the attention of this newspaper about a Business Training School on NW 76th St. that has not lived up to promises made to its students.

People seeking training as cashiers, clerks, stock clerks, etc. should check out the schools with the Chamber of Commerce or the Better Business Bureau to make sure the schools are certified and approved.

CLYDE KILLENS'
SIR JOHN HOTEL KNIGHT BEAT CLUB
"Home of The Stars"
— PRESENTS —
BIG DOUBLE ATTRACTION
FRIDAY and SATURDAY (ONLY) — APRIL 10th - 11th

Chickie "Effie Throckbottom" **Madam Horne**

ADMISSION: FRI. $1.50   SAT. $1.75

Plus The Famous
ALTHEA BRYANT
(300 lbs. of Blues)

COMING APRIL 17 - 18 - 19

Roy Hamilton

ROY HAMILTON
THE "GOLDEN BOY"
SUNDAY, APRIL 19th
BIG TEENAGE MATINEE
3:00 TO 6:00 P.M.
ADMISSION $1.00

Clyde Killens'
Miami is Ready for
"NIGHT IN NASSAU"
COMING APRIL 12th
At The Harlem Square Club
ADMISSION: ADVANCE $1.50   AT DOOR $1.75

Adm. Adv. $2.00 - Door $2.50

Shown Above: The "Nassau King" and "Nassau Clyde Killens" doing the BELLY DANCE, Night in NASSAU.

For Reservations Call FR 9-9272

| Charles Martin | Johnnie Williams |

Enjoy the best in entertainment
Music Furnished by DEWITT AND THE LANCERS
"Drinking with your favorite friends"

GOOMBAY
1900 N.W. 75th SREET

Opening April 10, 1964

| Chuck Locke | Wallace Robinson |

FIGURE 4.3 *Miami Times*, April 11, 1964, 5, http://ufdc.ufl.edu/UF00028321/00158.

schools to radio stations, how to find Black doctors and dentists, what's on offer from mom-and-pop stores and hair salons, the names and numbers of lots of psychics, and real estate possibilities in the enduring era of Jim Crow policies.[14] The history of the *Miami Times* is notable for the entertainment advertisements for Black performance venues (especially those taken out between the 1950s and early 1960s) in historic Overtown. These advertisements help to tell another story of Overtown and to imagine the publics never recognized or grossly misrecognized by all of Miami's news outlets. The advertisements give you a *physical sense* of the intense musical activity that shook and continues to shake its streets. All of the important artists on the jazz, soul, and gospel circuits inevitably show up in the ads, whether international stars such as Billie Holiday and Aretha Franklin or upcoming local groups such as the Miami-based Mar-vells and duo-supergroup Sam & Dave. Looking at the paper, whether turning its pages in microfilm or digitized forms, is like opening the doors to loud nightclubs. As Willie Clarke, one of Overtown's great sons and cofounder of Deep City Records said in an interview with Jacob Katel, "Overtown was a whole culture centered around entertainment," and you could say that its finding aids are the advertisements in the *Miami Times*.[15]

In this 1964 page alone there is a cryptic ad for "Watch for the big Costume Ball . . . get your costume ready" and a notice for a new club called GOOMBAY about to be opened in Liberty City. The mid-right panel shows the week's offerings from nightclub impresario Clyde Killens's "Knight Beat" Club in the Sir John Hotel. *In the same week*, patrons could hear protofunk from Chickie Horne, teenage matinees with Roy Hamilton, and blues from Althea Bryant.[16] Killens was originally from Valdosta, Georgia, and is one life among many in South Florida that tells a different story of the Great Migration.[17] Many Black families moved from the Lower South (mostly Georgia but also Alabama and South Carolina) to Miami because of employment opportunities in construction and service economies, climate, train lines, artistic curiosity, and proximity to familial networks, rather than head to the cold and gritty North.[18] It is hard to underscore—unless this sentence could play Bass—Killens's centrality to Miami music and performance histories. Killens's first job in Miami was as a drummer to accompany films in Overtown's historic Lyric Theater.[19] More the doyen of Overtown's music scene than a nightclub manager, Killens later became known as "Mr. Entertainment" or "The Glass" for his unfailing invitation for a toast, and his singular ability to call everyone inside to gather for a good time. To the lower left of the Knight Beat bill is an attached advertisement for "Night in Nassau," an annual event also invented and promoted by Killens, where Bahamians in name or ancestry or sensibility were given a heritage evening complete with the open invitation to "bring your Nassau food and invite him to your table."[20] The event was held at the very venue where Sam Cooke recorded his magnificent album *Live at the Harlem Square Club, 1963* more than a year earlier.[21]

As a nickname, "The Glass" suggested both Killens's hospitality and business acumen: he was able to entice Black performers to come play in Overtown after performing segregated gigs in Miami Beach. Yet for all his enterprising cordiality, Killens would bar certain kinds of entitled entry, not in recorded song as we heard in Eloise Lewis but through the printed word of the *Miami Times*. In a page from August 19, 1961 (see figure 4.4), we see a photo of Killens holding his trademarked extended glass (usually whiskey and water) next to his promotional ad for Dinah Washington's appearance at the Knight Beat. The *Times* made space for Killens to announce his "Special Policy for Dinah Washington." It reads: "Because of the unusually heavy demands for tickets and tables for the DINAH WASHINGTON shows, chiefly from members of the other race, Clyde Killens announces this week that he is forced to use a SPECIAL POLICY FOR THESE SHOWS, in order to accommodate all of the people who want to see and hear DINAH."[22] The instructions that follow are about the protocols of making reservations for specific show times—perhaps a revision of the club's usual less structured entry—yet the reader is still left to wonder how Killens was going to enforce this special policy. Like the open wink from Lewis's album cover, we have Killens openly advertising—extending to all—a once-in-a-lifetime performance experience, but also making sure that there would be enough space made for those who not only wanted but also had earned and *needed* to see Washington sing. Here Killens amplifies the function of the club promoter to a vital provider of community service, all of which depended upon his knowing and prioritizing neighborhood regulars and intimately understanding their needs. Here we sense that this "special policy" was a matter of public health. By curbing the onrush of white club slummers whose manifest destiny usually entitled them to occupy too much space, Killens said openly and secretly from the *Miami Times*: not all of this, not all of us, is for you.

Both of these *Miami Times* pages do and do not tell all of the devastating, confused signs of destruction happening in real time to Overtown after the genocidal placement of interstates 95 and 395 and their interchange straight through Overtown's heart and soul.[23] Overtown was long a prime

FIGURE 4.4 *Miami Times*, August 19, 1961, 9, https://ufdc.ufl.edu/UF00028321/00279/9j.

target of annihilation. It began with slum clearance in the early 1930s through deployment of racial panic over dilapidated housing conditions, which masked other motives for its convenient adjacency to downtown. Raymond A. Mohl states that choice among the weaponry was the "public health argument."[24] The successful chipping away at it, in increments that moved slow and then fast, would ensure its eventual eradication to expand the white business district and to disperse its community center for Black Miamians. White power brokers together with some of the area's property owners would eventually neaten their narratives of decay to clear it, openly, for highway construction. Spatial and economic arguments were made and naturalized.[25] The punitive and sadistic desire to fully suppress Black life, a sense of home, any commitment to educating Black students, and the relentless breaking apart of a very tight-knit community raising their kids together was and is brazen and ongoing.

At the time of the highway construction, the disciplining was especially detailed for Overtown's children. Dr. Dorothy Jenkins Fields tells the story of being a high school student on a field trip to the Dorsey Public Library and being told that they had "to write an essay on the highway in the sky . . . and when you're adults you will be riding on a highway on the sky. And so we want you to think about what that's going to be like and what you will do and how that would work."[26] Imposed destruction was turned into assigned, rote exaltation. No less serious or overt: these violences were also enacted to silence Overtown's music, which for many was the social and physical lifeline that defined this community. When listening to the live recording of Sam Cooke, for example, we get to hear the audience at the Harlem Square Club sing along and document their love for one another, their discordant buzzing togetherness, and their danced fight in the longer freedom struggle. Cooke's set made bookends of "Feel It" and "Having a Party." The highway's displacement pushed families that lived there for generations to "model cities" in Liberty City, Opa-locka, and Brownsville (advertised and editorialized in the former spaces that the *Miami Times* used for entertainment announcements). As integration was put into haphazard practice in Miami Beach, some Black performers would not make the trip to after-hours Overtown, and its audiences would start to frequent clubs there such as The Barn or other newly opened places such as the Tiki Lounge in Coconut Grove.

To move through the archives of the *Miami Times* is to see the slow and tragic disappearance of ads such as those that showcased Clyde Killens's curatorialship—and all that they held—as real estate interests continued to destroy and displace Overtown's venues, performers, and audiences throughout the 1960s. The fading out of these ads happened at roughly the same time the paper "repeatedly championed" the highway as cure for urban blight and (immediately broken) promise of prosperity, as N. D. B. Connolly has observed.[27] Yet in 1964, *still* (to return to Hurston's *still* back in chapter 1) parties are being thrown, big and small. In the 1964 ad, it is Killens who is pictured wearing a grass skirt and doing a belly dance. *Still* the island plural meets southern Georgia in Overtown. For Killens, 1964 was "the last really good year."[28]

The music of Overtown endures, and when it changes locations by force or by choice, it still makes anew. There are many who are invested (for a lot of different reasons) in what Connolly calls Overtown's metonymic function for "neighborhoods lost and white supremacy in action."[29] Connolly calls to attention the manifold uses for this story to stay told as is, and his unprecedented archival work undoes the facile assumptions that are compressed into its telling. I would add that the rhetoric of "Overtown" as total loss finds ready accomplices in the new businesses now gentrifying the neighborhood and who have imposed themselves there to celebrate "what it once was." When presumed lost, or written off as a complete(d) loss, there is the assumption that all lines have been broken between Overtown's past and its present in places such as Liberty City, Opa-locka, and Brownsville. I would also add, or at least turn up, how music troubles and trebles any narrative use of Overtown as demise. Listening closer to Overtown's music—not to make a cautionary function of it but to recognize its ability to build publics regardless—makes material continuity between generations even from under rubble or highways. Its long-developed musical traditions make it impossible for outsiders to amputate its remaining from its displaced residents or to fracture its downtown histories from its suburban figurations—even when the city of Miami (and the brutality of its ongoing place fables) is zealously invested in keeping them apart. Overtown's lines may be broken but are far from silent, and there is a different story that may be told of it, or felt of it, when following its music, when *assuming* that its music lives and continues to be transformed by visionaries in the projects and in the suburbs. The alternate stories that music gives us about what has been retained and restored require a different sense of mapping.

So strong are its musical traditions that Willie Clarke still narrates the former geography of Overtown through song. Although Clarke was born in Fort Gaines, Georgia, he recalls that the first time he heard Black music on the radio was as a four-year-old when his family arrived in Overtown in the early 1940s.[30] So began a lifetime of attaching sound to place. Turning back to his interview with Jacob Katel: "Overtown was beautiful. I used to leave home when I was too young to get in and stand outside and listen on 7th Street and NW 3rd Ave. in what they called a juke joint dancing their ass off to 'Who Threw the Whiskey in the Well.' I'm still crazy about that song. So funny."[31] And of the area a few blocks from his house, it was Louis Jordon's "'Saturday Night Fish Fries' and those kind of parties and get-togethers. . . ."[32] Such mapmaking, or making Overtown's coordinates through songs and dance, incorporates Lucky Millinder's natal Alabama and Chicago, and Louis Jordan's Arkansas. But not only. How to account for all the musicians, and what they brought with them *inside* these band-collectives and their recorded output? Note how Clarke uses the songs not only to mark location but also to set the mood or feeling or protocol in that location: What are the qualities of where one can dance one's ass off, and how is it made? Or what does Clarke mean, what open wink does he mean to shorthand by the phrase "those kinds of parties" that involve all of what's in play during the Saturday night fish fries? The 1949 hit song by Louis Jordon and His Tympany Five is considered among the first rock-and-roll records. The tune's venue is a house on Rampart Street in New Orleans, a jook that can be entered in a different way: "you don't have to pay the usual admission / if you're a cook or a waiter or good musician / so if you happen to be walking by / stop by the Saturday night fish fry." The narrator ends up in jail with his chick bailing him out, and the fish fry ends up as an invitation for a black eye, a night in jail, but also and no matter, for as the chorus repeatedly tells us, "it was rocking." These are all very specific things, tucked in and transported right close to Clarke's family home. A jook in New Orleans brought to a jook in Overtown. The song and the Overtown corner make a match in content and form in Clarke's memory and, by extension, to us here. Clarke's building this song into 7th Street and NW 3rd Avenue offers a suggestive wink, and if you actually listen to it, there is more information given about Overtown's swinging infrastructure, including the police harassment that tried to stop it. Although Clarke conveys Overtown's seclusion, he also insists that it is far from isolated from other Black cultural capitals such as New Orleans.

    The open winks from Lewis's cover and song, Killens's glass and program, and Clarke's palimpsestic jook corners all bear that galvanizing irreverence that the outside may have difficulty admitting. The difficulty may be in part caused by the control over who and where these performances let in and how—even as they may sound like they are available for everyone's freedom. The irreverence is spatial, raced, gendered, sexual, and temporal, and its outwardly performed abstractions alter familiarizing coordinates for music and mapmaking.

There is no curatorial deciding here (before visitation). Mine is not a project that seeks to know, or get, or sanction knowledge or movement about and into these spaces but to pick up a set of musical cues *as they are given, not as they are taken* to make a humble sinew in the longer collective telling of a story. The cues in these pages present true linkages between seemingly intermittent signals. The records here demand to be told as an unending, always amplifying story; they are not here as a select picking and choosing of Miami's greatest hits. Picking up these given cues is to honor their constant assignments for listening to elders and for the open curiosity that enables return to Obed Calvaire's beautiful counsel: "You could maybe get close" to saying something about Black Miami's bountiful musical legacies. There is no complete story of the before, during, and after Bahamian and lower south migrations to Florida or the "height" of Overtown's incredible nightlife because that would enforce colonial time and lane staying and it would assume that these migrations and this Overtown as place, as musics, as active legacies are over. Overtown remains, but it also, like the mobile New Orleans in song, moves to other places, putting its music on so many other corners.

To keep in and out of time with Willie Clarke's aural map, we imagine what songs he made of the intersections when his family left Overtown for Liberty City when he was in high school. And what did he take with him when he went to the historically Black Florida Agricultural and Mechanical University (FAMU) in Tallahassee, where he played tenor drum in its illustrious Marching 100 band? ("It still turns me on when I think about it.") What of this brassy, disciplined, technically and creatively magisterial collective did he bring back home with him? Of his training he shared this great bit with John Capouya: "All this training and studying about people as mental and physical beings got me thinking: 'Why do I like this song, why am I getting lost with this song?' And I figured out the hit songs are the ones I understand from beginning to end, the songs that make me want to sing along bob and weave and have a special feeling."[33] Clarke and fellow Miamian and FAMU student Johnny Pearsall would go on to cofound Deep City Records, named after a subterranean speakeasy in Tallahassee and Miami's profundity and vibe in the peninsula. Pearsall had a record store called Johnny's Records on the corner of 6th Street and 22nd Avenue in Liberty City, and the store's manager was a woman named Helene Smith, who would go on to sing on their first records and become Miami's "First Lady of Soul."[34]

The history of Deep City, Florida's first Black-owned record label, has been recently documented in a few places. There were the rereleases of original Deep City singles via Numero Records in 2005 and 2007 under the *Eccentric Soul* series, one that "documents lost soul music" in "lavishly packaged box sets."[35] And there is the 2014 documentary *Deep City: The Birth of the Miami Sound*, where we get to see some great interviews with some of its involved players, including Clarke. Note the shared if differently articulated aspiration of both right from their titular claims: recovering something that is lost and the assignation of origin. The producers and collaborators of these documentary efforts can be lauded for their labors of love, but I would like to offer some contributions to this history beyond its masculinist collector vibe. For example, the liner notes for the Numero collections, though respectful and earnest, still rely on archaeological hunting metaphors, saviorism, and hunger for the undiscovered to make curatorial selections for the connoisseur. Such desire is not unlike that implied by the 1951 brochure; in fact, Numero has also put out lavishly packaged rereleases of goombay music under its Cult Cargo series. What about those for whom this music was never lost? Those for whom "lavish" means something that can also be used and scratched rather than preciously displayed? As for the documentary, again, though important, it leans on a terrible plot device from many other music industry narratives: that which makes women responsible for messing everything up. In *Deep City* the faults are twofold: the label's decline was caused by a (manufactured) rivalry between its principal vocalists, Helene Smith and Betty Wright, and it suggests that Wright's desire for an enduring career also ruined everything. This plot device is used, unnecessarily and misogynistically, as the film's denouement.[36] In the words and ethos of DJ Uncle Al, I want to "Do it Different."

Here is another enticement for you to come—differently this time, for there is a reverse directional (see figure 4.5). This single features the promotional 45 plug side "A Woman Will Do Wrong" gorgeously sung by Helene Smith, produced by Deep City, and distributed by the Philadelphia-based label Phil-L.A. of Soul (pronounced fillet of soul).[37] Note the flood of locations within a seven-inch diameter: there are the embedded Overtown and Liberty City, the crucial additions of Philly

FIGURE 4.5 Helene Smith, *A Woman Will Do Wrong* (Phil-L.A. of Soul, 1967, vinyl). Collection of the author.

as a capital of soul and recording, and a Los Angeles way west but made so close as to appear right after the hyphen, here made into a wave, all underscored by a fish's skeleton.

The single reached the upper R&B chart in 1967 and was part of the extensive efforts of Clarke and Pearsall to try to move Miami, move this resolutely local but incredibly expansive voice of Smith's, and all the other voices she carried, out of state. The decision is written out for all: Plug side. Play this side on the radio. There is a countermovement of visitation associated with this shimmering artifact. It is not so much one that lures you to Miami, a "come here," that internal promotional. Instead, it is a push for Miami, for Black Miami especially, to reach up and out, to meet you at your place, to be in all those other venues with all those other people. To make social living. It is not an advertisement that asks for your voyeurism, waterfront development, and/or racked-up liquor tab. It is part of that geographic argument first established in this chapter by Lewis. The argument is actual and conceptual: the single argues for a place, this place, Overtown and Liberty City and the islands and upper Floridas inside them in the deeper soul tradition. It also reveals this place's ability to float elsewhere. It is as portable as New Orleans and asks for establishment on lots of other corners that want and need it. That this track in particular was among the early ones to break out of Miami as a hit for national R&B has much, if not all, to do with Smith's voice. Often described as "sweet," which it surely is, her voice resounds the serious heft of a prodigy experimenting with microphone and studio.

Smith recorded this single when she was twenty years old, and her melodic subtlety demonstrates a voice that asks you to meet her there. Something of this quality also happens when listening to João Gilberto and Aaron Neville. She and they inspire an unquestioned want to bend the ear toward the vocalist. Her vocal flutters just above the song's beautifully restrained arrangement by Arnold Albury (another FAMU alumnus who carried its verve and movement and metals into other musical structures). Smith's interplay with the ensemble, the organ, the incredible piano, and the backup vocals is so palpably collaborative—it is the kind of work that directs our eye and ear to that girl who doesn't want to be center stage but overtakes everything from far stage left. Smith's early influences include Baby Washington, Aretha Franklin, and Mary Wells, daughters of the northward migrations to Harlem and Detroit. Smith's voice is a south-to-north reintroduction of a sound that went the other way. The midway point of Philly made many reunions such as this, even if the musicians never actually met.

"A Woman Will Do Wrong" runs two-and-a-half minutes, and Smith's incredible maneuvers within the short form would find their fullest spectrum in the other recordings she made for Deep City over the following decade. While her records were short forms, they made long-form connectivity. "Willing and Able," one of her favorites, also reveals her sophisticated vocal ability to both hold back and move with the brassy FAMU cadence (she calls it "that full kick-butt sound"), as much as gently ground the give and take of Black Miami's vocal traditions as made in the church and experimented with in the clubs.[38] Her vocal line traces musical travel up and down the state of Florida, from Tallahassee and its stride into southern Georgia, and back down to its southernmost tip. Her voice and her interpretations also carry the history of FAMU's visitations to Miami and how they would shake the streets. Smith's fluency with and transposition of the FAMU and Overtown–to–Liberty City sound make her voice a vital archive for Florida's musical history. Smith is credited (rightly) as one of the pioneers of the "Miami Sound," and her performances demand that such a category needs to allow for air and movement outside of it. There are so many here, she sings.

Smith had priorities in addition to being a singer. Famously shy and growing increasingly tired with the rigors of the road, she drew back slightly from music to be a mother and a teacher. As Smith conveyed to John Capouya, "I was getting so into my family—wanting to have a child and then raising one—plus wanting to go to school." And of the music business, "There was just so much mess going on and people acting crazy. I just wanted to be a decent person, and have a good marriage."³⁹ The desire for a little corner of peace and quiet from touring and studio life did not mean the end of her musical legacy. It simply changed forms. Smith became a beloved teacher to many, an adoration we can imagine from her sheer affection for it: "I loved it. I taught everything: PE, Music, Art. And in those classes, you really have to teach." These classes are to some throwaway electives that distract from "real" curriculum such as math and language arts. But for so many others, they are a lifeline to other worlds desperately needed and reachable with body and mind. For Smith they are the places where teachers must bring their A game. Take this description of her innovative pedagogy: "When we were doing Science, sometimes I would teach them little songs about the water and the environment. We would sing it and they would love it. 'Let's sing it again!' Oh, yes."⁴⁰ In addition to her actual records, Smith's dedication to and innovative way with teaching has created musical institutions, especially for Miami, and, in an everyday way, for her neighborhood students. To tuck a micro-conservatory experience into a science class, to make rote exercises experiments in music, is precisely the way to study all water and surround. These kinds of informal but actual institutions built in the partial absence of Overtown's entertainment district, and the developing one in Liberty City, would train the next wave of young musicians and their audiences, whether they took their lessons in the classroom or in the studio or via radio.

IV. Many of Overtown's venues were mostly closed by the late 1960s, but there was so much music made in spite of the destruction over in Liberty City, where young artists such as Clarke, Pearsall, Smith, and many others were hard at work. I necessarily pause on Helene Smith and now, Betty Wright, because they both came of age in the Overtown–to–Liberty City era. They make a historical argument for collective musical innovation, their life experiences reveal how ongoing structures are built for music, and they do much to decenter dominant stories about labels and the men who built them.⁴¹ The much-adored musician Betty Wright, in addition to being one of Liberty City's own to make a huge national impact, was also one of the most important theorists about the transition of Overtown, how and where its musical legacies may have moved. Wright was born in 1953 to Rosa Lee Wright and McArthur Norris, one of Overtown–to–Liberty City's prominent musical families. Her mother, originally from Cairo, Georgia, moved to Perrine, Florida, and eventually landed in Overtown when she was in her twenties and became a pillar and beloved matriarch of music and community.[42] She was known to many as Nana and did much to help institute and flourish Black Miami's visionary gospel scene. Wright's father first owned a pool hall in Overtown and later a thriving landscaping business in Liberty City that helped showcase his talents in topiary.[43] They moved the family to the Liberty Square housing projects in the early 1950s and eventually to the El Portal neighborhood, where Flip Wilson lived right across the street.[44] Wright has made records of this in different forms of music and through her renowned support of the Liberty City and Overtown communities, especially nascent musicians.

Wright was roughly six years Helene Smith's junior and also made her debut on the Deep City label. A twelve-year-old Wright first met Pearsall and Clarke when she came to the store to pick up a copy of Billy Stewart's "Summertime" that she had won in a radio contest. While there, she sang a few lines of the song and eventually recorded a set of singles for Deep City, including "Good Lovin'/Paralyzed" and "Mr. Lucky/Thank You Baby" when she was fourteen.[45] This was far from a discovery of an unknown talent, for Wright had been performing with her family from the time she was three years old. But it was these singles that launched her into South Florida's and R&B radio's limelight. Wright's debut album, *My First Time Around*, was recorded on the Atco label and released in 1968. Held on the album are classic hits such as "Girls Can't Do What Guys Do," "He's Bad, Bad, Bad," and "The Best Girls Don't Always Win." United by Wright's vocally gifted maturity to sing the first heartbreaks of girlhood, the songs included some of South Florida's most esteemed session players, such as Clarence Reid (later known as "Blowfly"), Butch Trucks Jr. (later the drummer for the Allman Brothers), and Eddie Martinez (drummer for the South Florida supergroup the Birdwatchers). The album inaugurated an active and lauded early career that led to one of her greatest hits for which she is most widely known, the 1971 "The Clean Up Woman." This song was vitally accompanied by Willie Hale ("Little Beaver") on bass and rhythm guitars, and penned by Clarke and Reid on Henry Stone and Steve Alaimo's Miami-based label Alston when she was just seventeen years old. Her second album, the 1972 *I Love the Way You Love*, retained this company of Miami musical legends and added the talents of others such as Latimore and the incredible Snoopy Dean. Wright's rendition of Little Beaver's "I Love the Way You Love" is subtle, beautiful, and muscular storytelling, and it gives us a complete amorous history in three minutes.[46]

Betty Wright was one of the last acts to play at the Sir John Hotel before it was destroyed to make way for a new post office.[47] Twelve years later,

FIGURE 4.6 Still from a 1977 interview with Betty Wright. Miami Dade College Lynn and Louis Wolfson II Florida Moving Image Archives, September 13, 1977, CXN055: WCIX Newsfilm: Overtown—Betty Wright; Florida Memorial College; www.wolfsonarchives.org.

in 1977, Wright sat for an interview where she was asked to offer some reflection on having been the last performer to grace the stage there.[48] She gave the interview with her infant daughter, Namphuyo Aisha McCray, sitting on her lap (see figure 4.6).

In the interview, Betty Wright and her baby do everything to re-create for us a tangible impression of the importance of the Sir John Hotel. As Wright guides our entry to it, she also dismantles those expert postures and vocabularies that are called upon to transmit history, musical and otherwise. The scene opens on Wright and her baby girl looking at each other, taking the other in. Her unspoken conversation with her daughter, both completely alone in the presence of the other, even as they are in front of a camera and interviewer and unseen audience, gets us to see Wright's material restoration of the Sir John as she relays its tearing down. As she tells of her surprise discovery of the Sir John's undoing, happening by at the very moment they were demolishing it, Wright records her outrage at the burial site as she also demands to life those who built it. She lists with care, repeatedly, performers such as Barbara McNair, Flip Wilson, Sam & Dave, Jackie Wilson, Dionne Warwick, and the importance of these and her own solo-show performances, how they were given their own billing to show their publics what they could do in a singular night.

Although the venue was distinctive for the stylistic range of its invited players, it was not the mashed-togetherness of the variety circuit. For Wright, these individual performances within the medley of Overtown's local and visiting glitterati are remaining structures for the now-dispersed populations that once lived together there. They are foundations that children can identify and point to even if their stages were pulverized. At the same time, in addition to this difficult testimonial work, Wright offers an embrace of Overtown's improvisatory past and present.[49] Wright doesn't just say what it was; she tells you how to be there. At the Sir John, "You never knew just who was coming." She makes you want to operate now in the ways that made it what it was. In other words, to do any history of Overtown, and of its nursery for Liberty City and the Miami sound, is to leave yourself open to never knowing "just who was coming." Danielle Goldman has elegantly written that improvisation "is about moving where movement might not have seemed possible or in a way that, for whatever reason, no one could have imagined prior to its realization."[50] In the interview, Wright demonstrates moves where movement doesn't seem possible. She shows that the attempted destruction of Black life failed and its restoration happens in part by maintaining Overtown as a formative stop in the memories of and for many.

When watching the interview, there is a great sense of admiration of how calm, fed, and secure this baby is. Imagine all the logistical preparations, starting with the hours proceeding the interview, and back farther to what and who those past preparations make present. There are the many times Wright woke at night to feed and comfort her, felt in times like this interview, with likely the special-occasion bath given, and the outfit, even its cap sleeves perfectly ironed, with the good luck of a nap taken before the film crew came over. At the same time, in the midst of all this dexterity with the time and care of another, Wright put herself together perfectly. Her hair and makeup and outfit offer a polish to the scene, of holding herself together. And yet there isn't a sense of preciousness about her look; it is one that is not afraid of getting mussed up or thrown off by the baby's presence. Wright instead includes her baby into music history. It is humbling to take in how Wright manages to hold her for the duration, how she helps the baby to sit calmly and securely by a microphone without, for now, taking it into her hands or mouth. It is left there to pick up and experience when she's ready. Wright might be haunted by questions about her now and what's next as she reflects on Overtown's now and what's next: When will she be able to work, again, like she did before? What will her daughter and her cohort get to know about their history? But then again, she also might find assurance in the confident supplement that is being alone in the presence of another: her work will be better and more prepared than ever. When the interviewer asks her if she knew she was a star, Wright responds that she rather likens herself to the moon: "because a moon eclipses every now and then, but you always know it is coming back. And it's bigger and . . . I'm big at times, and I wane a little, you know, and I deviate."

At a later point in the interview, Wright encourages approaches to thinking about Miami beyond what she calls the "presupposed atmosphere" of Miami Beach. She says "presupposed atmosphere" in such a way that assumes the local in conversation. We know what it means: the blowing open of its postcard surface as touristic tropical paradise safely segregated and frozen in space and time. Pushing us to forgo all the dependables in the "presupposed atmosphere," which at their core are the blatant erasure of those who built the city, Wright takes away history's racist supports with this phrase. Wright peoples and narrates the creation and destruction of Overtown down to those everyday details about how communities make things happen and how imposed policies of separation actually work. How, for example, a discontinued bus route can tear communities apart as when she explains how its tightly knit residents used to take the 21 bus on the neighborhood's main artery to arrive together to listen. And later, after its citizens were displaced into housing projects in areas such as Opa-locka, Carol City, and Liberty City, audiences couldn't get there in the same way together. With the phrase, Wright does much to decalcify those "presupposed atmospheres" of music criticism more generally. As she remakes the foundations of this local history, Wright does not flash her rare vinyl still in its original wrapping. She refuses its data collection. Nor does she position herself as the renegade digger on an archaeological hunt but tells it from the insides, from its gatherings, from its dance floors. With her infant on her lap, Wright makes a case for Miami Sound as something that is identifiable and particular and capable, always, of new growth—and at the same time offers a mode for its criticism. I hear the Miami Sound somewhere between Betty Wright and her infant and back again, the lives and work that led them here and will continue to live and work away from here. With her, Wright says, with all.

FIGURE 4.7 Ms. B Records logo, taken from Betty Wright, *Mother Wit* (Ms. B. Records, MB-330, 1987, vinyl). Collection of the author.

Kurt "K. O. T. O." Curtis, whom we fondly remember from chapter 1, made a serious and painstaking catalog of Wright's discography by tracking her work throughout the 1970s. On her 1974 album *Danger High Voltage*, she was accompanied by Rick Finch and Harry Wayne Casey (of later KC and the Sunshine Band fame)—*and* Benny Latimore and Timmy Thomas, two of popular music's most unsung and innovative keyboardists. Featured there was another of Wright's signature tunes, "Tonight Is the Night," in which she sang out the interior monologue of a young woman losing her virginity. In 1981 Wright signed with Epic Records, with which she released *Betty Wright* and *Wright Back at You*, in addition to other work for the label such as singing backing vocals on Stevie Wonder's *Hotter Than July*. The major labels rejected "Pain," a song written by Wright in 1984 in the midst of her divorce. And so Wright decided to found her own label, Ms. B and Miami Spice Publishing Co. (see figure 4.7).

Betty Wright's Ms. B label is the collective ground for her self-produced and arranged album *Mother Wit*, released in 1987. It is in *Mother Wit* that I hear part of the reestablishment of Overtown, called for ten years prior in Wright's televised interview. Curtis reports that the single "No Pain, No Gain" was the first gold record earned by an African American woman on her own label.[51] And it also institutes Liberty City as a music capital, an important place where people were not only sent but continued to survive and make beautiful things in the transfer.[52] When taking in the album's lineup, it is, in her words, encountering the wondrous surprise of "you just never knew who was coming." In some ways, the personnel was expected, including the company of Wright mainstay collaborators such as Little Beaver and drummer Dennis Everheart. But here we also find a professional launching pad for upcoming vocalists such as Cynthia Calhoun, who later became part of the crucial backup vocal lines for Barry White, Steely Dan, Al Jarreau, and Gloria Estefan, among others. Calhoun credits Wright as the person who "introduced me to the music business."[53] The album also featured Myshjua Allen (daughter of the Nashville-born reggae roots singer Dhaima Matthews), who recorded hits for Kingston pioneer producer Joe Gibbs and who is now executive label manager for Tuff Gong International, as well as talented Freestyle vocalist Cynthia Roundtree.[54] Other reggae legacies on the album include Montego Bay–born and Miami Dade College alum Lancelot "Sir Lancelot" Hall, drummer for the band Inner Circle. Even resplendent Bobby Caldwell (!), whose Miami upbringing and musical training offer robust puncture into the simplistic category "blue-eyed soul," was featured in the vocal back line of *Mother Wit*. The lead vocalist takes a turn to be in background, to eagerly contribute to what he will do for love.[55]

The founding of Ms. B—"After the Pain" of its opening track—is thus a restoration, open opportunity, learning lab. On the sleeve, Wright includes the following after listing her acknowledgments of family and close friends and supporters:

"If I forgot your name this time, forgive me and sign upon the dotted line:

--."

This is an open signature line for all the known and unknown collaborators, neighbors, friends, teachers, fans, anyone at all to include themselves as part of this Overtown-and-after assembly. With this open line, Wright says: here is a place for you to write yourself into the record. From Wright's earliest recordings with Deep City to the founding of her own label to the later training she gave to contemporary stars such as Joss Stone, she brought Miami and everyone on the dotted line with her. But she always came home. The establishment that was her legendary Liberty City home on 10th Avenue shared with her third husband, the renowned Jamaican music pioneer Noel "King Sporty" Williams—perhaps best known for his innovative work with reggae and for writing "Buffalo Soldier" for Bob Marley, and more locally for doing much to facilitate the strong Bass character in Miami's music—gave shelter and comfort and creative inspiration to so many.

I return to the shore that began this section, with Wright holding her baby girl on her lap. I first came across that interview in 2011, even wrote and publicly delivered several papers about it, with the minimal context I was able to find about it from archivists or through asking friends and acquaintances. A paramount research question I had of this interview: Who of Wright's five babies was on her lap that day? Through more kinds of familiarity with Wright's life and career—a familiarity that took a lot of time, including the time it took having my own babies—I eventually found out that she was Namphuyo Aisha McCray. I was able to find her through her Instagram, and to give you an instantaneous sense of how generous she is, McCray agreed to speak with me just a few months after her mother's tragic passing at the young age of sixty-six. I told her I had been looking for her for a long time and opened up our talk by showing her the interview clip from 1977 when she was eight months old. I shared the deep impression I've always had about the calm and elegant curiosity of this baby, of this making together with her mother, to which McCray replied through an audible smile: "I was trained."[56]

McCray spent much of her childhood at her grandparents' home in El Portal, especially because her mother was often on tour. But for McCray, Wright was always materially present; she was "always with me" and "very, very involved in my life even when she was gone." Regardless of whether her mom was at home or away, McCray was very enmeshed in the musical living of Nana's house as it was a welcoming and generative home for many of Miami's great musicians. "It was nothing but music all the time," said McCray of her childhood. There was always someone walking around with a guitar (ever-present live performance), and all of the family members had incredible record collections (ever-present recorded archives). McCray was particularly drawn to her aunty Jeannette's collection, which held albums by Isaac Hayes, Chaka Kahn, Phyllis Hyman, Frank Sinatra, and Rufus; it was a part of the home conservatory that "really trained her voice." McCray was sometimes taken on the road with Wright, including a brief stint living in New Haven, where Wright worked as the librarian for the Lyman Wheeler Beecher Elementary School between gigs in New York. After moving back to Miami in 1985, Wright was hard at work building Ms. B and writing and recording her album *Mother Wit*, on which the young McCray sang backup vocals when she was ten years old. McCray would continue to sing locally but would not record again until she performed backup vocals on Gloria Estefan's 1991 *Into the Light*. Estefan's album was loaded with feelings of fall and recovery: it was recorded just after she was injured in a terrible bus crash while on tour. This album, many of us will recall, became used as a relentless soundtrack to post–Hurricane Andrew

Miami. It was Betty Wright who arranged the album's hit, "Coming Out of the Dark."

Note for note, the musical surround of McCray's childhood was matched by countless stories of Overtown. It was not the handing down of some nostalgic mythology but rather the material handing over of traditions. Hearing these traditions made it clear for McCray that Overtown, especially as a place for Black art, holds a spiritual and physiological set of histories necessary for present living. She mimics her grandmother's voice when recalling the time when "Aretha just called me to say she's keeping Betty for a bit longer." When I asked her what it was like to be growing up hearing these stories—stories that were passed down to her even as an eight-month-old in her mother's lap—McCray replied "I remember feeling left out." There is a different sense of loss here, one that can't be captured by the larger narration of a presumably lost Overtown. It is the kind of loss from one who would have been there, that makes one wonder about what they missed, how they missed it, why they couldn't be a part of it, and crucially, how to make it happen, now, in another kind of way. This myriad and devastating sense of being left out gave McCray the kind of determination and fury to make other continuations of Overtown. As McCray came of age, her dream was always to find a way to restore Overtown as a place for a living that honors the dead because "it was always really important to my mother."

In her 2020 single "So Many Ways," we hear McCray's voice in grown-up extension from that moment on her mother's lap and *Mother Wit*—and its other contours through her wildly prolific career recording with artists including Estefan, Jon Secada, Irene Cara, Trick Daddy, Joss Stone, and Pharrell Williams. You can hear Wright in her phrasing and timbre, but it is a voice that is all hers. Crisp and resonant, high and deep, McCray's voice bears an incredible control. She suggests additional voices you will hear in hers: Chaka Khan, Jennifer Holiday, Shirley Murdoch, Atlantic Starr, and Peter Cetera. To imagine all that McCray experienced in the particular intersections of people and places, and how this shores up not only in her voice but also in the aesthetic choices of a song's surround, is found in a visual counterpoint to that first filmed performance of hers in 1977. The video of "So Many Ways" is set in a 1950s diner, a location chosen by McCray given her ongoing attachment to the movie *Grease* ("I was Rizzo, of course"). In planning for the video, McCray asked her uncle Charles Wright about what old diners were like back then. When he told her that back then, they weren't allowed in diners, McCray knew that it was up to her to make up her own textured experience to them. She called on friends young and old to

FIGURE 4.8 Namphuyo Aisha McCray and her mother, Betty Wright, on the set of the video shoot for "So Many Ways," March 23, 2019. Filmed at MUSICTURISTA in North Miami. Courtesy of Namphuyo Aisha McCray.

help her stage it. And what she gives us in the spatial and sonic and danced argument of this video is a most-moving tutorial on what is required, and what inheritances are put into new forms, when imagining yourself as part of the story. Creative salvage (see figure 4.8).

Namphuyo McCray answered with a resolute "Yes" when I asked if her Nana had a Florida room. And what was it like? "It was everything. When I was a kid, it was *everything*. It was where my dog lived. It was my personal skating rink because when you're really little in a room that big, you know, I would put on music and skate around and around that room. It was where I played. We ate there. We had family reunions and birthday parties. It was everything. I mean, we even slept out there sometimes."[57]

V. Betty Wright transitioned to Heaven on May 10, 2020, but her funeral was still safely held and streamed so that all her beloveds could be with her and her family to accompany her spirit's passing. At the live-streamed funeral, held during the quarantine, one of Liberty City's most famous native sons, Luther Campbell, said this: "If you have ever been to [Wright's] house, you got the best of both worlds . . . you got Sporty, who's going to give it to you blood raw, and Betty telling you it's going to be all right." By the strength of the umhms of agreement in the socially distanced service, it was clear that there is no way we can know the sheer numbers of those who may have passed through and who still move through the House of Betty Wright, and over five decades' worth of songs, telling them all it is going to be all right.

There are so many others here listening and making anew. Luther Campbell, who McCray told me was Betty Wright's best friend, brings his own lines to the Overtown–to–Liberty City history. His mother, Yvonne Galloway, was born in Overtown in 1933 and raised there.[58] She was the daughter of a Bahamian father and one of the sisters together known as the beautiful "Galloway Girls." In 1954 she met and married Stanley Campbell, the child of Jamaican émigrés, and they lived in a small apartment in the neighborhood. The young family left Overtown when they began clearing it for the interstate and moved to Liberty City after seeing an ad in the *Miami Times*. Two years later, in 1960, the Campbells would give birth to Luther. Luther, once known as DJ Luke Skyywalker before George Lucas took it away, thereafter Luke, and sometimes, with the comforts of middle age, "Uncle Luke," is an all-in-one name you may instantly recognize as the head MC and producer of 2 Live Crew, a pioneering group in a music genre called Miami Bass.[59] Campbell's career is often made reducible to the 2 Live Crew moment or as the plaintiff in a famous federal copyright law case, *Campbell vs. Acuff-Rose Music*, which established that commercial parody qualifies as fair use and won for his misuse of Roy Orbison's "Oh, Pretty Woman." He is what some may call a difficult figure for the ways he is both adored and reviled. All of this is important, and important to this chapter's story, yet I do not want to turn Campbell into a narrative function for the larger race and sex panics of the late 1980s and early 1990s. Nor do I want to get mired in the more controversial details around his public personality or inconsistencies in the various tellings of his biography. Instead, I turn to Campbell as another vital historian of Black Miami in tandem with music. He is of the generation that inherited all of who and what came before, with, and after the rise of Deep City, the careers of Smith and Wright (including their self-made entrepreneurial practices that were so rooted in Overtown and Liberty City), in a Miami that would do anything to prohibit their success. With this, with them, there are also Campbell's aesthetic inheritances that carried him from before he was even in the womb. Campbell has documented these inheritances with prolific acuity in music and with the written word. Whether through his column in the *Miami New Times* or his 2015 autobiography, *The Book of Luke: My Fight for*

Truth, Justice, and Liberty City, Campbell is a writer who is incredibly adept at putting the local in a larger national context, as if he were spinning records together. In *The Book of Luke* he suggests that this faculty has much to do with his upbringing, his emphasis on the formative work ethic of both parents, and especially from the teachings of his politicized uncle, Ricky Stirrup. I would add that it is his aesthetic innovations—what he was able to do with turntables, audio equipment, party making, *doing*—that make him one of the great theorists and historians of Miami.

All these qualities were on full display during a 2014 interview with Campbell at Bokamper's Sports Bar in Miramar on the day President Barack Obama officially normalized relations with Cuba.[60] While we spoke in that booth, person after person across the age, gender, and color lines would approach "Luke" (using his first name, local statesman style) to tell them how much they loved him and how he saved their life. I asked him about his parents:

> [My father] grew up in Jamaica. They met in Cuba. They were there partying. My great-grandmother is Cuban, so I assume they were visiting her. They ended up falling in love and having all these kids. He used to tell me all these stories about Cuba. They just lifted a large part of the embargo yesterday. They used to tell me stories about partying over there during the Batista days and how a lot of musicians from the States would go over there and perform and how it was just a great party town. They'd always brag about how the Bahamas was like Cuba used to be. It was about going to Cuba and enjoying yourself. I used to like hearing those stories. My mom was from Nassau, and her mother's mother was from Cuba. On the weekends it was about partying.[61]

The 1951 brochure with which I opened this chapter has now been blasted open to involve, despite its intended commercial intentions, Black tourism and pleasure.[62] From Miami, this is not the sort of itinerary that gives one pause but is a banal part of the city's family business, especially Miamian pioneer families like Yvonne Campbell's. These historical migrations have not always been for work, and even if it was and is migration for work, Luther Campbell insists upon traditions of pleasure, on the making-a-lot-of-kids ethos, on a good time, on the complaints that may arise about any ordinary visit to relatives near and far. Campbell's "partying"—and it must be clarified that parties are not always, if ever, about forgetting the pain of the everyday but perhaps also a playful suspension of it—is an invitation to imagine the aesthetics developed while enjoying oneself even as your work, or lack of it, would suggest that you can't.

Campbell then went on to talk in more detail about his mom, Yvonne, who eventually opened her own salon in Northwest Miami called the Beauty-Rama.[63] His earliest musical memories came from his boyhood sweeping up of the salon floor, where his mother and her clients would turn up the radio to singers such as the brazen Millie Jackson, whose direct address raps mid-disco gave uncensored comfort and gumption to the jilted throughout the 1970s. And when Luke would return home, his father seemed to always be playing Burt Bacharach. He said, "I learned more about Burt Bacharach and Millie Jackson than anybody. It was a combination of that." The Bacharach fixation woke him up every Saturday morning as his father would play, compulsively, Dionne Warwick's version of "I'll Never Fall in Love Again." As he relayed this to me, Campbell did not refer to the song by name but sang it out loud. Luke's was a voice I only knew through his gravelly call-and-response screams. That day he translated Warwick's conservatory soprano into a vulnerable tenor. Now, whenever I hear Luke, I also hear Dionne Warwick. And vice versa. Campbell's "combination of that" puts together seemingly incongruous things such as Bacharach and Millie Jackson. I can actually hear Campbell's "combination of that" beyond this sentence through the shape he draws for us of Nassau, Havana, Kingston, and Miami. Both partying and "combination of that" offer inspiring navigational lines to activate the bottom, the sonic environmentalism from below those crossed imperialisms that have taken hold of the area for centuries.

In listening to his stunning autobiographical disclosures I hear some anticipatory feedback (through Jackson and Warwick) to the violent misogyny, particularly against Black women, in the lyrics of Luke and his 2 Live Crew. The galvanizing call for an intersectional Black feminist sensibility to the larger "case" of 2 Live Crew was urgently articulated by Kimberlé Williams Crenshaw in the early 1990s. Crenshaw was not satisfied with legal arguments about obscenity or with Henry Louis Gates Jr.'s spirited defense of 2 Live Crew's work as racial humor in the op-ed pages of the *New York Times*. For Gates, the corrective of 2 Live Crew's misogyny lies in "the emergence of more female rappers to redress sexual stereotypes."[64] Crenshaw's work and, I would argue, various recorded (hear out the Coochie Crew and Repo Crew) and unrecorded responses that many girls and women have enacted on dance floors everywhere recognize that facile correctives never work. I hold on to these critiques and responses now as much as I did then as a teenager on those dance floors. What is really important to mention here is that 2 Live Crew and their lyrics are just *one* part of this robust entity called Miami Bass. Exclusive attention to the lyrics has long made possible a totalizing and moralistic disavowal of the musical aesthetics, which we know all come from somewhere.[65]

Impossible to define as a genre, Miami Bass is something that is learned through hearing rather than telling.[66] For Miami Bass makes *not* hearing it impossible. It is a sound that enters you. A tremble, a tremor, all over the city and anywhere it's played. In clubs, in front of schools, at the mall, in the cars that go boom. It messes up any equivalency between land and rights by those who have been denied both. It bears brilliant formal inventions of the unpropertied. Miami Bass makes deep guttural sounds, bolstered by speakers and wiring and conch shells, with some strident rapping atop it. It has room for everything that has made Miami, and what's more, it resounds up, northward through the peninsula, to make new communion with the Deep South hip-hop coming out of southern Georgia. Up there it is slower than down here. In Miami it is faster; it is a chase; it asks for pageantry under pressure. The dancing planes are low to the ground; bodies are inverted. You will hear traditions from all over the islands tucked into it, Latinate and Calypsate, steel pan and clave and goombay drum organic or transposed into other technologies. Further shaped by innovative technologies made in Liberty City, such as the arts of speaker manipulation from a group of Rastafarian Jamaicans who lived across the street from Campbell's childhood home, Bass's heart and mechanics owe much to all these other islands and spiritualisms.

All right: in some Miami Bass recordings the lyrics are really terrible and become harder to tolerate should you happen to have daughters. Lots of brazen straight man–centered fantasies of unlimited and available pussy and anal sex. Lots of titty shaking. All of that. For many of Miami Bass's practitioners, those lyrics were both truth documents and pure fictions. I do not ever want to minimize the gender violence in the lyrics. Yet there is a history of dancing below them, and while down there, of turning a collective ear to bass's aesthetic inheritances, ancient and current. What joy it gave and gives for dance, for our daughters who are (as we once were) savvy enough to know the lyrics aren't about them.[67] In my discussions with many women who came of age with Miami Bass—including the daughters of Overtown and Liberty City's musical dynasties, such as Namphuyo McCray and Leah Jackson (the glorious singer Gwen McCrae's daughter)—"beautiful" and "so beautiful" have been the words to describe that sound.[68] And many will recall that Bass was and is an ongoing opportunity to feel and press against the limits of the body, especially while dancing. Many will fixate on Miami Bass, across the ideological positions, as a soundtrack only worthy of prohibition. Sectors of respectability—abounding in Florida—that have long implemented their constraints on young people experimenting with self and other, are particularly ruffled by Miami Bass. Bass is the ultimate in counter-uplift in a city that has forever made racist linkage between Black people's behavior and sanitation/cleanliness.[69]

Outright dismissal or censorship of Miami Bass as illicit garbage severs creative connections to the early Black populations that established Miami, a disavowal of the rich spatial and musical swirl of the Antilles and Lucayan archipelago and the US South, and the aesthetic practices developed there to keep things alive. Bass, and this geographic area's desire for it, includes the rumble up from the oceanic grave from those who lost their lives in the passage. Its eruptive repetitions remind that there are a lot of people and things below—Overtown's rubble, condo-ed over cemeteries, and the Miami Circle are all living hard in the subterranean and submarine—that demand your attention in body and mind. Listening to Lewis, Killens, Clarke, Smith, Wright, McCray, and the records chosen and played by Yvonne and Stanley Campbell, the greater Beauty-Rama, and what young Luke heard there allows me to wade into bass another way—meaning, I'm entering it, not explaining it. It is an offer of an open though tangible set of origins. Entering by way of these pioneers is to sense its echolocational profundity, its unrelenting deep-sea qualities that resurrect all that lies on the ocean floor, to hearing into those itineraries that opened these pages. The bottom. In its rumble there is a perceptible platform for Black health, a crucial environmental movement for the city of Miami that has historically and insistently made calls for Black death. In Bass I hear a reparative sound to the decimating trawl of this under-theorized channel of the Atlantic, an activation of what we can't and shouldn't forget. All better put by this wonderful formulation offered by Dave Tompkins: "Bass is green."[70]

VI.

Bass makes you come. For all its fullness, for all its robust ability to shake and disturb the surround, it is perhaps the sound that arrives after everything is taken away. Luther Campbell was an up-and-coming DJ in Liberty City with the Ghetto Style DJs, a very influential crew that had enough heart left over to arrange, upon Campbell's initiative, dance parties for neighborhood kids so that they would have a place to go and, as Earl Lovelace once put it, "dance to the hurt."[71] They would offer a much-needed community service, especially after the Miami rebellions of 1980 following the acquittal of the five policemen who murdered Arthur McDuffie, a friend to many in Overtown and Liberty City.[72] The devastation of Liberty City was near totalizing and permanent, and resources pledged to its redevelopment were instead infamously funneled to Latino and white business and property owners. According to Campbell, "There were no real restaurants, no good bars. Our dances were the only entertainment lots of people had, the only thing to lift people's spirits."[73] And so Ghetto Style DJs would play free parties in African Square Park. Campbell and his crew would rig up their equipment using the socket of a neighboring lightbulb plug and play their innovative sounds. The crew also brought their temporary gigs to more-permanent establishments. Through Campbell, the crew made their own wildly successful alcohol-free music parties under the name the "Pac Jam Teen Disco," first held at the Sunshine Roller Rink down south in Homestead. In early 1984 Campbell eventually decided to move the function back to Liberty City, on the corner of 54th Street and 12th Avenue, and call it Pac Jam II. As Campbell recalls of that time, "The kids knew it was a safe space, as safe as we could make it in a place like Liberty City. Parents knew that, too. We had a lot of support from the community. Weekends, that place was *packed*. It was a place for all the Liberty City groups to play their music, and the little jitterbugs were a great audience to try out new stuff. It was the perfect place for me to break records." These parties primed Campbell to build, sound by sound, party by party, sell by sell, his own label, Luke Records, which would go on to define what Miami Bass became for the rest of the world.[74] His were the records carried to Rio by a young DJ Marlboro while vacationing in Miami to add in the development of that gorgeous Brasilian intercession of baile funk.

Here is an early record put out by Luke Skyywalker Records, one that readies you for another kind of trip. Recorded by Anquette, the name of the group and also the name of its front-woman rapper, Anquette Allen. The other members are Keia Red and Ray Ray. Allen was one of the only young women MCs known in the location of Miami Bass (in addition to Lady Tigra and Bunny D of L'Trimm's "We Like the Cars That Go Boom"). Allen also happened to be Luther Campbell's cousin. She had just graduated from high school when she was recruited to make a follow-up song to 2 Live Crew's enormously successful 1986 "Throw the D" (Throw the Dick), to which Anquette's song response was "Throw the P" (Throw the Pussy). It was a bold challenge to unchecked and unidirectional penetration on the airwaves and dance floors. Part of why Anquette is so fundamental in this story is to counter the erasure of women and girls from Miami Bass histories.

FIGURE 4.9
Anquette, *Ghetto Style/Shake It (Do the 61st)* (Luke Skyywalker Records, GR-107, ca. 1986, vinyl). Collection of the author.

Even in the absence of woman-helmed recordings, it is their dancing that is foundational to how it came to sound the way it does—whether at the Pac Jam Teen Disco, middle-school dances, family parties, or strip clubs. Anquette (the group) was also known for its incredible twin set of anthems: "Respect," an update of Aretha Franklin's classic, and "Janet Reno," a galvanizing songspace that paid homage to the then prosecutor of Dade County, who actively pursued fathers who didn't pay child support. The record cover of Anquette (see figure 4.9) was photographed on the *Bounty*, a re-creation of the 1789 ship built for the 1962 movie *Mutiny on the Bounty*, which was docked in Miami's Bayside until the threat of Hurricane Andrew made it move along in 1992. In their crisp and matching (and then highly coveted) Benetton jersey polos and white culottes, Keia Red and Ray Ray peek out from and pose with the ship's steering wheel while Anquette bends over its spindle, one hand cradling her cheek with the other hidden in her pocket. Everything about it is perfect, heartwarming, inspiring, badass. One imagines what it may have been like to be a young girl when this record came out. What did they do to take this ship's command? And: I want to come too! The B side of this album featured Anquette's "Shake It (Do the 61st)," which after all the places we've gone in *The Florida Room* can now be felt and heard as a remix of Hurston's "Proposed Recording Expedition to the Floridas" back in chapter 1. It is a soundtrack to Katherine McKittrick's theorizations about black women's geographies that "signal alternative patterns that work alongside and across traditional geographies."[75] It is also an extension and amplification of Willie Clarke's sonorous cartography, the teenage modeling of Knight and Wright, and the kind of living and posing within the promotional that bears a beautiful irreverence.

To my ear, there is no better argument than this song that figures the state, and especially Miami, as a critical hallucinogenic we can all be eager to take when asking, "What happened? Who's here? Who's coming?"[76] A sped-up riff of Bobby Byrd's "I Know You Got Soul" opens up a complicated network of affiliation. Anquette then begins to rap, "Hold up wait a minute let us put some boom in it." The heavy boom is a proposal for how to hear what is to come. Anquette then raps the following in perfectly spaced and paced succession:

61st
The Bahas
Carol City
Scott Projects
The Pork n' Beans
The Village
New Orleans
Knight Manor
The Graveyard
Atlanta . . .

African Square
Liberty City
Overtown
The Blueberries
50 Ave.
Nashville
62nd
Brown sub
Sugar Hill
Larchmont
Little Haiti
Little Havana

Alabama
L.A. . . .

And they continue shouting out places from Fresno to Virginia. These kinds of maps are common in Latinate musics, where shout-outs to countries of origin, and in hip-hop, where shout-outs to neighborhoods of origin, are a standard convention. However, it's rare to hear this kind of vocal mapping in the cadence of a young woman's voice. It is a map that insists on lots of girls on the move. There are kernels of this movement laced throughout this chapter. In the song there is that psychedelic swirl of Lewis's uneasy Caribbean, and there is another kind of Overtown restitution with Miami Bass. A restoration that aids in making central all the uncredited that made and composed it in part by dancing to it. The song brings a who else and where else was there to make it "combinations of that." Through Anquette we relive and remember the cheers and responses from girls and women's participation, from their good time, from their hurt, so often edited out. Hold up wait a minute. Anquette did all of this in the studio for Luke Skyywalker Records and not just as respondents to some dick being thrown around. What I want to keep emphasizing to the ear are the traceable and long-established traditions that Anquette picks up and makes their own. From the open invitation by "The Glass" to an especially profound connection to Clarke's mobile jook intersections. Teachers such as Smith, or other voices on the radio or in the classroom who may have taught them to make up songs to learn geography. There is Wright's mode of memory and McCray's making anew. Anquette makes sure that we know the names and locations that have made survivalist dance floors in the embers of urban renewal.

Anquette's style is not one of mere execution of an arbitrary list but of expedited transformation of the surround. Its vocal contouring of the United States is an alternate cartography in the sound of daughters and the islands and elsewheres they come from. It is also rare to hear shout-outs that compress, in the space of a stanza, both the resolutely local and the outerspatial. The opening two stanzas first situate themselves in the nurseries of Miami Bass before moving their pulsations to the elsewhere. Pork and Beans must be heard *before* other countercultural deltas such as the Village and New Orleans. Anquette makes housing projects interchangeable with other cultural capitals—especially those capitals of the recorded-music industry (even Fresno), which in turn bring their own dynamic racial and ethnic histories into the fore. Cities are not singular. Miami is not only Miami but also Little Haiti and Little Havana. And then there is also the amazing multiple play that these names evoke via these hyper-regional spaces, locations that might be in Miami but are also locatable elsewhere. The Sugar Hill to which she refers could be in Miami or northern Harlem. I could go on and on. Many who were born and raised in Miami and who now live elsewhere in the North will generally refer to going to any location as going "up to ___." From New York, they might say: I have to go up to New Jersey today. Or I have to go up to Los Angeles. This is not a tic per se but an ever-present orientation that lives in our bones. This sense of location is in Anquette and in Miami's music—across many genres—even as it radiates everywhere. It is an ever-present orientation from the heavy, bottom up, regardless of where one travels to.

Work with Miamian aesthetics can thrive in the futuristic ellipses that Anquette sets down in the recording. And it is the incredible compact creativity of the producer of the track, David Hobbs (also known as Mr. Mixx, one of the founding members of 2 Live Crew, who is not from Miami but Santa Ana, California), that gives the women beautiful playas to play in. Between the stanzas, the song gives way to danceable beaches that mix together James Brown's "Get on Up" and "Get into It," some altered synthesized braiding from the German electronic supergroup Kraftwerk's "Numbers," and what Detroit house's Juan Atkins was also doing to them too. Hobbs makes Detroit's presence here so strong in sound that perhaps Anquette didn't need to name it outright. The song is rounded out, heavily, by Motor City's Felix and Jarvis's "Jam the House," and it is thanks to them we get "Are you ready to throw down?" on repeat. There are even palpable traces of the Real Roxanne (Brooklyn's Adelaida Martinez). Throughout the stanza's reprieves—the places to bust a move, to bring wherever the dancer's place is to the circle—Anquette relentlessly offers "Hey hey hey hey hey hey hey hey." The heys are to and for anyone who is listening to *do it*, regardless of where they're located or where they're from. This is different from asking you or demanding you to come. They are callings. The heys are also hellos, a reaching out to the listener to bring whatever they have and leave the rest. Put some boom in it. Above and beneath it all is that heavy, bien heavy bass, a deep thundering kind of Miami clave that, like all claves, doesn't seem like it can make sense as a structure but does. And that Bass holds everything in the song together: Anquette's voice, the regional and national locations, the alternate cartography of Bobby Byrd's (Georgia) and James Brown's (South Carolina) soul. The Bass is a provisional, quick, and carefully articulated answer to Hurston's lingering question: How do all these recorded parts and proposals, those of this chapter and *The Florida*

Room, connect? How does this finale song, after Lewis, reconceptualize wreckage practices? Daphne Brooks says it all here: "Black women's musical practices are, in short, revolutionary because they are inextricably linked to the matter of Black life. Their strategies of performance perpetually and inventively philosophize the prodigiousness of its scope."[77] Anquette's song, recorded in Miami almost fifty years after Hurston's proposal, gives us some sense of the quality and pervasive matter that can animate future assemblies. The southernmost tip is as heavy with life, still.[78] Anquette reveals how these historically brought and wrought aesthetics extend an old-new geographic thought from the Americas, from a lower peninsular shape, from a set of overlapping neighborhoods that animate its bottom, direct from an intersection on 61st Street.

AFTERWORD

I am here because of a surprising convergence in Gainesville between my mother (from Ormond Beach, Florida) and my father (from Havana, Cuba) while they were students at the University of Florida and its eventual fruition in Miami. My writing life that includes and prefigures *The Florida Room* might be a working through (with my own symptoms) their deep and resolute attachments to the state and to the island. Being born into this fascinating melancholy is part of what trained me to listen out of place with strong feelings of being in place. I was raised in the listening arts of transference. The Floridian convergence offers a skill set to hear songs such as Duane Allman's "Please Be with Me" and Archie Shepp's "Invitation," together with Los Van Van's "Soy Todo" and N. G. La Banda's "Los Sitios Entero," as a spiritual and material home in this extended, and to my stubborn heart, temporary away time in New York and New Jersey.

Some cannot leave Miami because the structure won't allow it. Others who do may leave it because of proclivities for what Little Beaver suggested in both parts of "Party Down." Others have long fled for political reasons or for a general inhospitality to their misfit sensibilities. Still others need to leave to find work. Those who leave, for whatever reason, often have a hard time staying alive while away. There are also those who move for the ordinary curiosities shared by those in other island nations about what else and who else is out there, up there. My reasons are a mix of these, and life on the road has meant a collection of fragments that spoke to my ambivalence to this place I never, in truest body, left. The unrelenting longing and more-fleeting revulsions for Miami were mirrored in other cutaways and found in the unlikeliest of places. One of my favorites involves the Frankfurt school, a foundational place of exile and theory. Miami unbelievably and expectedly appears in Theodor Adorno's correspondence to his parents after they had fled Germany, and while living in the first phase of their exile in Havana. In a 1939 letter he gave them the following warning: "I would urgently advise you against Miami, one of the most ghastly places I have ever seen, a desert littered with house palm-trees and rip-off bars . . . [do] not spend more than 24 hours in Miami." And then, an outward change of heart. Just over a year later, Adorno wrote to them again, now in Miami, "We are now seriously considering spending our holidays with you in Miami . . . it would be lovely if we could come. . . . We would like to know if you would be able to find someone who would drive us around in the car a little for some money and kind words, and if you could advise us regarding clothing (elegance? Will we need warm clothes? How are the nights?)."[1] The pivot from horrified disgust to the appeal for some much-needed togetherness, dressed to impress with loved ones, is what many Miamians, those of the past and present, feel whether we are living there or not. It is a pastime of many, especially those who remain, to talk about how much they revile Miami. There is much to discuss: its terrifying politics, the continued apartheids made of race and real estate, the stripping of public institutions, the traffic, the violence, the starkness of unlivable poverty and the most brazen wealth locally and internationally extracted, the environmental destruction, and other strange events that seem unique to there. But they keep staying, and we keep going home.

Part of the internal conflict that made the writing of this book take so long, was that question that nags so many who can't live where they're from: How to write from the trenches if you can't actually be in them full-time? But then a directed imperative to *do it*, on so many of the musicians' and interviewees' cues threaded throughout *The Florida Room*. Directives were everywhere actually, even appearing while walking down the street in my New Jersey town. I was wearing a Miami Heat shirt that day when a Legba figure approached me and asked, mid-stride, "You like the Heat?" I answered, "That's my hometown." He said: "Miami?" Me: "Yep." As he walked away, he fully roused the spirits with this aural gift, "Go with it! Go with it!" I went with it. Because of Miami's history of everyday razing and amnesia, there was an urgent composite portrait I needed to put together and share, all at once, like this. I can barely recognize where I'm from, even as I visit for extended periods several times a year. Writing with and through and despite the disorienting buildup has given me all the more reasons to set some things down for the collective record.

The Floridian convergence is a baroque altar that gave me the great fortune to be in so many places at once. The annual experiencing of Daytona's Bike Week and Miami's Calle Ocho in the same month. Concerts at Bayfront Park with typical lineups that included KC and the Sunshine Band, Santana, and Celia Cruz. Joe Walsh forgetting the lyrics at Metro Zoo. Parking-lot Bass in the dancing outer bands of the party inside Luke's. Prince's Glam Slam club when South Beach started to figure out the cover charge. Underage nights with New Order in the Grove at Upstairs. Funk at Rose's Bar. Disco nights at the Cameo. Roller-skating sessions to "Boogie Shoes" at the Kendall Skating Rink and, later, Pretty Tony's "The Party Has Begun" at Hot Wheels Skating Center. Eddie Mix spinning at South Miami Junior High. DJs opening stores at Dadeland. The Dade County Youth Fair and its jammed signals between the patrons' Freestyle and the ride operators' classic rock. The Super Q commercial jingle, the Opa-locka/Hialeah theme song. The jukebox and concession at Bird Bowl. Tropical Park Bass dance-offs. These are not signposts for nostalgia but marks of my generation *still*. The city that bursts with nightlife in multiple languages, even in the daytime, remains fast and strong. Those who remained and those who keep arriving continue to add to its ongoing shanty. They are creating even more dimensions for the greater Florida room, conceptualizing it differently and beautifully in ways and spaces far beyond the million-dollar condos with the art to match, or the clubs with bottle service. Making do with the makeshift is their only structural code.

ACKNOWLEDGMENTS

The spatial imaginary of *The Florida Room* had the unanticipated effect of becoming real. This has all to do with the people who shared their stories with me and with the many more who have long offered lively hospitality. This book holds well over two decades of concert going, written fragments, interviews with artists, public lectures, parts of short essays or longer articles, many students and seminars, research in archives that have moved or changed personnel. All of those activities—in addition to those that involved actually being from Miami—were helped along by a lot of kindness and humor and support. Every step was an extended search for a form. The Florida room was the provisional structure that wanted to hold everything. The visits to it, over all this time, demanded to be written out with considerable urgency during the quarantine of 2020. To borrow from Wilson Harris, "The dance of place had begun" in that mandatory period of social isolation. It lent new immediacy to the project, and writing it in the close company of others—regardless of distance—kept me alive. A reminder to self and everyone: talking to people not only nuances the scholarship but also has medicinal qualities.

    I first want to thank those who took the time to story this book. Some of these interviews took place over years, and some others, equally intense, were compressed within a short span of time. In order of their appearance, I send all gratitude and blessings to Daniel Tommie Ochehachee for his stunning reflections on his history and earthworks. To Linda Williams for her deep telling of Coconut Grove Village West and our standing lemonade appointment. To Robin Gore for recounting her moving genealogy of the Mariah Brown family. To Sandra Riley for being the crossroads figure between myself, Williams, and Gore. To the mighty Patsy West for being a wonderful teacher about South Florida's Indigenous histories and for her example of staying with the long view. West generously and tirelessly went out of her way to help me get it the way it wanted to be. I thank Juan Valadez for being with the Everglades, for taking me to the water from the distance, for drawing the manatee in a deep dive. Benny Latimore offered the deepest model for weaving philosophy and history. My conversations with Leah Jackson and Gwen McCrae taught me much about making intergenerational care while talking about music. To Felix and Caridad Sama for bringing the song lines together. To Desmond Child and the Child family for giving us occasions to gather in music, *everywhere*, and actual gatherings in the somewhere of New York. Gracias a Frank Ferrer a luminary at the Cuba–rock-and-roll crossroads. To Guillermo García Rodiles for the unexpected surprise of his congas off the spoils. To Dafnis Prieto for training me to take the time. To Obed Calvaire for giving four-country texture to this place we're from. To Yosvany Terry for always opening up the cosmologies. To Jacob Katel for his commitment to go where the stories take him and for transmitting those stories out to all. To Luther Campbell for his spacious sense of the local. And especial thanks to Namphuyo Aisha McCray, who gave to this project in so many ways. One day we will make that summit.

This book holds over twenty years of conversation with Shane Vogel. His singular encouragement of the ideas, writing, and style did everything to give it heart and soul. Vogel's inspiring model and commitment to thinking and listening helped me—at *every* stage, joyful and frightening—to get this into print. The hand that helps you cross the water is everything. Daphne Brooks's transformative work and its deep material impact on the social, *and* her tireless efforts to make the social import material in all our work, encourage every line of this text. Brooks's creative and magnificent ability to push thought and music to the precipice, and letting it live there, gives us all enduring and gorgeous assignments for living. Antonio López's brilliant prescient-ancient work on the intersections between Indigenous, Black, and Cuban South Florida laid the foundations for this book, and his deep local and everywhere knowledge has done so much to improve these pages: from catching the Flanigan's typo to encouraging the chickee. His company is a most hilarious and illuminating seminar. Karen Shimakawa made the infrastructure possible for this writing: her brilliant sense for theory and space expanded my time and place for theory. What a blessing to live among incredible intellectuals and friends. Kandice Chuh, Deb Vargas, and Erica Edwards, all formidable theorists of the local, have given me unfailing support and health and company in the exquisite challenges of making work and making home. Mary Pat Brady's powerful spatial imagination has long been a profound influence on me, and her generous read of the manuscript during some doldrums offered some much-needed merriment and perspective. Richard T. Rodriguez brought his post punk soundtrack to renew my listening life just when I needed it most. Gisela Fosado, my editor at Duke, has made this a magical experience from our first meeting. Fosado's instant openness to this project and her elegant mode of encouragement made me want to keep writing. *Imagínate*. I cannot thank her enough for that gift. Her visionary stewardship of Duke University Press is an inspiration to many. Alongside Fosado, Ale Mejia and Susan Albury did everything to transform the usual fits and starts of publication into the smoothest ride possible from start to finish. Thank you to Cathy Hannabach for arranging the index. Robust applause to Matt Tauch and his cover design that leaves everything open. The wondrous Amna Farooqi heroically stepped in to help with some late-stage research assistance so that I could teach at my job and teach in my home during the era of remote learning. For Farooqi, no person was too hard to find, no source was too hard to track, no request was too bizarre to take on. Such was the depth of her involvement that she is now an official Floridian.

There are many more who gave a lot of time and resources and work so that these ideas could be refined at home and on the road. Thanks to a faculty fellowship from NYU's Center for the Humanities, and especially the efforts of Uli Baer and Molly Rogers, I was able to get traction on the manuscript. What a total thrill it was to gather with the following folks, all ideal interlocutors and hosts, who offered formative rehearsal spaces for *The Florida Room*: Caitlin Marshall, Patricia Herrera, Marci McMahon, and Iván Ramos for their Revolutions in Sound at the University of Maryland School of Theater, Dance, and Performance Studies; Daphne Brooks, Brian Kane, and Van Truong for everything that is the experience of Black Sound and the Archive at Yale University; Malinda Lowery, Elizabeth Engelhardt, and pride of the 305 Maria Estorino at the UNC–Chapel Hill Southern Summit; Matt Sandler and Frances Negrón-Muntaner at Columbia University's Center for the Study of Ethnicity and Race; Suzanne Cusick and Martha Feldman for their bold invitation to the American Musicological Association; Soyica Colbert, Doug Jones, and Shane Vogel for the Race and Performance after Repetition Symposium at Indiana University Bloomington; C. Riley Snorton, Hentyle Yapp, and Johanna Burton for Saturation at the New Museum; Frances Aparicio and Veronica Dávila for making Soundscapes of Latinidad at Northwestern; Maria Sonevytsky and Alex Benson and their musical imaginaries at Bard College; Ramón Rivera-Servera and Alejandro

Madrid and their Mapping Sound at Cornell University; Kandice Chuh and the Revolutionizing American Studies Initiative at CUNY's Graduate Center; Gus Stadler and the American Studies Working Group at Haverford College; Carter Mathes and the Critical Caribbean Studies Research initiative at Rutgers University; Tim Watson, Lillian Manzor, Donette Francis, the departments of English and American Studies, and the Cuban Heritage Collection at the University of Miami; and finally, a very robust thank-you to the "What's Left of Cuba?" series curated by Ana María Dopico, Jill Lane, and José Esteban Muñoz at NYU Center for Latin American and Caribbean Studies.

I thank the following archivists for their indefatigable dedication to holding up the past and for their bountiful directives while I got to visit over the span of many years. Maria Estorino, then at UM's Cuban Heritage Collection and now director of the Wilson Library at UNC–Chapel Hill; Verónica González at FIU's Diaz-Ayala Cuban and Latin American Popular Music Collection; Dawn Hugh, archivist at History Miami (who has recently retired after thirty-three years there); Patsy West and the Seminole/Miccosukee Archive; and Timothy Barber at The Black Archives History and Research Foundation of South Florida. Thanks also to Jeff Ransom and Sarah Cody of the Office of Historic Preservation of Miami-Dade County for their overview of the Miami Circle. The Department of Performance Studies is another place of invigorating holdings. Who could have imagined that faculty meetings could be places for experimentalism and philosophical thinking? Hardiest abrazos to my beautiful colleagues André Lepecki, Karen Shimakawa, Diana Taylor, Ann Pellegrini, Barbara Browning, Fred Moten, Malik Gaines, Michelle Castañeda, Allen Weiss, Deborah Kapchan, Laura Fortes, Allison Brobst, Nicole Cusick, and especially Noel Rodríguez for making the workplace a funplex.

To my hometown that stays and moves around. I sing it loud and often: South Miami Middle School set the tone, and my high school, New World School of the Arts, made everything possible thereafter. From that special place, the everlasting friendship of Natalie Gold, whose soul and spirit are motivation to be my best self. Her cheerleading of this book from the sidelines, with her special Miami sensibility, makes this book feel all the more like a collective head. And I would be lost without the rest of the Miami misfit crew: Liz Kapplow, Maggie Baisch, Michael Aranov, Erik Lieberman, Juan Valadez. Matt Sandler is a vitalizing partner in the arts of being away. Maggie and David Schmitt gave a whole lot with that record collection. To Jorge Ignacio Cortiñas and Ana Dopico, my fellow Miami Cubans in northern exile, I owe so much to their brilliance and getting it before I had to. José Esteban Muñoz, I am, as ever, looking up to you.

Talk about a Florida room! The following friends form a mega-mix of time, place, and companionship. Gracias a Jacqueline Loss, Armando Suárez Cobián, Lauren Arcis, Katia Rosenthal, Alina and Ela Troyano, Sandy Plácido, Ricardo Ortiz, José Nestor Marquez, Ana M. López, Elizabeth Alexander, Ann Lane, Ricardo Montez, Christine Bacareza Balance, Germán Labrador Mendez, Sandra Ruíz, Licia Fiol-Matta, Lena Burgos Lafuente, Hypatia Vourloumis, Danielle Goldman, Christina León, Emilio Pérez, Laura Harris, James Stoeri, Jean Vitrano, Scott Herring, Albert Laguna, Matt Jacobson, Marc Robinson, Alicia Schmidt-Camacho, Steve Pitti, Katie Lofton, Van Truong, Peter Hudson, Siobhan Somerville, Laura Kang, Heather Love, Nadia Ellis, Lindsay Reckson, Sonya Postmentier, Adrienne Brown, Juana María Rodriguez, Rosa Marquetti, Josh Chambers-Letson, Tavia Nyong'o, Alejandra Bronfman, Tim Rommen, Josh Javier Guzman, Summer Kim Lee, Roy Perez, Josh Green, Matilde Fidler, Marissa Barlin, Jennifer Pfeiffer, Joanna and Peter Ahlberg, Norbert and Michelle Butz, Jodi Gall, Joanna Dunlap, Sarah Olivier, Elana and James Nanscawens, Sydney and Paul Reisen, Vanessa and Tony Trombino, Valentina Centrangolo, Lucia Mazzarella and family. Thunderous lines of acknowledgment go to the music-writing crew from Seattle and beyond: Dave Tompkins and our Bass Mountain School, Sonnet Retman, Gayle Wald, Josh Kun, Ann Powers, Isabelia Herrera, Masi Asare, Eric Weisbard, Eric Lott, Karen Tongson, Tim Lawrence, Gus Stadler, Kandia Crazy Horse, Garnette Cadogan, and Josh Jelly Schapiro. I am extremely grateful for all my students and would like to especially thank Cy Citlallin Delgado Huitrón and Camila Arroyo Romero for their virtuosic interlocutions, senses of humor, and assistance during the final stages of the book's writing.

My mother, Virginia, once picked up the phone while observing a wood stork rookery. It has been my long-standing plan to extend her everyday, beautiful relation to Florida's fauna and flora into a most-loving offering in writing. What a blessing to be raised by this incredible teacher of staying with the surround. My mom tirelessly opened up her knowledge base to others and, with her keen sense for always finding the right teachers, gave me unimagined horizons for thought. I once asked my father, Manuel, to transcribe the lyrics to a rumba I had been writing about, and while he typed, he made subtle rhythm with his shoulders. This capacity for bringing body to mind, and his capacious sense of music from large church choirs to Motown to Broadway standards, did much to give me a radio mind. I'm so glad, too, that Lisa Delmonte has joined our family. The book bears a strong attachment to my sister Tory Vazquez, whose feeling and wonder for Florida grounds my everything. Tory was and is my lovable and funny backseat partner in the long trips up and down the peninsula, and perfect harmonic co-witness of all the sights and sounds. My sister Nicole Mestre, always with a book in her hand, has been a wise teacher that models reading everything and everyone. What a total joy it is to hear her craft her own stories. And my little sister Terry Vazquez, with our special connectivity over DJ Uncle Al and many other danceables, has unfailingly opened my eyes to Miami's here and now, however much it changes or stays the same. I treasure the way music falls on us both. Maria Hortensia, I hear you and know you are listening. Dolores and Shane Maxwell, Ceci and Gabi Mestre, you got this.

I'm grateful to our celestial pit bull, Blanca Rosa, and our new chicken friends Carmela, Tomasa, Gigi, Corndog, and Balloony, for giving my family a lot of laughter and fascinating narratives to follow. Vincenzo Amato is my long view, and after such an endearing collaboration, there is always the miracle of new stories and affection and admiration. Our unspoken and active agreement about what matters has taken many forms and, in every instance, more surprise. To Lucia and Manuela—the best things that have ever happened to me—I offer this past and present so you may take it by the hand, in your own way. To be a mother of daughters is imagining the impossible: a happiest life.

NOTES

PREFACE

1 This book is founded in music, but that is not to say it does not recognize the robust and hard-fought scholarly foundations about a field we might call "Miami Studies." There are dozens of scholars—whom you will find threaded throughout the book and as sentinels in the bibliography—who have profoundly shaped my thinking. Their work has been as important to my training in the writing about history as they have been in my listening to it. They have made both activities, by necessity, feel closer. They thrum throughout this book, especially those figures who skate the scholarly/literary/musical continuum, such as Zora Neale Hurston, in all ways the field's prescient chair. You will hear from noncanonical voices who self-publish their words because no one else will. You will hopefully meet many others you weren't expecting.

2 Miami *is* perhaps a "Gone City," in the sense of the manic song masterpiece written in 1949 by Arturo "Chico" O'Farrill for Machito and his Afro-Cubans. O'Farrill is among the most important and prolific Cuban composers, and his influence is as palpable in jazz as it is Cuban music. I must note that O'Farrill first fell in love with the trumpet and big-band jazz when he was sent to military school in Florida. See "Chico O' Farrill" in Radamés Giro, *Dicciónario enciclopédico de la música en Cuba*, vol. 3 (Habana: Letras Cubanas, 2007), 167–68.

3 See Michele Currie Navakas's great book, *Liquid Landscape: Geography and Settlement at the Edge of Early America* (Philadelphia: University of Pennsylvania Press, 2017). The first lines of Navakas's study say it all: "What does it mean to take root in unstable ground?" (1).

4 "Cubans" play an especially strong role in the larger geopolitical story of good and evil in and out of Miami. This monolithic Cubanity (sometimes true, sometimes false) is circulated by Right and Left, and does much to obliterate what José Esteban Muñoz calls a "sense of brown." See José Esteban Muñoz, *The Sense of Brown*, ed. Joshua Chambers-Letson and Tavia Nyong'o (Durham, NC: Duke University Press, 2020).

5 Lorna Goodison, "Deep Sea Diving," in *To Us, All Flowers Are Roses* (Urbana: University of Illinois Press, 1995), 55–56.
6 For some of my earlier writing on mangroves, and a bibliography that helped me to get there (and here), see Alexandra T. Vazquez, "Learning to Live in Miami," *American Quarterly* 66, no. 3 (September 2014).
7 Severo Sarduy, "The Beach," in *For Voice*, trans. Philip Barnard (Pittsburgh: Latin American Literary Review Press, 1985), 15–16.

CHAPTER ONE: THE FLORIDA ROOM

1 *Oxford English Dictionary Online*, "jalousie, n.," accessed July 18, 2019, https://www-oed-com.proxy.library.nyu.edu/view/Entry/100677.
2 *New Oxford American Dictionary Online*, "Florida room, n.," accessed July 4, 2019, https://www-oxfordreference-com.proxy.library.nyu.edu/view/10.1093/acref/9780195392883.001.0001/m_en_us1247871? rskey=JD56tM&result=1; *Oxford Dictionary of English Online*, "Florida room, n.," accessed July 4, 2019, https://www-oxfordreference-com.proxy.library.nyu.edu/view/10.1093/acref/9780199571123.001.0001/m_en_gb0304450? rskey=JD56tM&result=3; *The Canadian Oxford Dictionary Online*, "Florida room, n.," accessed July 4, 2020, https://www-oxfordreference-com.proxy.library.nyu.edu/view/10.1093/acref/9780195418163.001.0001/m_en_ca0025631? rskey=JD56tM&result=2.
3 Other literatures that mention a Florida room include Claudia S. Slate's "Florida Room: Battle for St. Augustine 1964: Public Record and Personal Recollection," *Florida Historical Quarterly* 84, no. 4 (2006): 541–68; and Carlos Victoria, "Comentarios De Un Oidor o Lorenzo García Vega En Su Florida Room," *Encuentro De La Cultura Cubana*, nos. 21/22 (2001): 48–51, which is an encounter with the Cuban author all staged from a Florida room (!). On small mentions of other architectural histories, often around the decline of the Florida room, see Albert C. Manucy and St. Augustine Historical Society, *The Houses of St. Augustine: Notes on the Architecture from 1565 to 1821* (St. Augustine, FL: St. Augustine Historical Society, 1962); Barbara Marshall, "Reviving the Florida Room: New Exhibit Recreates, Modernizes State's Iconic Home Fixture," *Palm Beach Post*, February 14, 2014, www.palmbeachpost.com/article/20140214/LIFESTYLE/812058992; and Eric Barton, "The Quiet Demise of Florida's Room," September 15, 2020, www.flamingomag.com/2020/09/15/the-quiet-demise-of-floridas-room.
4 Donald Fagen, "Florida Room," by Donald Fagen and Elizabeth "Libby" Titus, on *Kamakiriad*, Reprise Records, 1993, compact disc.
5 See Craig Thompson Friend, "Editor's Preface," *Florida Historical Quarterly* 81, no. 3 (2003): 253.
6 Elizabeth Dustin, "Doings of Women: Mrs. Quintan of the Indian Association . . . ," *Los Angeles Times*, February 22, 1891, 14, accessed July 9, 2019, http://proxy.library.nyu.edu/login?qurl=https%3A%2F%2Fwww.

proquest.com%2Fhistorical-newspapers%2Fdoings-women%2Fdocview%2F163563875%2Fse-2%3Faccountid%3D12768. ProQuest Historical Newspapers.

7 After Dustin's introduction, we find traces of the Florida Room in classified ads advertising the state's mid-century building boom. In a 1952 ad in the *St. Petersburg Times*, we're presented a home that boasts a Florida room "built for outdoor living Florida Style" (a style which means shielded from the actual elements), a place screened in and topped with an insulated roof. *St. Petersburg Times*, January 4, 1952, 35.

8 See "Paul Rudolph—A Life of Art and Architecture," Paul Rudolph Heritage Foundation, accessed January 13, 2020, www.paulrudolphheritagefoundation.org/biography.

9 Joseph King, "Twitchell and Rudolph," in *Paul Rudolph: The Florida Houses*, ed. Christopher Domin and Joseph King (New York: Princeton Architectural Press, 2002), 22–56. For more in-depth work on specifically Floridian vernacular architecture, see Dorinda K. M. Blackey, "Defining Vernacular through the Florida Vernacular—the Cracker House," student paper, American Architectural History, College of Architecture at the University of Florida, 1982, https://ufdc.ufl.edu/UF00103303/00001/1j.

10 This premise and accompanying aesthetics that forge what Ross Gay has succinctly identified as "the not-so-good old days," is something that the poet initially suspected, "as a kind of aesthetic assimilation, questioning I realized was actually a centering of whiteness when I remembered my Papa's house in Youngstown with the rhubarb plants out back, mid-century par excellence. Aunt Butter's more or less the same." Ross Gay, *The Book of Delights* (Chapel Hill, NC: Algonquin, 2019), 139.

11 Of Rudolph's Floridian buildings, C. Ford Peatross notes his "ability to explore and develop the spatial richness, complexity, and interrelationship of the interiors and exteriors of his buildings, their sites, their natural surroundings, and their climate." Also, "It was in Florida where Rudolph developed many of his bold and brilliant techniques of graphic representation. . . ." And so, the hereafter of Rudoph's Florida Room period did much to alter how spaces were represented on the page. C. Ford Peatross, "Preface," in *Paul Rudolph: The Florida Houses*, ed. Christopher Domin and Joseph King (New York: Princeton Architectural Press, 2002), 9.

12 Robert Bruegmann, "Introduction," in *Paul Rudolph: The Florida Houses*, ed. Christopher Domin and Joseph King (New York: Princeton Architectural Press, 2002), 15–16.

13 Alison A. Elgart, "The Animal Interments at the Miami Circle at Brickell Point Site (8DA12)," *Florida Anthropologist* 59, nos. 3–4 (2006): 179–90. For a play-by-play about the site in the public imaginary and how it was transformed into place for scientific inquiry, see Ryan Wheeler's informative and engaging "Miami Circle Reflections" for the Robert S. Peabody Institute of Archaeology, April 22, 2020, https://peabody.andover.edu/2020/04/22/miami-circle

-reflections-part-1-the-journey-begins. Wheeler wrote this as the first of a series of blog posts he began on the subject.

14 The Miami Circle is (justifiably) a place of intense scholarly focus. For example, it was the feature of three special issues of *The Florida Anthropologist* between 2000 and 2006. See also National Park Service, *Miami Circle: Special Resource Study* (Washington, DC: US Dept. of the Interior, 2007).

15 Robert S. Carr, *Digging Miami* (Gainesville: University Press of Florida, 2012), 237–38.

16 Ryan J. Wheeler and Robert Carr, "It's Ceremonial Right? Exploring Ritual in Ancient Southern Florida through the Miami Circle," in *New Histories of Pre-Columbian Florida*, ed. Neill J. Wallis and Asa R. Randall (Gainesville: University Press of Florida, 2014), 203–22. See also Elgart, "The Animal Interments," 179–90.

17 Carr, *Digging Miami*, 241–42.

18 Carr, *Digging Miami*, 243. See Jacqueline Eaby Dixon et al., "Provenance of Stone Celts from the Miami Circle Archeological Site, Miami, Florida," *The Florida Anthropologist* 53 no. 4 (2000): 328–41.

19 For all about these ways of living and how I was trained in "being with," see Kandice Chuh et al., "Being with José: An Introduction," *Social Text*, no. 4 (2014): 1–7; and José Esteban Muñoz, *Cruising Utopia: The Then and There of Queer Futurity* (New York: NYU Press, 2009). This concept "being-with" extends from Jean-Luc Nancy, *Being Singular Plural*, trans. Robert Richardson and Anne O'Byrne (Stanford, CA: Stanford University Press, 2000).

20 I came to the term *i:laposhni:cha thli:* from two sources. The first was Daniel Tommie Ochehachee. People of Mikasuki-speaking heritage may formally belong to either the Seminole Tribe of Florida, the Miccosukee Tribe of Indians of Florida, or the Independents. In my attempt to use the names chosen by the people themselves, I follow the example of Patsy West in her *The Enduring Seminoles: From Alligator Wrestling to Casino Gaming* (Gainesville: University Press of Florida, 1998). West states that "Mikasuki (in many different spellings, including Miccosukee) referred originally to the large late-eighteenth-century town east of Tallahassee in northwest Florida, where the forebears of these people lived" (1–2). West's use of these peoples own term of identity (which at the time of her book's publication was *i:laponathli*) was made in consultation with Mikasuki-speaking elders.

This dynamism of self-naming was documented in another of West's articles, "Abiaka, or Sam Jones, in Context: The Mikasuki Ethnogenesis through the Third Seminole War" (*Florida Historical Quarterly* 94, no. 3 [2016]: 367n1), West specifies that "Mikasuki persons who have been taught their traditional culture call themselves 'i: laponathli,' a contraction meaning 'the people,' and 'ilaposhni cha thi'; that literally means 'the people who speak,' which could be seen to refer to their early Southeastern roots." West has recently re-consulted with Jeanette Cypress (granddaughter of Susie Billie), and the preferred term of identification is now *i:laposhni:cha thli:*. West's findings emerge from her historical research, oral interviews, and involvement with the i:laposhni:cha thli: for more than five decades. West has an exhibition. "The i:laposhni:cha thli: Saga: An Untold Florida History," (HistoryMiami April 2022) that specifically addresses the complexities of naming. As of this writing, Jeanette Cypress has instructed West to use i:laposhni:cha thli: (and this spelling) and, together with my own discussion with Daniel Tommie Ochehachee, I follow their collective instruction here. Daniel Tommie Ochehachee in discussion with the author, November 29, 2021.

In Buffalo Tiger's 2002 autobiography, which heavily informs chapter 2, he uses "Eelaponke" and it is hard to know if this orthography is his or Harry A. Kersey's. For more sources on broader Seminole histories, readers may refer to my bibliography.

21 This beautiful line, an "y mas na'" line, is from a very short section called "Our Names" in Tiger's autobiography. In its last paragraph, Tiger more directly schools the reader, "It is important for you to know what we call the Everglades. 'Everglades' is not in our language, but it is where we have always lived. Some of our people call it *Paheyaoke*—'River of Grass.' Some people call it *Ashaweayaoke*—'Where the Cypresses Are.' And others call it *Chooyayaoke*—'Where the Pines Are.' Pine trees grew on the sandy soil." That this phrase, "what is important for you to know," is decidedly not used when he describes the names of people, is profound instruction. Buffalo Tiger and Harry A. Kersey Jr., *Buffalo Tiger: A Life in the Everglades* (Lincoln: University of Nebraska Press, 2002), 38–39.

22 William C. Sturtevant and Jessica Cattelino, "Florida Seminole and Miccosukee," *Handbook of North American Indians*, vol. 14, *Southeast*, vol. ed. Raymond D. Fogelson, general ed. William C. Sturtevant (Washington, DC: Smithsonian Institution, 2004), 438. For a deeper dive into the chickee, its construction, and its aesthetics, see Carrie Dilley, *Thatched Roofs and Open Sides: The Architectures of Chickees and Their Changing Role in Seminole Society* (Gainesville: University Press of Florida, 2015).

23 Daniel Tommie Ochehachee (Bird Clan) in discussion with the author, January 11, 2021. Ochehachee describes Tucker's skill as particularly extraordinary because he was able to precut all of the pieces for the chickee in the field "so that he wasn't wasting time on the job." Tucker was "efficient, he didn't waste time, he was generous, and he was serious about his work."

24 Some scholars, such as Maskókî-speaking Seminole historian Willie Johns (Wildcat Clan), have argued that the contemporary chickee (from at least the time of the Seminole Wars) was strategically designed to be built relatively quickly, so if a family group needed to run, it could do so. Johns also notes that his ancestors lived in log-cabin–like structures before their relocations (forced and chosen) to different parts of the peninsula. The chickee, or as Johns put it, "survival huts," were harder for settlers to detect. Willie Johns and Stephen Bridenstine, "'When Is Enough, Enough?': Willie Johns on Seminole History and the Tribal Historic Preservation Office, the Creek Perspective," in

We Come for Good: Archeology and Tribal Historic Preservation at the Seminole Tribe of Florida, ed. Paul N. Backhouse, Brent R. Weisman, and Mary Beth Rosebrough (Gainesville: University Press of Florida, 2017), 6. See also Dilley, *Thatched Roofs and Open Sides*, 53. For another history of the chickee, the intense shift in clan formations, and the effects on the culture's matrilineal structure and gender roles in the transition to concrete housing, see Jessica Cattelino, "Florida Seminole Housing and the Meaning of Sovereignty," *Comparative Studies in Society and History* 48, no. 3 (2016): 699–726.

25 Ochehachee discussion, January 11, 2021.
26 It is impossible to date the chickee according to the norms of Western time and its accompanying archaeological science, but there is tacit agreement that it is a design handed down over a long period of time. See Dilley, *Thatched Roofs and Open Sides*, 53–55. Some of the ongoing debates about the i:laposhni:cha thli: presence in the southern part of the peninsula revolve around when these populations actually began to live there. The histories often told of the Seminole rely on a familiar narrative of people being pushed down from the ancestral lands now known as southern Georgia, Alabama, and northern Florida by colonial violence. These narratives make migration strictly a *reaction to*. This is of course partly true, but there are other histories—as handed down by the i:laposhni:cha thli: themselves—that insist on their much, much longer stewardship of these lands. As Buffalo Tiger tells us, "We know Florida as the 'pointed land.' Years and years ago people were always looking for which way to go because it was not easy for Indian people to find food and the right place to live for their people. So the wise people were sitting around all night figuring which way to go. At that time, they saw a beautiful tree standing with its limb pointing south, and that meant something . . . they found out that the 'pointed land' was a beautiful place to live, so that's when they started moving down this way. So we know that's how we got here years ago." Tiger and Kersey Jr., *Buffalo Tiger*, 35.
27 Ochehachee in discussion with the author, January 12, 2021.
28 James E. Billie, "Life in a Chickee on 'Tahl-Chobee Yo-Gee,'" *Seminole Tribune*, April 29, 2015, https://seminoletribune.org/life-in-a-chickee-on-tahl-chobee-yo-gee, emphasis mine.
29 Ochehachee discussion, January 11, 2021.
30 City of Lake Worth, Florida, *Architectural Styles and Building Traditions* (Lake Worth, FL: n.d.).
31 Jane S. Day and Sarah E. Eaton, "Mariah Brown House: Designation Report 3298 Charles Avenue," Report of the City of Miami Preservation Officer to the Historic and Environmental Preservation Board on the Potential Designation of the Mariah Brown House, n.d. According to Marvin Dunn, the Brown House is likely Dade County's oldest Black dwelling (built in the mid-1880s). In Marvin Dunn, *Black Miami in the Twentieth Century* (Gainesville: University Press of Florida, 1997), 36.

32 For a foundational resource on Bahamian migration to Miami, see Raymond A. Mohl, "Black Immigrants: Bahamians in Early Twentieth-Century Miami," *Florida Historical Quarterly* 65, no. 3 (1987): 271–97. Bahamian migration to South Florida (and more bibliographic resources) will be listened to and discussed further in chapter 4. For more on the history of Kebo, see Dunn, *Black Miami in the Twentieth Century*, 36. See also "The Mariah Brown House," AT&T Miami-Dade County African-American History Calendar, 1996, Black Archives History and Research Foundation of South Fl (1996_005a_Mariah_Brown_House).

For more about details about Mariah Brown culled together from settlers' journals, see Sandra Riley's "Mariah Brown and Coconut Grove's African-Bahamian Village on the Bay," *Journal of the Bahamas Historical Society* 29 (2007): 33–41. Riley notes that the house was built with Dade County Pine.

33 As Graylyn Marie Swilly-Woods has written, "Over the last century, residents of Overtown and West Coconut Grove have had little or no control over developments in their communities or how mainstream tourism leaders make their investments." See her experienced and community-based overview of the difficult histories and possibilities of West Grove and Overtown as heritage tourism: Graylyn Marie Swilly-Woods, "Glocalizing Community Heritage Tourism in Two African-American Communities in Miami" (PhD diss., Antioch University, 2019).

34 All of the information and story here is from Linda Williams in discussion with the author, January 20, 2021, and through various follow-ups in the weeks following. Throughout our first call I got to overhear several people in the neighborhood come up to her and chat. She said: "This is what we do. People pass by; people say hello." Toward the end of the call I could hear the bells ring at Christ Episcopal Church, built in 1901 by Bahamian immigrants.

35 The Fairchilds, as in David Fairchild, the botanist who brought hundreds of thousands of exotic species to the US. Also, the Pancoast family is one of South Florida's famous architecture families (the father, Russell, was one of Miami Beach's principal architects and the son, Lester, a guru of the neo-mid-century home).

36 Linda Williams in discussion with the author, January 28, 2021.

37 Williams was careful to note that they did not seek the "Community-wide historical designation" because it would have created a lot of financial burden on residents should they want to change something like a doorknob in a style that might not match up with the original home. Williams discussion, January 20, 2021.

38 Williams is openly critical about how long it has taken the committee to restore the Brown House. She says, "I don't have this kind of time."

39 Robin Gore in discussion with the author, January 21, 2020.

40 Riley was Coral Gables Senior High's International Baccalaureate English and theater teacher and, after retiring, formed her theater company. In the later stages of the writing of this book, Sandra Riley became one of those six-degrees

figures, as in "Have you talked to Sandy?" I first found her on the Crystal Parrot Players website. See https://crystalparrot.org. Riley then put me in touch with Linda Williams, who then put me in touch with Robin Gore. As Gore said of Riley, "She is the sweetest person I know." Riley also has an important connection to Patsy West, who is an important figure in chapter 2.

41 Sandra Riley, "Mariah Brown," in *Bahamas Trilogy* (Miami: Parrot House, 2017).

42 Gore discussion, January 21, 2020. I want to stress the importance of field trips here. I am far from alone when I say that my own intense attachment to much of South Florida's histories and ecosystems can be traced directly from field trips such as those imagined by Williams and Gore.

43 For a recent photographic essay that includes these formal inventions in various architectures, see Germane Barnes, "Black Miami's Resiliency: A Photographic Essay," *Anthurium* 16, no. 1 (2020): 3. This was featured in the wonderful special issue "Looking for Black Miami," coedited by Donette Francis and Allison Harris.

44 Overtown, what N. D. B. Connolly once called "a little corner of the Atlantic World," will be met in more musical and historic detail in chapter 4. In N. D. B. Connolly, "Colored, Caribbean, and Condemned: Miami's Overtown District and the Cultural Expense of Progress, 1940–1970," *Caribbean Studies* 34, no. 1 (2006): 3–60. Overtown has been known in past iterations as Miami's "Central Negro District" and, starting around the 1920s, as "Colored Town." "Overtown" became the name generally used for the area starting in the 1940s.

45 Interview with Purvis Young by Hans Ulrich Obrist (2005) in *Purvis Young*, ed. Juan Valadez (Miami: Rubell Museum, 2018), 24. According to Dorothy Jenkins Fields, Good Bread Alley stands between Northwest Twelfth and Fourteenth Streets and between Third and Fourth Avenues, and was "an area that began evolving prior to 1920 and was so named because some of the women baked and sold bread in their homes. In the 'alley' there were more than three hundred shot-gun houses with less than five feet between them. The front porch of one house was directly in front of another, divided only by a path or alley" (329–30). Good Bread Alley was destroyed by the expressway construction that trampled Overtown, a devastating event that will be further analyzed in chapter 4. See Jenkins Fields, "Tracing Overtown's Vernacular Architecture," *Journal of Decorative and Propaganda Arts* 23 (1998): 323–33. See also N. D. B. Connolly's great collation of oral histories about Good Bread Alley in his "Colored, Caribbean, and Condemned," 19–21.

46 See Juan Valadez's catalog *Purvis Young*, and especially his "Introduction," in *Purvis Young*, ed. Juan Valadez (Miami: Rubell Museum, 2018), 12–14.

47 Gean Moreno, "Writing the Glyph," in *Purvis Young*, ed. Juan Valadez (Miami: Rubell Museum, 2018), 40.

48 For brilliant new work on dissent against scale, see Mary Pat Brady, *Scales of Captivity: Racial Capitalism and the Latinx Child* (Durham, NC: Duke University Press, 2022).

49 Purvis Young is one of the most famous and recognizable of Miami's artists and is also perhaps one of the most circulated names in the "Miami art boom" that expedited the commodity making of artists, their works, and formerly "undesirable" areas of the city in the late 1990s. For more on Young and the speculation of his work, see Nathan Connolly's "Speculating in History," *Anthurium* 16, no. 1 (2020): 9. Juan Valadez's *Purvis Young* is a notable exception of critical literature that attends closely to the artist's work and his relationships with people.

50 David Whiteis, "Latimore: Some Things You Can't Fake," *Living Blues: The Magazine of the African American Blues Tradition* 49, no. 5 (2018): 10–20, emphasis mine.

51 On Hurston's work for and the publication history of *The Florida Negro*, see *The Florida Negro: A Federal Writers', Project Legacy*, ed. Gary W. McDonogh (Jackson: University Press of Mississippi, 1993).

52 Stetson Kennedy, "Florida Folklife and the WPA: An Introduction," State Archives of Florida, n.d., accessed January, 15, 2020, www.floridamemory.com/onlineclassroom/zora_hurston/documents/stetsonkennedy. Original essay appeared in Jill Inman Linzee, *A Reference Guide to Florida Folklore from the Federal WPA Deposited in the Florida Folklife Archives* (Tallahassee: Florida Department of State, Division of Historical Resources, Bureau of Florida Folklife Programs, 1990).

53 For a brilliant and comprehensive reading of the WPA guide series, the conditions of labor behind the Florida guide, Hurston's presence within it, and Florida in the American interwar imaginary, see Sonnet H. Retman's "'The Last American Frontier': Mapping the Folk in the Federal Writers' Project's Florida: A Guide to the Southernmost State," in *Real Folks: Race and Genre in the Great Depression* (Durham, NC: Duke University Press, 2011).

54 Zora Neale Hurston, "Negro Mythical Places," in *Go Gator and Muddy the Water: Writings by Zora Neale Hurston from the Federal Writers' Project*, ed. Pamela Bordelon (New York: W. W. Norton, 1999), 108.

55 Federal Writers' Project of the Works Progress Administration for the State of Florida, *Florida: A Guide to the Southernmost State, American Guide Series* (New York: Oxford University Press, 1939), 431.

56 As Retman sagely puts it, "These stories have yet another function: they point to the unmappable—a subversive space of imagination, desire, and agency—a space that resists the fixing gaze of the tourist and the state." Retman, "The Last American Frontier," 150–51.

57 Zora Neale Hurston, "Negro Mythical Places," in Federal Writers' Project, *Florida: A Guide*, 431. I've included here the original text as Hurston wrote it. The FWP guide heavily edited the original, which became the following: "Beluthahatchee is a country where all unpleasant doings and sayings are forgotten, a land of forgiveness and forgetfulness" (431).

58 Zora Neale Hurston, "Proposed Recording Expedition into the Floridas," May 1939, manuscript/mixed material, Library of Congress, accessed February 17, 2014, www.loc.gov/item/flwpa000213. The finding aid gives us the

following context for the piece: "Hurston's essay was written in preparation for the visit of Herbert Halpert (director of the folk song department of the National Service Bureau, Federal Theater Project) on the Joint Committee on Folk Art and Library of Congress–sponsored southern recording expedition. According to Dr. Corse, 'His trip was cut short so that only a few of these recordings were made. Zora Neale Hurston completed contacts for Negro recordings at the turpentine camp in Cross City and in Tampa before she was called to Philadelphia.'"

59   Hurston, "Proposed Recording Expedition into the Floridas."

60   Hurston, "Proposed Recording Expedition into the Floridas."

61   The critical literature on Hurston and Florida is as vast as its rivers of grass. However, as this introduction reveals, I hope to move attention on Hurston's Florida from conventional readings of literary setting and into performative doing. For one important resource that sought to specifically focus on the Floridian substances in Hurston's work, see *Zora in Florida*, ed. Steve Glassman and Kathryn Lee Seidel (Orlando: University of Central Florida Press, 1991, distributed by University Presses of Florida).

62   As Daphne Brooks, one of the greatest theorists of Hurston, has written, "Her performance doubly inscribes the self-making dreams and imagination of the Black collective whose voices she preserves, as well as her own present, active, independent reception as a woman with her ear to the ground and her voice to the wind" (159). Brooks's chapter, "'Sister, Can You Line it Out?' Zora Neale Hurston Notes the Sound," on Hurston, nestled within her majestic work *Liner Notes for the Revolution: The Intellectual Life of Black Feminist Sound* (Cambridge, MA: Harvard University Press, 2021), is required reading.

63   On the invitations made possible by the conceptual difficulty of Hurston's work, I am very much inspired by the stunning correspondence between Barbara Johnson's writing on Hurston featured in her *A World of Difference* (Baltimore: Johns Hopkins University Press, 1987) and Hortense J. Spillers's reading of it all in "A Tale of Three Zoras: Barbara Johnson and Black Women Writers," *Diacritics* 34, no. 1 (2004): 94–97.

64   From Camille T. Dungy's "Before the Fetus Proves Viable, a Stroll Creekside in the Sierras," *Callaloo* 34, no. 3 (2011): 787.

65   By this mode of working I need to invoke Spillers's reading of Johnson's work on Hurston when she writes that "Johnson gives us a *relative* that becomes, in Ralph Ellison's aesthetic logic, an *ancestor* with an idea that in turn opens a tradition of writing not as a *monument* or mausoleum, but as a *practice*" (Spillers, "A Tale of Three Zoras," 96).

66   There is also an ecological sense here as Hurston witnessed much of the laboring in and of the state of Florida that made raw materials for the United States. See Susan Scott Parish's wonderful "Zora Neale Hurston and the Environmental Ethic of Risk," in *American Studies, Ecocriticism, and Citizenship: Thinking and Acting in the Local and Global Commons*, ed. Joni Adamson and Kimberly N. Ruffin (New York: Routledge, 2013), 21–36.

67 Henry Stone, "Foreword," in Kurt "K.O.T.O." Curtis, *Florida's Famous and Forgotten: History of Florida's Rock, Soul and Dance Music, the First 30 Years: 1955–1985*, vol. 1, *A to M* (Altamonte Springs, FL: Florida Media, 2005), 17.

68 "Personal Interviews" from Curtis, *Florida's Famous and Forgotten*, vol. 2, M to Z, A1–A2.

69 Killens plays a central role in chapter 4.

70 Benny Latimore in discussion with the author, October 15, 2021. "Benny Latimore aka Latimore Talks Miami Soul: 'I Lived Overtown at the Sir John Hotel,'" an interview with Jacob Katel featured in Jacob Katel and Henry Stone, *The Stone Cold Truth: Inside the Music Biz* (Henry Stone Music USA, 2016), 172–74. For more on Latimore, see John Capouya, "Blues Hall of Famer Benny Latimore Calls Riverview Home but Never Takes the Stage Here," *Tampa Bay Times*, May 25, 2017, accessed January 28, 2020, www.tampabay.com/news/humaninterest/blues-hall-of-famer-benny-latimore-calls-riverview-home-but-never-takes/2325159. Capouya's *Florida Soul: From Ray Charles to KC and the Sunshine Band* (Gainesville: University Press of Florida, 2017) will figure heavily in chapter 4.

71 Curtis, *Florida's Famous and Forgotten*, 1:423–24.

72 As of this writing (January 21, 2020), you can find the song here: "Latimore Let's Straighten It Out," YouTube video, posted by Aud, November 9, 2010, www.youtube.com/watch?v=aRctq68MGxM.

73 Capouya, "Blues Hall of Famer." In another interview with Capouya, Latimore has this to say of the song: "In my life I used to tell people: 'Evidently something has gotten crooked. We need to straighten it out.' But my idea was you have to sit down and straighten out any kind of relationship you have . . . it doesn't have to be a man-woman relationship. It could be with your brother, uncle, boss, or your friend. With any two human beings there's going to be a little bit of clash and you have to straighten it out. I say that onstage a lot." In Capouya, *Florida Soul*, 296.

74 *More More More* was produced by Steve Alaimo.

75 Andy Vineberg, "Levittown Bass Player Ron Bogdon Made Lasting Impression," *Burlington County Times*, July 14, 2015, accessed January 28, 2020, www.burlingtoncountytimes.com/article/20150714/LIFESTYLE/307149693.

76 Vineberg, "Levittown Bass Player Ron Bogdon Made Lasting Impression."

77 Benny Latimore in discussion with the author, October 15, 2021. Little Beaver biographical data has been culled from Curtis, *Florida's Famous and Forgotten*, 1:444–48. See also Alexandra T. Vazquez, "You Can Bring All Your Friends," *Small Axe* 49 (2016): 185, for a closer reading of Little Beaver's extraordinary recordings *Party Down I* and *Party Down II*.

78 You can find the incredible "Super Funky" here: "Thunder, Lightning & Rain—Super Funky (parts 1 & 2)," YouTube video, posted by DJ Weego, April 22, 2011, www.youtube.com/watch?v=V28aZYY-BeE.

79 Whiteis, "Latimore: Some Things You Can't Fake," 10–20, emphasis mine.

80 *Oxford English Dictionary Online*, "colon, n.2," accessed January 22, 2021, www-oed-com.proxy.library.nyu.edu/view/Entry/36513?result=2&rskey=zCgViO&.

81 "Latimore/Let's Straighten It Out," YouTube Video, posted by Kazuharp, December 11, 2010, www.youtube.com/watch?v=DgFRxaSk5yA.

82 Leah Jackson and Gwen McCrae, email message to the author, January 25, 2021.

83 "Gwen McCrae, Let's Straighten It Out," YouTube video, posted by Neil Allen, July 2, 2011, https://www.youtube.com/watch?v=8Ck5gsAUTF4.

84 Gwen McCrae and Leah Jackson in discussion with the author, July 3, 2020.

85 Gwen McCrae knows little about her father: he died when she was a baby. There are few details I can include here other than the fact that he was born in Pensacola. Jackson and McCrae email message, January 25, 2021.

86 McCrae and Jackson discussion, July 3, 2020.

87 George McCrae's single "Rock Your Baby" would be one of the greats in the catalog of what came to be known as the "Miami Sound."

88 Henry Stone is the force and music industry "iron fist" through which any study of South Florida musical history must pass. As the founder/promoter/distributor of some of the area's most important independent music labels, he figures largely in the history and manufacturing of the "Miami Sound." I want to acknowledge and honor the important infrastructure he made possible for Miami musical production, but my focus here will stay with the artists because their stories are often subsumed, like all musicians, by the stories of their labels. I do not want to shorthand their musical contributions under the catchall names of the labels they worked for—for example, the "TK days," or, as has been done elsewhere, "Motown," "Fania," etc. In the press about Stone's various labels, artists are very often referred to as being part of his "stable." There is ample literature on Stone, and I refer readers to Katel and Stone's *The Stone Cold Truth*; Curtis's entry on Stone in his *Famous and Forgotten*, 2:769–72; and this excellent web resource: www.henrystonemusic.com.

89 McCrae and Jackson discussion, July 3, 2020. Note how Latimore puts the work of the company (not The Company) this way in 1975: "Hell, I've recorded everywhere. New York, L.A., you name it, I've been there. All of those cats in all those places all they're really interested in is overdubbing 75 horns or how many strings they can bring in and things like that. Well all that's only icing on the cake. Here at TK we don't worry about no icing. Here we just bake the cake!" Jon Marlowe, "TK's Here to Bake the Cake, but That's Not All That's Cookin," *Miami News*, January 16, 1975, 3.

90 Deborah R. Vargas, "Punk's Afterlife in Cantina Time," *Social Text* 31, no. 3 (2013): 57–58. Gwen McCrae and Latimore recorded a version of "Let's Straighten It Out" together in 2006.

91 Felix Alexander Sama and Caridad Sama in discussion with the author, January 24, 2021.

92 Felix Alexander Sama in discussion with the author, January 22, 2021.
93 For more about mobile DJs and their arts, a must-read is Christine Bacareza Balance's *Tropical Renditions: Making Musical Scenes in Filipino America* (Durham, NC: Duke University Press, 2016).
94 *Liberty City* and its "Mega Mix" is available on most music platforms. For now, you can also find it here: "Mega Mix," YouTube video, posted by DJ Uncle Al-Topic, November 8, 2014, www.youtube.com/watch?v=nBA7TiGdgAg.
95 For some of my earlier writing on DJ Uncle Al, see Alexandra T. Vazquez, "How Can I Refuse?," *Journal of Popular Music Studies* 23, no. 2 (2011): 200–206. For an important piece on DJ Uncle Al and his incredible work, including heartbreaking lines from his son Albert Moss Jr., see Dave Tompkins, "An Oral History of the Miami Mobile DJ Scene," September 23, 2019, accessed December 2019, https://daily.redbullmusicacademy.com/2019/09/miami-bass-mobile-djs-regulating-oral-history. For another source on Moss by fellow DJs, see the section on him in the documentary *Music Regulators*. The Uncle Al segment may be accessed here: "Music Regulators—DJ Uncle Al 3," YouTube video, posted by SFLA80S, May 16, 2019, www.youtube.com/watch?v=PiDUq_boiaM.
96 Moss Jr. offered these touching words of tribute to his father in the documentary *Music Regulators*, which also includes footage of Uncle Al in action. See Music Regulators—DJ Uncle Al 3."
97 Here I am very much influenced by Shane Vogel's concept of the "elsewhen." See his incredible chapter "Working Against the Music: Geoffrey Holder's Elsewhen," in Shane Vogel, *Stolen Time: Black Fad Performance and the Calypso Craze* (Chicago: University of Chicago Press, 2018), 163–205.

CHAPTER TWO: MIAMI FROM THE SPOILS

1 This superlative is mentioned on a bronze signpost (those that mark important locations of Florida's early history) found in the Barnacle Historic State Park in Coconut Grove.
2 See Charlie Hailey's wonderful *Spoil Island: Reading the Makeshift Archipelago* (Lanham, MD: Lexington, 2013), xiii–xiv. For Hailey's specific work on the spoils in Miami's Biscayne Bay, see his chapter "Rational and Irrational: Developing Biscayne Bay's Lagoon," 173–96. And for other resources on the history and restoration efforts in Biscayne Bay, see Gary R. Milano, "Island Restoration and Enhancement in Biscayne Bay, Florida," in *Proceedings of the Twenty Sixth Annual Conference on Ecosystems Restoration and Creation*, ed. P. J. Cannizzaro (Tampa: Hillsborough Community College, 2000), 1–17; and Donna J. Lee and Anafrida B. Wenge, "Estimating the Benefits from Restoring Coastal Ecosystems: A Case Study of Biscayne Bay, Florida," in *Coastal Watershed Management*, ed. Ali Fares and Aly I. El-Kadi, 283–98 (Southampton, UK: WIT Press, 2008).
3 Hailey, *Spoil Island*, 2.

4 Quoted in Samantha Riepe, "Living Like Crusoe," *Miami Herald*, April 4, 2004, 1B. Riepe is, to my knowledge, the first to report on Montaner.
5 Quoted in Abby Goodnough, "Miami Journal; A Paradise of Detritus (Plus Ducks)," *New York Times*, April 12, 2004, www.nytimes.com/2004/04/12/us/miami-journal-a-paradise-of-detritus-plus-ducks.html.
6 Quoted in Riepe, "Living Like Crusoe," 1B.
7 See Kathleen Sullivan Sealey, Ray King Burch, and P.-M. Binder, *Will Miami Survive? The Dynamic Interplay between Floods and Finance* (Cham, Switzerland: Springer International, 2018).
8 E. V. Blackman, *Miami and Dade County, Florida: Its Settlement, Progress and Achievement* (Washington, DC: Victor Rainbolt, 1921), https://archive.org/stream/miamidadecountyfooblac#page/n13/mode/2up/search/board. Though among the "first" histories, it was a part of a general flurry of the narrative use of Miami in and for the US racial imaginary. See the grotesque novella by Hanson Brock, *Down Miami* (Miami: Tropic Press, 1920), http://hdl.loc.gov/loc.gdc/scd0001.00022293497.
9 Blackman, "Author's Foreword," *Miami and Dade County*, n.p.
10 Perrine was born in New Brunswick, New Jersey. A partial biography of Perrine was published in 1885 and written by his son Henry E. Perrine: *A True Story of Some Eventful Years in Grandpa's Life* (Buffalo, NY: Press of E. H. Hutchinson, 1885). The manuscript is held in the US Work Projects Administration, Federal Writers' Project: Folklore Project, Life Histories, 1936–39. See Henry E. Perrine, *Grandpa's Life*, Florida, manuscript/mixed material, www.loc.gov/item/wpalh000428.
11 T. Ralph Robinson, "Henry Perrine, Pioneer Horticulturalist of Florida," *Tequesta* 1, no. 2 (1942): 17–18.
12 The transaction is not about replicating the familiar and the flora from the North but rather to replicate the tropical South. The area's pinelands, from the outside, somehow did not match the climate. It needed more green and more color. Blackman provides the excerpt in his book. For the full proceedings, see US Congress, *An Act to encourage the introduction and promote the cultivation of tropical plants in the United States*, act of July 7, 1838, 25th Cong., 2nd sess., ch. CLXXXVIII, statute II, www.loc.gov/law/help/statutes-at-large/25th-congress/sesson-2/c25s2ch188.pdf.
13 Perrine, *A True Story*, 6–8. See also James W. Covington, *The Seminoles of Florida* (Gainesville: University Press of Florida, 1993), 99.
14 Robinson, "Henry Perrine," 16–24. Across the critical literature on Perrine, one gets the sense that because it so happened that South Florida's climate matched other parts of the Caribbean and the Yucatán, specifically, that a human intervention was needed to make it all line up.
15 Chakaika, of Mikasuki-speaking heritage, was part of a group known in wartime annals as the "Spanish Indians." For more on Chakaika and his role in the raid on Indian Key, see William C. Sturtevant's "Chakaika and the 'Span-

ish Indians': Documentary Sources Compared with Seminole Tradition," *Tequesta* 2, no. 13 (1953): 35–74. Sturtevant makes clear the deep mythologies that surround this event—for example, the various versions told by settlers and native peoples. In his article, he is sure to include them all, making no distinction in value between written and oral histories. For more early scholarship on the occupation of Indian Key, see Dorothy Dodd's "Jacob Houseman of Indian Key," *Tequesta* 1, no. 8 (1948): 3–20. Indian Key lies between Cape Florida and Key West, and it was eventually developed by the infamous wrecker Jacob Housman after he acquired it, in that dubious way, from two men who had been squatting on it. The island was a depot of sorts for wreckers of the era, and Housman profiteered off of its commerce. Indian Key even served as the newly formed Dade County's temporary seat in 1836. At the onset of the Second Seminole War, Housman fortified the island. While Perrine waited for his parcel of land to be designated on the mainland, he took his family (and plant collection) to Indian Key until it would be possible for him to enact his horticultural plans. Housman, "an autocratic ruler," found in Perrine a supporter of his plan to turn Indian Key into a port of entry. Just after Perrine's arrival, Housman's finances began to dwindle, so in 1840, as a way to generate income for himself, he made a proposal to the US government "to catch and kill all Indians of South Florida, for two hundred dollars each." Dodd, "Jacob Houseman," 14.

16 For an extended study on the Second Seminole War, see John K. Mahon, *History of the Second Seminole War, 1835–1842* (Gainesville: University of Florida Press, 1967).

17 Blackman, *Miami and Dade County*, 16–17.

18 As I stated in chapter 1, because of the continual displacements and reenplacements of its heterogenous and multilingual populations, scholarship on the Seminole is vast, often contradictory, and difficult to parse out, and there remains an important call for other ways for telling it. *Seminole* was the term used to describe all indigenous people of Florida until the mid-twentieth century. However, the people it is meant to describe emerge from distinct language groups and cultures. For two bountiful entries into these histories, see Betty Mae Tiger Jumper's autobiography, an important literary and historical work on the mid-nineteenth- to twentieth-century histories of those who came to be formally known as Seminoles, and on reservation history written from the perspective of a Mikasuki-speaking woman. Betty Mae Tiger Jumper and Patsy West, *A Seminole Legend: The Life of Betty Mae Jumper* (Gainesville: University Press of Florida, 2001). As a way into the Mikasuki-speaking populations who came to be known under the political entity of the Miccosukee Tribe of Indians of Florida in 1962, see Buffalo Tiger and Harry A. Kersey Jr., *Buffalo Tiger: A Life in the Everglades* (Lincoln: University of Nebraska Press, 2002). For a general historical overview that includes the clans in their Mikasuki and "Creek" names, see William C. Sturtevant and Jessica Cattelino,

"Florida Seminole and Miccosukee," in *Handbook of North American Indians*, vol. 14: *Southeast*, vol. ed. Raymond D. Fogelson, series ed. William C. Sturtevant (Washington, DC: Smithsonian Institution, 2003), 429–49. See also John K. Mahon and Brent R. Weisman, "Florida's Seminole and Miccosukee Peoples," in *The New History of Florida*, ed. Michael Gannon (Gainesville: University Press of Florida, 1996), 183–206; and Covington, *The Seminoles of Florida*.

19 In Patsy West, "Abiaka, or Sam Jones, in Context: The Mikasuki Ethnogenesis through the Third Seminole War," in *Florida Historical Quarterly* 94, no. 3 (2016): 393–94. As West shows though her work on Abiaka and the Mikasuki people, this "indicates . . . a fallacy that should not be continued" (393). See Patricia R. Wickman, *The Tree That Bends: Discourse, Power, and the Survival of the Maskoki People* (Tuscaloosa: University of Alabama Press, 1999), 71. This was also the history told by Buffalo Tiger.

20 Refer to chapter 1, note 20, for more on my use of i:laposhni:cha thli:.

21 Blackman, *Miami and Dade County*, 33.

22 *The Florida East Coast Homeseeker*, February 1908, HathiTrust, https://babel.hathitrust.org/cgi/pt?id=nyp.33433007772399&view=1up&seq=46&q1=magic.

23 A fascinating double: Birmingham, Alabama, is also known as "Magic City," and the term arrived around the same time as Miami's. Listen to Sun Ra and his *The Magic City*, echoing the Birmingham (his hometown) version of the phrase in 1965. "Magic City" is also a TV show from 2012 and a recent song by Gucci Mane.

24 As N. D. B. Connolly argues of Miami's many glossy nicknames, "South Florida's exotic labels also served to conceal the brutality and racism so often required to create and preserve one of the nation's most celebrated tourist destinations." N. D. B. Connolly, *A World More Concrete: Real Estate and the Making of Jim Crow South Florida* (Chicago: University of Chicago Press, 2014), 5.

25 Even if those strains aren't recalled by you, let us lean on the national familiarity with "Old Folks at Home," the terrible 1851 minstrel standard and Florida's official state song. The song was composed by Stephen Foster, who never actually saw the Suwannee River but turned it into a primary hook for tourism. It has been an embroiled song in many battles. In 2007 Governor Charlie Crist forbid the use of the song at his inauguration and, together with Florida's Black Caucus, commissioned a new song that became not the state's official song but *anthem*: "Florida (Where the Sawgrass Meets the Sky)." It was a reluctant two-song solution to appease northern and southern reaches of the state.

26 LeBaron was a librettist who wrote the book for more than ten Broadway musicals and ended up being a prolific Hollywood producer of films, including *Cimarron* (1931).

27 Versions were recorded by Joseph C. Smith's Orchestra (1919), Edward Allen (1919), Maz Fells' Della Robbia Orchestra (1920), Fritz Kreisler (1920), Jules Levy Jr. (1919), Prince's Dance Orchestra (1919), Campbell & Burr (1920), and

Carl Fenton's Orchestra (1920). Tony Martin's version of 1940 features musical Hawaiiana (!). It also features in a 1924 film titled *Miami*, starring silent-movie star Betty Compson.

28 For a wonderful overview and analysis of theatrical productions and early films that use Miami as backdrop, see Julio Capó Jr.'s fantastic *Welcome to Fairyland: Queer Miami before 1940* (Chapel Hill: University of North Carolina Press, 2017). See especially his important chapter "Miami as Stage," where he discusses "Miami as a fairyland for white pleasure. It advertised the city through oozing sensuality, Caribbean exoticism, and black subservience. Theatrical performances helped women and men—residents and visitors alike—navigate the edges of their fantasies and imagine Miami as a site of exploration and conquest" (157).

29 Here is Fritz Kreisler's version (1920): "Kreisler Plays 'On Miami Shore' by Victor Jacobi," YouTube video, posted by VictrolaCredenza, March 31, 2009, www.youtube.com/watch?v=R26fsuJA1WI.

30 "Fritz Kreisler plays Chopin—Mazurka No. 4 Op. 67 posth," YouTube video, posted by Daniel Kurganov, violinist, April 29, 2012, www.youtube.com/watch?v=xdf86FrXQpY.

31 "Apple Blossoms" (1919) also involved William LeBeron as lyricist, was an operetta based on "Un marriage sous Louis XV" by Alexandre Dumas (Fritz Kreisler cowrote the music), and starred performers such as Fred and Adele Astaire. See "Apple Blossoms Has Unusual Music and a Good Story," *New York Clipper*, October 15, 1919, 16. Brief mentions of Jacobi can be found in Andrew Lamb's *150 Years of Popular Music Theatre* (New Haven, CT: Yale University Press, 2001), 146; and Gerald Martin Bordman's *American Musical Theater: A Chronicle* (Oxford: Oxford University Press, 1978).

32 Victor Jacobi and William LeBaron, "On Miami Shore (Golden Sands of Miami): waltz song," 1919, Vocal Popular Sheet Music Collection, score 1111, https://digitalcommons.library.umaine.edu/mmb-vp/1111.

33 This work was later reprised, with alterations, in English under the title *Rambler Rose*.

34 The most comprehensive bibliographical account of Jacobi that I have been able to locate in English is by Kurt Gänzl in his *The Encyclopedia of the Musical Theater*, vol. 2, 2nd ed. (New York: Schirmer, 2001), 1005–7. All of this information on Jacobi comes from his entry.

35 Gänzl, *Encyclopedia of Musical Theater*, 1005–7.

36 Gänzl leaves us with this amazing anecdote under the "Miami" entry in his encyclopedia: "Apparently a title that is considered more evocative outside America than in, *Miami* has been used as the name of musicals in Britain, France and Hungary, but not in the United States of America." He adds, somewhat sardonically, "a number which had already managed to get itself interpolated into not one but two Australian musical productions. . . ." Gänzl notes the Australian productions were *Theodore & Co.* and *Yes, Uncle!*

37 Obituary for Elena 'Mimi' Casals, *New York Times*, May 13, 2012, https://archive.nytimes.com/query.nytimes.com/gst/fullpage-9A07EEDD1F3AF930A25756C0A9649D8B63.html. See also her obituary in *El Pais:* Mauricio Vincent, "Elena Casals, bolerista cubana del desengaño," *El Pais*, March 25, 2012, https://elpais.com/cultura/2012/03/25/actualidad/1332709646_578554.html.

38 Desmond Child in discussion with the author, January 18, 2018. See also Jordon Levin, "Cuban Poet, Songwriter Elena Casals Dies at 85," Repeating Islands, March 21, 2012, https://repeatingislands.com/2012/03/21/cuban-poet-songwriter-elena-casals-dies-at-85.

39 Desmond Child interview with Craig MacNeil. For a great live interview with Child, hear the whole of Craig MacNeil's interview on his *Whimsically Volatile* podcast: Desmond Child, interview by Craig MacNeil, *Whimsically Volatile*, podcast audio, December 29, 2019, http://whimsicallyvolatile.libsyn.com/73-desmond-child.

40 Desmond Child in discussion with the author, February 2018.

41 Child discussion, January 18, 2018.

42 According to Desmond Child, Casals hired Marlow Rosado, a Puerto Rican composer and former schoolteacher, to help arrange and record her songs, which gave us this version of "Magic City." Rosado's later salsa album, *Marlow Rosado y La Riqeña Retro*, won a Grammy for the best Tropical Latin Album in 2013. Desmond Child, email message to the author, February 13, 2020.

43 Vincent, "Elena Casals."

44 Roberto Ledesma, "Muchísimo," n.d., on *Orquesta de Pepe Delgado-Para Enamorados Volumen II* (Gema Records, LPG-3028, vinyl); and Roberto Ledesma, "Triste" and "Que Seas Feliz Con Tu Dinero," n.d., on *Adoro* (Gema Records, LPG-3054, vinyl). Both albums were recorded with the Orquesta de Cuerdas de Pepe Delgado. Exact recording dates are unknown but likely were in the early 1960s. Another widely available song of hers was featured on the last album Olga Guillot recorded: "Doña Tristeza," May 9, 2001, on *Faltaba Yo* (Warner Music Mexico, compact disc). Casals's name is misspelled when credited on this Guillot album. It has her as Helena (and not Elena) Casals.

45 Of his twelve years in Liberty City, Child recalls how every family member who came from Cuba would stay with them; never were there fewer than seven people living in their tiny apartment. When he was growing up, "Cuban songwriters in exile were crammed in there sitting on the floor in a circle singing their latest songs that would later turn into hits." Of his musical surround, he recalls that on the shared swingset which he shared with "kids of all colors" they had a transistor radio that would play everything: Brill Building pop, rock, rockabilly, Aretha Franklin, Motown. But "Latin was played inside on the record player, especially Cuban Boleros like my Tia Olga Guillot who was married to my mother's brother Tio Bebo. They would visit us from Mexico when she was on tour in Miami." As you now see, this text exchange had to be shared. Desmond Child, text message to the author, January 7, 2021.

46 Child, interview by MacNeil. Spoiler alert: Miami Beach High is also the alma mater of Luther Campbell, who is one of the subjects of chapter 4. A project for someone *please*: Tego Calderón is also a graduate of Beach High.

47 Desmond Child has also given us the beautiful gift of publishing his mother's poems and boleros in *Elena Casals: Mis Cajas de Carton/Elena Casals: My Cardboard Boxes*, ed. Armando Suárez Cobián, trans. Jodi Marr and Desmond Child (Nashville: Deston Entertainment, 2021).

48 Minute 11 in Child, interview by MacNeil, emphasis mine.

49 Child, interview by MacNeil.

50 Desmond Child interview by Dale Kawashima, "Desmond Child Continues Great String of Hits, from Aerosmith & Bon Jovi to Ricky Martin," *Songwriter Universe*, July 4, 2001, www.songwriteruniverse.com/child.htm.

51 "I Was Made for Lovin' You," performed by KISS. https://www.youtube.com/watch?v=12fJAnaif34. Provided to YouTube by Universal Music Group.

52 Emma Trelles, "Steven Tiger, 57, Rock Musician," *South Florida Sun Sentinel*, July 1, 2006, www.sun-sentinel.com/news/fl-xpm-2006-07-01-0606300422-story.html. Lee Tiger remembers his brother as an artist who infused his paintings and music with the tenets of the tribe: "My brother was one who did use all the elements as far as trying to retain tradition and culture, while at the same time moving through the modern world. That's why he wrote the song Space-Age Indian. But he also tried to keep the tranquility of the Everglades and the harmonistic idea that the Miccosukees have about living with nature." See Patsy West and Lee Tiger, "'Tiger Tiger': Miccosukee Rock 'n' Roll," in *Southern Cultures* 14, no. 4 (2008): 127–40. And for more on Tiger Tiger, see Kurt Curtis's entry "Tiger Tiger," in Kurt "K.O.T.O." Curtis, *Florida's Famous and Forgotten: History of Florida's Rock, Soul, and Dance Music, the First 30 Years: 1955–1985*, vol. 2, M to Z (Altamonte Springs, FL: Florida Media, 2005), 800–802; and Harry A. Kersey Jr.'s work and interview with Buffalo Tiger in "Florida's Indians: Their Journey from Backwoods to Big Time," *Forum: The Magazine of the Florida Humanities Council*, January 31, 2007, https://issuu.com/flahum/docs/forum_2007spring.

53 "Because of the Night," YouTube video posted by Tiger! Tiger!—Topic, December 25, 2014, https://www.youtube.com/watch?v=VX8bvWrwmZU&list=OLAK5uy_kWnHGcydzGS3xCw3B3C2ZUz-GrTp5s0cI.

54 West and Tiger, "Tiger Tiger," 129.

55 For an insightful, brief overview of Shusei Nagaoka, see Nate Patrin's "A Tribute to Graphic Designer Shusei Nagaoka," *Red Bull Music Academy*, August 4, 2015, https://daily.redbullmusicacademy.com/2015/08/shusei-nagaoka-feature.

56 José Esteban Muñoz, *Disidentifications: Queers of Color and the Performances of Politics* (Minneapolis: University of Minnesota Press, 1999), 189.

57 Gerald Vizenor, "Aesthetics of Survivance: Literary Theory and Practice," in *Survivance: Narratives of Native Presence*, ed. Gerald Vizenor (Lincoln: University of Nebraska Press, 2008), 1.

58 Covington, *The Seminoles of Florida*, 257–58.

59 For more about the federal termination era and what it meant to the Seminoles and Miccosukee, see Harry A. Kersey Jr., *An Assumption of Sovereignty: Social and Political Transformation among the Florida Seminoles, 1953–1979* (Lincoln: University of Nebraska Press, 1996); and Harry A. Kersey Jr.'s "Afterword" in Buffalo Tiger and Harry A. Kersey Jr., *Buffalo Tiger: A Life in the Everglades* (Lincoln: University of Nebraska Press, 2002), 137–47.

60 Covington, *The Seminoles of Florida*, 260.

61 Covington, *The Seminoles of Florida*, 263. Refer to Tiger's autobiography for his narration from the inside of all of this: Tiger and Kersey Jr., *Buffalo Tiger*, 78–86.

62 Tony Gieske, "Indians Ask 3 Nations to Help Claims," *Washington Post*, November 19, 1958, B8, ProQuest Historical Newspapers, http://proxy.library.nyu.edu/login?qurl=https%3A%2F%2Fwww.proquest.com%2Fhistorical-newspapers%2Findians-ask-3-nations-help-claims%2Fdocview%2F148945864%2Fse-2%3Faccountid%3D12768. "Tribe on Wrong Trail: Appeals in Vain for 3 Foreign Envoy's Aid on Land Claims," *New York Times*, November 19, 1958, ProQuest Historical Newspapers, http://proxy.library.nyu.edu/login?qurl=https%3A%2F%2Fwww.proquest.com%2Fhistorical-newspapers%2Ftribe-on-wrong-trail%2Fdocview%2F114502654%2Fse-2%3Faccountid%3D12768.

63 For a comprehensive read on the dizzying years leading up to Miccosukee independence and their interaction with Castro in Havana, see Harry A. Kersey Jr.'s "The Havana Connection: Buffalo Tiger, Fidel Castro, and the Origin of Miccosukee Tribal Sovereignty, 1959–1962," *American Indian Quarterly* 25, no. 4 (2001): 491–507. The article not only reproduces the documents exchanged between the two but also contains incredible interview material between the author and Buffalo Tiger. Beverly Bidney reports that the US government gave the Miccosukee recognition on the promise that they would not return to Cuba until relations would be normalized. Reflecting on the bold move a half a century later, son William Buffalo Tiger Jr. said, "The trip to Cuba was so far out of normal, I don't know if I'd be brave enough to do that." Beverly Bidney, "Former Miccosukee Chairman Buffalo Tiger Passes at 94," *Seminole Tribune*, January 29, 2015, http://seminoletribune.org/former-miccosukee-chairman-buffalo-tiger-passes-at-94.

64 Kersey Jr., "The Havana Connection," 503.

65 Musa Isle was initially founded in 1907 by John Roop, who later leased a section of this land to Willie Willie, a Seminole who with his father, Charlie Willie, would bring "animal commodities" from their trading post west of Miami to Musa Isle for sale. Willie would encourage other Seminoles to trade in and around Musa Isle during the winter tourist season. The Willies were among the Seminole's first entrepreneurial architects for the touristic economy, where they would sell objects and activities.

66 Tiger and Kersey Jr., *Buffalo Tiger*, 60–61. There was so much promised by "Musa Isle, Home of the Seminole Indian." Across its myriad promotional materials visitors could enjoy per the promotional brochure in the 1960s (author's collection): "Seminole Indian Trading Post—Alligator and Crocodile

Farm—Museum and Zoo—Wishing Well—A Place of Beauty and Interest for 35 Years—As You Enter the Village You See Tropical Foliage of Every Kind, Such as, the Royal Palms, Bamboo, Citrus Trees and Guava. Guide on Duty."

67 West and Tiger, "Tiger Tiger," 132.
68 Bidney, "Former Miccosukee Chairman."
69 Bidney, "Former Miccosukee Chairman."
70 West and Tiger, "Tiger Tiger," 129–30.
71 West and Tiger, "Tiger Tiger," 130.
72 For more on Lee Tiger's contemporary entrepreneurial work on behalf of the Miccosukee, see Dennis Weidman, "Global Marketing of Indigenous Culture: Discovering Native America with Lee Tiger and the Florida Miccosukee," *American Indian Culture and Research Journal* 34, no. 3 (2010): 1–26. In Buffalo Tiger's autobiography, it is interesting to see how he narrates his sons' lives on the road: "After they grew up they had ideas, their own minds. I didn't agree with them. I thought they were better off growing up with what they had to be. I told them they had to leave. They were gone for two years. They went to New York and California and returned home. They had different feelings and we got along fine." Tiger and Kersey Jr., *Buffalo Tiger*, 70.
73 West and Tiger, "Tiger Tiger," 135.
74 "Ingresan Al Robinson Crusoe De Miami En El Hospital Jackson," *El Nuevo Herald*, May 5, 2004, 2A, NewsBank: Access World News—Historical and Current.
75 For more on Guillermo García Rodiles and his incredible story, see his self-published memoir, *From War to Rock 'n' Roll* (Miami: Rodiles, 2017).

CHAPTER THREE: DRUMS TAKE TIME

1 David Scott, "The Re-Enchantment of Humanism: An Interview with Sylvia Wynter," *Small Axe* 8 (2000): 124.
2 As one of the great theorists of the Caribbean and the multiple worlds held in it, Wynter's rural time demands our attention partly because it moved the writing of her novel-turned-play *The Hills of Hebron*, which prepared her later critical work. Novel and play composition offered early formal stages for the dynamism of her thinking. This writerly experimentation, I hasten to add, was taken up around and after Wynter resided in London as a member of Boscoe Holder's midcentury dance company "The Caribbean Dancers." All this rehearsal in other forms, on different stages and with other bodies, proposes performance as rehearsal for future thought. It is hard to know when performance—whether everyday gesture or structured arrangement—will offer some temporary crystallization of an idea that will honor and give back to it. But performance assures the fact of its return.

Wynter began to dance with Holder while she was a student at University of London, "I would leave my lectures at Kings College and go across to his studio to begin to dance with him, right. That's how I came to dancing." Sylvia Wynter, "Sylvia Wynter: An Oral History," interviewed by Natalie Marine-Street, Stanford Historical Society Oral History Program interviews, November 27, 2017, https://purl.stanford.edu/kd232zm4370. This oral history is incredible for the amount of performance studies details, still overlooked and undertheorized, in Wynter's oeuvre. I also want to note from this interview that Wynter's mother, in addition to running a boarding house, was an actor in one of Jamaica's most successful radio soap operas (!) For further reading on Wynter the artist, see Imani Owens's important essay, "Toward a 'Truly Indigenous Theater': Sylvia Wynter Adapts Federico García Lorca," *Cambridge Journal of Postcolonial Literary Inquiry* 4, no. 1 (2017): 49–67.

3. Kofi Agawu, *The African Imagination in Music* (Cambridge: Oxford University Press, 2016), 179, emphasis mine.
4. María del Carmen Mestas, *Pasión de Rumbero* (Barcelona: Puvill Libros, 1998), 6.
5. Dafnis Prieto, *A World of Rhythmic Possibilities: Drumming Lessons and Reflections on Rhythms* (Miami: Dafnison Music, 2016), 49.
6. Prieto, *A World of Rhythmic Possibilities*, 49, emphasis original.
7. Prieto, *A World of Rhythmic Possibilities*, 81.
8. *Oxford English Dictionary Online*, "lapse, n.," accessed April 25, 2020, www.oed.com/view/Entry/105775.
9. For Prieto the lapse has an origin and an open end point. It began when he was a ten-year-old studying at the Olga Alonso School of Fine Arts and culminated when Prieto was thirteen when a teacher let him know that there were indeed instructions to the book.
10. Dafnis Prieto in discussion with the author, May 17, 2020.
11. Throughout his teaching and writings, Prieto makes constant reference to Stone's exercises.
12. Prieto discussion, May 17, 2020.
13. Also known as the grand poinciana. These were introduced to South Florida by David Fairchild. "Poinciana," a song written in 1936, has become a standard of the Latin jazz repertoire (based on "La Canción del Árbol"). Please hear the live 1958 version by Ahmad Jamal.
14. This Instagram video was posted on his account dafnisonmusic on March 30, 2020. It has been viewed (as of April 23, 2020) 1,966 times. Dafnis Prieto [@dafnisonmusic], "Example from the Book Rhythmic Syncronicity," Instagram video, March 30, 2020, accessed April 23, 2020, www.instagram.com/p/B-XCGFeAeav/?igshid=y7bsw0evp943.
15. Prieto discussion, May 17, 2020.
16. Agawu, *The African Imagination in Music*, 158.
17. Take another of Prieto's quarantined entries on Instagram: "Tile Playing in 6/8! Any Place Is a Good Place!," where we see Prieto's hands tap out on that white-tiled kitchen countertop found all over Florida. Dafnis Prieto

(@dafnisonmusic), "Tile Playing in 6/8!," Instagram video, April 17, 2020, https://www.facebook.com/dafnisprieto/videos/653031482186759/" https://www.facebook.com/dafnisprieto/videos/653031482186759.

18 Dafnis Prieto, "Regresar: Back in Cuba," dir. Saleem Reshamwala (KidEthnic), prod. Lindsay Evans, YouTube video, posted by Dafnis Prieto, October 31, 2019, www.youtube.com/watch?v=uUnL-mu95cw.

19 I'm thinking here about Jamaica Kincaid's use of Wordsworth's "I Wandered as a Lonely Cloud" (aka "Daffodils") as a way to name the imposition of "repulsive" colonial cosmologies in the new world, especially in her *Lucy: A Novel* (New York: Farrar, Straus and Giroux, 2002). See also her continued ambivalence with the daffodil as she planted it in her Vermont garden: Jamaica Kincaid, "Gardens: Dances with Daffodils," *Architectural Digest* 64, no. 2 (April 2007): 78–82.

20 Dafnis Prieto in discussion with the author, July 7, 2019.

21 Prieto discussion, July 7, 2019.

22 Prieto discussion, July 7, 2019.

23 Chucho Valdes had his New York premiere there. Yosvany Terry in discussion with the author, June 3, 2020.

24 In addition to Yosvany Terry on saxophone and chekeré, and Prieto on drums, the principal members of the group included Venezuelan pianist Luis Perdomo and the Puerto Rican bassist John Benitez. Revolving members and guest stars abound, including Miguel Zenón, Pedrito Martínez, and other New York–based musical prodigies. But there were also more established jazz musicians that played there, such as Steve Turre and Roy Hargrove, who were also eager to play (and did) on a consistent basis by Terry's invitation. For an interview with Terry about his pioneering work at the Jazz Gallery, see "Jazz Cubano and Beyond: The Music of Yosvany Terry" by Amical Navarro, YouTube video, posted by FivePassion, April 6, 2012, www.youtube.com/watch?v=_x4HPfWBNns.

25 Obed Calvaire in discussion with the author, May 6, 2020.

26 Obed Calvaire in discussion with the author, May 6, 2020.

27 I had the great fortune of first meeting Calvaire when I invited the Yosvany Terry Quintet to come play at Princeton University in 2013. I discuss this briefly at the end of the chapter.

28 Obed Calvaire in discussion with the author, May 6, 2020.

29 His maternal grandmother, though the mother of seven with her husband, took in seven of his children by other mothers and raised them together with her own. Baradé is also known as the French Baradéres. Ktalove Bertrand, "Baraderes: Mystical Venice of Haiti," *Haiti Observer*, April 11, 2017, www.haitiobserver.com/blog/baraderes-mystical-venice-of-haiti.html. Baradéres figures heavily and lyrically in Dany Laferriére's 2013 *Enigma of Return*, when the author returns to his father's birthplace in the wake of his passing. Regarding Rara, I like this capacious definition put forward by Elizabeth McAlister:

"The phenomenon of Rara is both fun and profound. It is at once a season, a festival, a genre of music, a religious ritual, a form of dance, and sometimes a technique of political protest." Elizabeth McAlister, "Rara: Vodou, Power, and Performance," Smithsonian Music, https://music.si.edu/story/rara-vodou-power-and-performance.

30 Obed Calvaire, email message to the author, May 25, 2020.

31 Obed Calvaire, email messages to the author, May 21 and May 25, 2020.

32 Calvaire, email messages to the author, May 21 and May 25, 2020. For more on Colas, see this series of documentaries by Roupy Productions, available on YouTube: "Biographie de Roger Colas, chanteur, peintre, tailleur, musicien, compositeur @ Roupy Productions TV," YouTube video, posted by Roupy Productions TV—RPTV, July 31, 2016, https://www.youtube.com/watch?v=fNjQifFGY8o. One detail I would like to hold on to: one of Colas's best-known albums is a collection of boleros by Mexican composer Agustín Lara (1971).

33 Here is what I love about people: I was able to track down Fritz Calvaire's CD from Wagmarlove Online Music Store based in Queens Village, New York City, "the most visited online Haitian music store." When my package arrived with the CD, placed on top was a burgundy pocket monthly planner and ballpoint pen etched with the store's business information. It wasn't just the inclusion of these handy gifts, but *the ways they were placed in the package* for the receiver so that when you opened it, you were given an experience. Like Christmas in July. This mail order—anonymous epistolary contact—offered reflection on elegant forms of curation. Visit and support Wagmarlove Music Store, www.wagmarlovemusicstore.net.

34 Fritz Calvaire would organize and host concerts of Haitian and Caribbean gospel music at places like Barry University and other venues. They would always sell out. Calvaire discussion, May 6, 2020.

35 Obed Calvaire, formerly a self-described "horrible student" who had spent a lot of time in detention for whatever mischief before high school, knew that he had to do what he had to do (maintain a 3.5 grade-point average) in order to stay there. Of his time before New World, Calvaire says that "it wasn't as if I wasn't smart enough; I just didn't care."

36 Calvaire discussion, May 6, 2020.

37 You can access the performance here: "Dave Holland/Chris Potter/Obed Calvaire—Good Hope," YouTube video, posted by Jazz and More, November 18, 2017, www.youtube.com/watch?v=IyyRuS2BadY.

38 See, for example, "Obed Clavaire—Focus," YouTube video, posted by No Logo, April 19, 2017, www.youtube.com/watch?v=r9BEI8ayo8A. See also "Artist Spotlight: Obed Calvaire | SF Jazz Collective," YouTube video, posted by Vic Firth, April 9, 2014, www.youtube.com/watch?v=T5BsLCRJdBg.

39 Calvaire discussion, May 6, 2020.

40 "Artist Spotlight: Obed Calvaire | SF Jazz Collective."

41 Calvaire discussion, May 6, 2020, emphasis mine.
42 See my initial theorization of this Miamian mode in Alexandra T. Vazquez, "You Can Bring All Your Friends," *Small Axe* 49 (March 2016): 185–93.
43 Calvaire discussion, May 6, 2020. And of playing with him onstage, "There's so much going on, that as a drummer, there's no need to go mayhem; you can just cruise and have dialogs with Pedrito."
44 Prieto calls songo "a style of music that has many 'variations/combinations.' When we talk of songo we are not only talking about a single pattern, but a whole musical style that has a vast repertoire of patterns and a great deal of rhythmic adventures." Prieto, *A World of Rhythmic Possibilities*, 88.
45 Emphasis in original. Prieto, *A World of Rhythmic Possibilities*, 89.
46 José Luis Quintana and Chuck Silverman, *Changuito: A Master's Approach to Timbales*, Book & CD (Los Angeles: Alfred Music, 1998).
47 Quintana and Silverman, *Changuito*, 12.
48 Flight is central to African folklore in the New World, and and there is an abundance of materials to be found across literary, artistic, and many other forms. This is an impossible bibliography to include here. For two entry points see Virginia Hamilton's *The People Could Fly: American Black Folktales* (New York: Knopf Books for Young Readers, 1993). See Soyica Diggs Colbert, "Flying Africans in Spaceships," in *Black Movements: Performance and Cultural Politics* (New Brunswick, NJ: Rutgers University Press, 2017), 23–57; Toni Morrison, *Song of Solomon* (New York: Knopf Doubleday, 2004).
49 Yosvany Terry in discussion with the author, June 3, 2020.
50 Yosvany Terry in discussion with the author, November 14, 2013.
51 Terry discussion, June 3, 2020.
52 I wrote about the Terrys, especially Yosvany and Don Pancho, in Alexandra T. Vazquez, *Listening in Detail: Performances of Cuban Music* (Durham, NC: Duke University Press, 2013).
53 Terry discussion, June 3, 2020.
54 Terry talks about this in the *Return to Havana* documentary. See Fabien Pisani, dir., *Return to Havana* (Cuban Joint Production, 2020). The movie premiered on May 28, 2020, on gladyspalmera.com. For a write-up on and a link to the movie, see the mighty Rosa Marquetti's "Yosvany Terry presenta *Return to Havana*," Gladys Palmera, May 28, 2020, https://gladyspalmera.com/actualidad/yosvany-terry-presenta-return-to-havana/2020. Terry also mentioned it in discussion with the author, various dates.
55 *Return to Havana*.
56 Terry discussion, June 3, 2020.
57 *Return to Havana*.
58 Agawu, *The African Imagination in Music*, 179.
59 Terry discussion, June 3, 2020. There is an echo here in Cuban music with the expression "Clave goes with everything" (Clave va con todo).
60 Agawu, *The African Imagination in Music*, 179.

61 Also including Osmany Paredes, who is a frequent and central Prieto and Terry collaborator.
62 Masa is a really important link here—the Chilean linkage—and was also mentioned at length in the Prieto discussion, July 7, 2019.
63 For a chapter-length study on Rodríguez, see the first chapter of Vazquez, *Listening in Detail*, 43–92. In one of our interviews, Prieto tells the amazing anecdote of going out to dinner with Rodríguez in Paris and without any fanfare, Rodríguez pulled a banana out of his coat pocket to eat with his spaghetti. Prieto discussion, July 7, 2019.
64 See this overview of Terry's work and biography in Ted Panken, "For Saxophonist-Composer Yosvany Terry's 45th Birthday, a Jazziz Feature from 2014, Two Interviews from 2013, and a Downbeat Profile (and the Interview for That Profile) from 2013," *Today Is The Question: Ted Panken on Music, Politics, and the Arts* (blog), May 31, 2017, https://tedpanken.wordpress.com/2017/05/31/for-saxophonist-composer-yosvany-terrys-45th-birthday-a-jazziz-feature-from-2014-two-interviews-from-2013-and-a-downbeat-profile-and-the-interview-for-that-profile-from-2013.
65 Bueno is another gifted composer and musician who requires way more time and space beyond "Bailando." While now based mostly in Miami, he continues to work in and with island-based artists. He was the leader of other foundational groups in the United States such as Yerba Buena.

CHAPTER FOUR: BASS IS THE PLACE

1 Please read Katherine McKittrick's, *Demonic Grounds: Black Women and the Cartographies of Struggle* (Minneapolis: University of Minnestoa Press, 2006). See also Tim Cresswell, *Geographic Thought: A Critical Introduction* (Malden, MA: Wiley-Blackwell, 2013).
2 See Suzanne Césaire, *The Great Camouflage: Writings of Dissent (1941–1945)*, ed. Daniel Maximin and trans. Keith L. Walker (Middletown, CT: Wesleyan University Press, 2012).
3 The Eloise Trio, "Come to the Carribbean," track A1 on *Come to the Caribbean and Meet the Exciting Eloise Trio* (Decca Records, DL 4293, 1962, long-play record). The song "Come to the Caribbean" was written by Freddy Munnings and Billy Cooke (on the album their names are erroneously spelled, as too often happens on "exotica" records), https://youtube.com/watch?v=DHLp9DrnxpQ. I share a bit of the sleeve notes: "To invite you to 'Come to the Caribbean,' knowing we can't actually send you a ticket for the next sailing, we'd have to be either slightly touched, or have a might potent ace up our sleeve. Our ace is the Eloise Trio. For if anything on earth can lift you right out of your armchair and transplant you onto a gay and fabulous tropical island, the fiery rhythms and dynamic showmanship generated by Eloise, Bucky and Bert can."

4   Timothy Rommen comes to similar vocal conclusions in his important *Funky Nassau: Roots, Routes, and Representation in Bahamian Popular Music* (Berkeley: University of California Press, 2011), 88.
5   Rommen, *Funky Nassau*, 88.
6   For a much more nuanced and full sense of goombay, see Rommen, *Funky Nassau*, 24–25. On the history of goombay, junkanoo, and its principal performers, see musician and scholar Christian Justilien's important web resource, "Bahamas Entertainers," accessed April 29, 2020," https://www.bahamasentertainers.com/copy-of-featured-artists. For the perplex that is Calypso and in particular the ways it circulated outside of the postwar Caribbean, see Shane Vogel's *Stolen Time: Black Fad Performance and the Calypso Craze* (Chicago: University of Chicago Press, 2018).
7   See Raymond A. Mohl, "Black Immigrants: Bahamians in Early Twentieth-Century Miami," *Florida Historical Quarterly* 65, no. 3 (1987): 271–97. See also Melanie Shell-Weiss's important essay, "Coming North to the South: Migration, Labor and City-Building in Twentieth-Century Miami," *Florida Historical Quarterly* 84, no. 1 (2005): 79–99. Howard Johnson points to Bahamian migration to Key West as early as 1820 and sees Bahamians as part of what made the area a "wrecking center." His study of Bahamian migration, especially from 1880 to 1920, and the early remittance economies between Miami and the Bahamas, is a must-read. Howard Johnson, "Bahamian Labor Migration to Florida in the Late Nineteenth and Early Twentieth Centuries," *International Migration Review* 22, no. 1 (1988): 84–103.
8   For a really helpful context for the greater Bahamian-Floridan connections in the longer history of wrecking or wracking, an eco-critical inquiry, and also a great synthesis of extant scholarship, see Devin Leigh's excellent "Between Swamp and Sea: Bahamian Visitors in Southeast Florida before Miami," *Florida Historical Quarterly* 93, no. 4 (2015): 511–37.
9   For more on wrecking in the longer history of Bahamian maritime arts, see Michael Craton and Gail Saunders's important work *Islanders in the Stream: A History of the Bahamian People*, vol. 1, *From Aboriginal Times to the End of Slavery* (Athens: University of Georgia Press, 1992), 86–87. As Craton and Saunders state, "It was, almost by definition, hazardous work," and the hauls, whether big or small, offered quick and temporary assets to penniless Bahamian mariners. For a thorny read on the procedures of wrecking from the vantage point of a political scientist in the early twentieth century, see the brazen linkages made between wrecking (or "salvaging") and African and African-descended Bahamians and criminality by James M. Wright: "They were an uneducated class, whose members had been brought up at sea from childhood and were generally content to become and remain 'hardy and intrepid' children of the sea. Seaworn in countenance and uncouth in costume they took pride in preserving certain outward traits of their lawless seventeenth century predecessors, for instance of carrying big knives in their belts." James M. Wright, "The Wrecking

System of the Bahamas Islands," *Political Science Quarterly* 30, no. 4 (1915): 618–44. I must also mention that Abiaka, the resistance leader of the Second Seminole War, was, according to Patsy West, "well seasoned to the art of wrecking, [and] kept his resistance movement well supplied with its bounty." In Patsy West, "Abiaka, or Sam Jones, in Context: The Mikasuki Ethnogenesis through the Third Seminole War," *Florida Historical Quarterly* 94, no. 3 (2016): 374.

10 See Laura Harris's making different of these pirate narratives in her wonderful "What Happened to the Motley Crew? C. L. R. James, Hélio Oiticica, and the Aesthetic Sociality of Blackness," *Social Text* 30, no. 3 (2012): 49–75.

11 In Paul Gilroy, "'Not a Story to Pass On': Living Memory and the Slave Sublime," in *The Black Atlantic: Modernity and Double Consciousness* (Cambridge, MA: Harvard University Press, 1993), 21.

12 In an important interview with Garth Reeves (Henry Ethelbert's son), we learn that his father began his career as a master printer in the Bahamas working at the *Nassau Guardian*. He eventually left Nassau for Miami in 1919 and settled his family there soon after. Reeves was instrumental in the early desegregation wade-ins of Miami's beaches and would eventually helm the *Miami Times* in 1970. "Garth Reeves (The HistoryMakers A2013.183), Interviewed by Larry Crowe, June 5, 2013," The HistoryMakers Digital Archive, www.thehistorymakers.org/digital-archives. See also Dr. Dorothy Jenkins Fields and her oral histories of the Reeves family: "The Origin of the Miami Times," *Update* 5, no. 5, June 1978. See also Leslie G. Streeter's "70th Anniversary: Perseverance Linked to a Dream Led to Launching of The Times as a Voice for Black Community," *Miami Times*, September 2, 1993. For another study of the *Miami Times*, see Yanela G. McLeod's *The Miami Times and the Fight for Equality: Race, Sport, and the Black Press, 1948–1958* (Lanham, MD: Lexington, 2019).

13 N. D. B. Connolly makes vital critiques of the political conservatism to be found in the *Miami Times* (particularly under the leadership of H. E. S. Reeves) and its occasional complicity with the plans for highway construction. See N. D. B. Connolly, *A World More Concrete: Real Estate and the Remaking of Jim Crow South Florida* (Chicago: University of Chicago Press, 2014), 249. Connolly crucially points out the paper moving its headquarters out of downtown and to the suburbs in 1957. I want to hold on to these critiques. Yet I also want to linger with the advertisements that make another kind of noise in plain sight (including the one from 1964) and many of the locally reported stories that nevertheless may offer counternarrative signals to the paper's uplift sensibilities. This chapter listens to those many instances of what Connolly observes: "Black people found ways to assert their own claims over South Florida's land through cultural practice and creative appropriations of state power." Connolly, *A World More Concrete*, 102.

14 Connolly's *A World More Concrete* explains the behind-the-scenes contexts of the property advertisements that appeared in the *Miami Times* and elsewhere. There are worlds of difficult stories held in these advertisements, and Connolly's book tells them.

15 Here is the full statement: "Overtown was a whole culture centered around entertainment. There were nightclubs everywhere. . . . Everything was right there. We were the definition of a prosperous, energetic, motivated race of people. It didn't matter black, white, green, yellow, we were too busy being educated and satisfied with each other listening to music, partying on the weekend, football games, parades." Jacob Katel, "Interview with Willie Clarke 2013," in *A People's History of Overtown*, vol. 1 (2016), 131–32.

16 The Sir John Hotel was first owned by Sam Rabin, son of Russian refugees who came to Miami during the pogroms. See "Sonny Rabin on the Lord Calvert and Sir John Hotel," interview with Jacob Katel on October 29, 2011, in Katel, *A People's History*, 106. Ms. Rabin is the niece of the president of Lord Calvert whiskey distillery, which had a distributorship in Miami, where her father worked. In this interview, Rabin tells of constant police harassment because of the Lord Calvert's integrated audiences. According to Sam Moore (of Sam & Dave), "The Knight Beat was right on the floor, not a high stage. Just about a step up, like a sidewalk, maybe a little higher. It was circular and you had people standing all around and in back of wherever you were. After the show you could have chicken or fish or drinks and when the show started you had the entertainers getting dinner right next to you." In Jacob Katel, "Interview with Sam Moore 2015," in *A People's History*, 146. For more on the vitality of Overtown's nightclubs, see Marvin Dunn's *Black Miami in the Twentieth Century* (Gainesville: University Press of Florida, 1997), 143–54.

17 Revisit, always revisit, Farah Jasmine Griffin's *"Who Set You Flowin'?": The African-American Migration Narrative* (New York: Oxford University Press, 1995) for the hard and beautiful tellings of these movements.

18 On this undertheorized southern story of the Great Migration, see Raymond A. Mohl's "Miami, Florida," in *The Great Migration: A Historical Encyclopedia of the American Mosaic*, ed. Stephen A. Reich (Santa Barbara: Greenwood, 2014), 206–9. Mohl points us to W. E. Vickery's *The Economics of the Negro Migration 1900–1960* (New York: Arno, 1977); and Emmett Jay Scott's *Negro Migration during the War*, rev. ed. (1920; repr., New York: Arno, 1969). For a general history of Black populations in Miami across the twentieth century, see Marvin Dunn's foundational *Black Miami*. So many performers were born in Georgia, such as Sam Moore (from the luminous duo Sam & Dave).

19 Bea L. Hines, "Overtown: Rich History, New Hopes," *Miami Herald*, June 1, 1980, 10.

20 See ad in the *Miami Times*, April 15, 1961, 4.

21 In the album *Live at the Harlem Square Club*, Sam Cooke opened with "Feel It," as in don't fight it. He asks the crowd, "Is everybody in favor of getting romantic?" right before singing his majestic "It's All Right" medley.

22 Elsewhere, Killens referred to white patrons as "people from the other side." Gayle Pollard, "Black Clubs Jumping, but Few Whites or Superstars Are Making Scene," *Miami Herald*, May 9, 1975, AAA1.

23 N. D. B. Connolly points out how H. E. S. Reeves was in support of the highway construction, revealing the complicity of property owners and "modernization." Connolly quotes Reeves in the *Miami Times* in 1957: "The expressway will, perhaps, cut into our already limited living space displacing some poor people, but with the expansion and progress of a city, there is little you can do about it." Connolly, *A World More Concrete*, 214.

24 Raymond A. Mohl, "Trouble in Paradise: Race and Housing during the New Deal Era," in *The Making of Urban America*, ed. Raymond A. Mohl (Wilmington: SR Books, 1988), 218. *Really* important to note here is the familiar playbook of the "public health argument," as used against the Indigenous populations in South Florida. For example, in Betty Mae Tiger Jumper's autobiography, she and Patsy West show how Seminole camps in the 1920s were often targeted with the same "concern" over public health for the "Indians," and all the more so to contain their contaminating threat to whites. See Betty Mae Tiger Jumper and Patsy West, *A Seminole Legend: The Life of Betty Mae Tiger Jumper* (Gainesville: University Press of Florida, 2001), 47.

25 For detailed histories of the destruction of Overtown and the ruthless and enduring real estate apartheids of South Florida, again see Raymond A. Mohl, "Race and Space in the Modern City: Interstate 95 and the Black Community in Miami," in *Urban Policy in Twentieth-Century America*, ed. Arnold Richard Hirsch and Raymond A. Mohl (New Brunswick, NJ: Rutgers University Press, 1993), 100–158. Mohl writes that Overtown's population of approximately forty thousand was reduced to ten thousand. Of the highway construction specifically, Mohl gives a sense of the destructive scale of the project on the neighborhood: "Groundbreaking for the monster Miami midtown expressway interchange occurred in September 1966. The eight-lane, four level interchange rose in some places as high as a seven-story building. The interchange also destroyed nearly eighty-seven acres of housing and commercial property at the heart of Overtown . . ." (134). Antonio López, Chanelle N. Rose, Melanie Shell-Weiss, Nathan Connolly, Tameka Bradley-Hobbs, Monika Gosin, and Tatiana McInnis all revive and contribute to this important scholarship—*and* provide a new school of South Florida Black studies that takes into difficult account the intersection of Blackness, immigration, property laws, and intraethnic tensions in Miami's enduring freedom struggle. See Antonio López, *Unbecoming Blackness: The Diasporic Cultures of Afro-Cuban America* (New York: New York University Press, 2012); Chanelle N. Rose, *The Struggle for Black Freedom in Miami: Civil Rights and America's Tourist Paradise, 1896–1968* (Baton Rouge: LSU Press, 2015); Melanie Shell-Weiss, *Coming to Miami: A Social History* (Gainesville: University Press of Florida, 2009); Connolly, *A World More Concrete*; Monika Gosin, *The Racial Politics of Division: Interethnic Struggles for Legitimacy in Multicultural Miami* (Ithaca, NY: Cornell University Press, 2019); and Tatiana Danielle McInnis, "Missing Miami: Anti-Blackness and the Making of the South Florida Myth" (PhD diss., Vanderbilt University, 2017).

26 "Dorothy Fields (The HistoryMakers A2006.024), Interviewed by Tracey Lewis, February 17, 2006," the HistoryMakers Digital Archive, session 1, tape 5, story 6. Dorothy Fields describes how Florida's I-95 expressway displaced Black residents in Miami's Overtown neighborhood.
27 Connolly, *A World More Concrete*, 2.
28 Quoted in Pollard, "Black Clubs Jumping," 1.
29 Connolly, *A World More Concrete*, 282.
30 John Capouya, "Willie Clark and Deep City Records," in *Florida Soul: From Ray Charles to KC and the Sunshine Band* (Gainesville: University Press of Florida, 2017), 194–97.
31 In Katel, *A People's History*, 134. "Who Threw the Whiskey in the Well?" is a song originally recorded in 1945 by Lucky Millinder and His Orchestra with Wynonie Harris on vocals. In his *Florida Soul*, Capouya also includes Millinder as a vital conduit for Florida music not only for his performances done in Florida but also for his formative rejection of none other than Ray Charles for a gig at the Sunshine Club in Orlando in the mid-1940s. Capouya, *Florida Soul*, 40.
32 Katel, *A People's History*, 134.
33 Capouya, *Florida Soul*, 200.
34 Smith started working at Johnny's Records when she was in tenth grade and would eventually marry Johnny Pearsall. They originally met as middle schoolers at Brownsville Junior High. See "Helene Smith: Miami" in Capouya, *Florida Soul*, 211–13.
35 *Eccentric Soul: The Deep City Label* (2005); *Eccentric Soul: The Outskirts of Deep City* (2007). See the liner notes by Ken Shipley, Rob Sevier, and Tom Hunt (October 2005) and Ken Shipley (September 2007), or perhaps you will see what I mean when reading, in full, the Numero Group's mission statement:

> In the growing noise of the so-called reissue field, The Numero Group remains distinct in its quality: deeply researched, expertly resuscitated and lavishly packaged box sets, playlists and ephemera of historic music from the 1950s–1990s. Founded in Chicago in 2003 by Rob Sevier and Ken Shipley, for more than 15 years Numero has committed to unearthing precious lost sounds for new audiences, with an unparalleled ear for potential and spirited eye for detail.
>
> With hundreds of titles in our diverse catalog of LPs, CDs, cassettes, 45s, 12-inch singles and playlists, each Numero production illuminates the often herculean efforts of individuals who sang, played, recorded and peddled their art to little fanfare in its day. Through intense research and wild ideas, these songs find new life in streaming, lovingly packaged media and placement in film and television. By self-imposed law, everything assembled by Numero is a stunning new artifact of sound, image and word."
"About the Numero Group," www.numerogroup.com/etc.

36 Capouya helps verify my intuition: "Smith does take issue with some of the assertions about her rivalry between her and Betty Wright in the 2014 documentary *Deep City: The Birth of the Miami Sound*." Capouya, *Florida Soul*, 212. For another great entry on Smith, see Sir Shambling's entry "Helene Smith," Sir Shambling's Deep Soul Heaven, www.sirshambling.com/artists_2012/S/helene_smith/index.php.

37 "A Woman Will Do Wrong" was written by Paul Kelly and Clarence Reid in 1966; https://www.youtube.com/watch?v=sd1nNDexGTQ. Phil-L.A. of Soul was an R&B label founded in 1967 by Larry Cohen, who changed from being in charge of promotions for the Artic label (one of many under the umbrella of the Jamie label, which was founded by Harold Lipsius in 1955). See A. D. Amorosi, "Early Philly Soul Label to Release Its Forgotten Archives," *My City Paper*, March 20, 2013, accessed July 15, 2020, https://mycitypaper.com/Early-Philly-Soul-Label-To-Release-Its-Forgotten-Archives.

38 Her description of FAMU is from, again, Capouya's wonderful interview in *Florida Soul*, 216.

39 Capouyua, *Florida Soul*, 220.

40 Capouya, *Florida Soul*, 220.

41 This is a sad truism for so many histories written about "race record" labels from Motown to Fania Records. The women musicians are usually fully written out of the story with the exception of very few, or sometimes even just one—for example, Diana Ross and Celia Cruz and, in the case of Miami scene, both Helene Smith and Betty Wright. However, there is zero imagination and rigor used when writing about these key women players.

42 Yes, the Perrine that I refer to here is the very Perrine land grant discussed in chapter 1.

43 Namphuyo Aisha McCray in discussion with the author, December 29, 2020. As McCray put it, "Everyone called Norris to do their yards" and also added that she used to work with him for her ice-cream money: "He did some big jobs where he sculpted animals out of wire and bush."

44 Across two long interviews I was blessed to conduct with Wright's firstborn daughter, Namphuyo Aisha McCray, she conveyed, over and over again, how much music surrounded her as a young girl from her grandparents and aunts and uncles. "Everyone was always playing something in that house." Namphuyo McCray in discussion with the author, August 7, 2020, and December 29, 2020. Rosa Lee Wright, Betty Wright's mother, was an especially important musician in Overtown history as a musical fixture in the First Born Church of the Living God. With her children she formed the gospel band "Echoes of Joy." Betty Wright began performing and recording with the group when she was three years old. Rosa Wright was born in 1925 in Cairo, Georgia, and moved to Miami in 1936. She lived in and raised her family in the James E. Scott housing complex in Liberty City from 1950 to 1972. She then moved the family to the El Portal neighborhood. See also Robert Beatty, "Gospel Pio-

neer Dies at 85," *South Florida Times*, September 10, 2010, www.sfltimes.com/uncategorized/gospel-pioneer-dies-at-85.

45 Kurt K. O. T. O. Curtis, "Betty Wright," in *Florida's Famous and Forgotten: History of Florida's Rock, Soul, and Dance Music, the First 30 Years: 1955–1985*, vol. 2, M to Z (Altamonte Springs, FL: Florida Media, 2005), 902–11. See Betty Wright's appearance on *Soul Train* when she performed "Clean Up Woman" and "Babysitter": "Betty Wright—Clean Up Woman & Babysitter," YouTube Video, posted by Jamarkus Hall, March 26, 2020, www.youtube.com/watch?v=4nK6YJH1kmk.

46 For the early career of Wright in the Miami press, see this article by Mel Ziegler, "Just Plain Betty White Has a Hit on Her Hands," [sic] *Miami Herald*, July 26, 1968, B1. In the article, there is this great statement from Willie Clarke, listed as her manager: "She has strength in ther voice, feelin' [sic]; she has the soul. She isn't afraid at all. She goes right out there and sings a song like it ought to be sung."

47 The death knell of the Sir John is articulated most forcefully and cynically in the *Miami News* on October 1, 1976, under a little editorial subsection called "Around the Town." It explains it this way: "The federal government has purchased the Sir John Hotel on N. W. 6th St. for the site of the new downtown post office. The Postal Service contracted with Metro's Department of Housing and Urban Development to assist in the relocation of five businesses and 34 individuals. General Services Administration also acquired properties on the west side of the federal courthouse/post office complex on N. E. 1st Ave. for the new courthouse annex. This will require relocation of seven businesses, 97 individuals and six families. It's all in the name of progress." In "Around the Town," *Miami Times*, October 1, 1976, 12A.

48 Betty Wright interview, https://www.youtube.com/watch?v=J-thfb6BFwo. The Sir John Hotel, built by Ben Danbaum in 1951, was originally known as the Lord Calvert Hotel.

49 In this way I situate her and it in Daphne A. Brooks's porous genealogy of Black Women's musical avant-garde cultures. See Brooks's *Liner Notes for the Revolution: The Intellectual Life of Black Feminist Sound* (Cambridge, MA: Harvard University Press, 2021).

50 Danielle Goldman, *I Want to Be Ready: Improvised Dance as a Practice of Freedom* (Ann Arbor: University of Michigan Press, 2010), 142.

51 Curtis, *Florida's Famous and Forgotten*, 904.

52 It is important to note here that Liberty City was not the only place for Overtown's displaced refugees and also to say that for many, the early Liberty Square projects (like many model housing projects/developments around the US) were seen as an opportunity for better housing, functioning plumbing, and upward mobility until rampant federal and local neglect of the facilities, coupled with growing poverty and crime. As a result, it is where Liberty City's nickname of "Pork n' Beans" came from, given that this was all people could afford to eat.

53 At the time of writing this particular section in 2018, this was taken from "Biography" on Cynthia Calhoun's official website, www.cynthiacalhoun.com /Cynthia/Bio.html. However, the site has been discontinued.

54 Roundtree made the beautiful vocal on one of Freestyle's greatest hits, "Got to Be Next to You." For more on Freestyle, see my article, Alexandra T. Vazquez, "Can You Feel the Beat? Freestyle's Systems of Living, Loving, and Recording," *Social Text* 28, no. 1 (2010): 107–24. As proof of her later participation in the Overtown–to–Liberty City matrix, she was also the model featured on Lang Cook's important album, *She's Hot with 2,000 Watts*.

55 Take this great detail from an interview Caldwell once gave on NPR, May 19, 2005: "Always had it because most of my childhood was spent in Miami, which was a dumping ground for all kinds of music—Haitian, reggae, Latin, pop, R&B, culture. I mean, it was really a diversified city. But my mom, who was a real estate broker, sold Bob Marley his home in Miami, and I became friends with Bob Marley through friends and we became close enough to where I actually had felt as though I had been to Jamaica." See Ed Gordon, "Bobby Caldwell: 'Perfect Island Nights,'" NPR, May 19, 2005, accessed May 1, 2019, www.npr .org/templates/story/story.php?storyId=4657970.

56 McCray in discussion with the author, August 7, 2020, and December 29, 2020.

57 McCray in discussion with the author, December 29, 2020.

58 Part of these details of Yvonne Campbell's story were told in conversation with Luther Campbell in discussion with the author, December 2014, and as told in Luther Campbell's autobiography, *The Book of Luke: My Fight for Truth, Justice, and Liberty City* (New York: HarperCollins, 2015), 10. Others are taken from the obituary "Stanley Victor Campbell Dies at 90," *Miami Times*, October 28, 2015, www.miamitimesonline.com/obituaries/stanley-victor-campbell-dies-at-90 /article_97b02a68-9098-11e6-bcd6-10604b9ffe60.html. See also this great article about her from 1990: Liz Doup, "Mom's Lament: A Bad Rap," *South Florida Sun Sentinel*, May 13, 1990, www.sun-sentinel.com/news/fl-xpm-1990-05-13 -9001080221-story.html. And this: Chuck Philips, "Businessman with a Nasty Rep: Rap: 2 Live Crew's Controversial Luther Campbell Says He's 'Just a Hard-Working Guy Marketing a New Product," *Los Angeles Times*, July 25, 1990, www .latimes.com/archives/la-xpm-1990-07-25-ca-1217-story.html.

59 Their album "As Nasty as They Wanna Be" was among the first to receive the parental advisory stickers from Tipper Gore's Parents Music Resource Center. This led to the famous arrests of record store clerks for not checking IDs.

60 This interview was co-conducted with Dave Tompkins, author of *How to Wreck a Nice Beach: The Vocoder from World War II to Hip Hop* (Chicago: Stop Smiling Books, 2011).

61 Campbell discussion, December 2014. As often happens with families, it can be hard to keep track of who was born here or there, so I don't think Campbell didn't know the details of his parents' stories here, for they show up slightly differently in his published autobiography. But in the interview there may

have been a kind of shorthand. A "this is where they're also really from" type of reflex that one often hears (and uses!) in places like South Florida.

62 For more on this, see Matthew Rodrigue, "The Search for Anti-racial Exoticism: Black Leisure Travel, the Caribbean, and Cold War Politics, 1954–1961" (MA thesis, Temple University, 2010).

63 Yvonne Campbell was hairdresser to some of Overtown and Liberty City's stars. See mention of a few of her clients in Stanley Campbell's 2015 obituary in the *Miami Times*: "Yvonne [Campbell] was beautician to Ms. Meeks, Ms. Range, Ms. Littles (of the *Miami Times* Reeves family) and a host of other influential women of Miami." I love to imagine that they were listening to Millie Jackson. "Stanley Victor Campbell Dies at 90."

64 Henry Louis Gates Jr., "2 Live Crew, Decoded," June 19, 1990, www.english.upenn.edu/~jenglish/Courses/gates.htxx. "Much more troubling than its so-called obscenity is the group's overt sexism. Their sexism is so flagrant, however, that it almost cancels itself out in a hyperbolic war between the sexes. In this it recalls the intersexual jousting in Zora Neale Hurston's novels. Still, many of us look toward the emergence of more female rappers to redress sexual stereotypes. And we must not allow ourselves to sentimentalize street culture: the appreciation of verbal virtuosity does not lessen one's obligation to critique bigotry in all of its pernicious forms." See also George Lipsitz's dismissive reading of 2 Live Crew and Miami in "World Cities and World Beat: Low-Wage Labor and Transnational Culture," *Pacific Historical Review* 68, no. 2 (1999): 213–31. Some flippancy is also detectable in Andrew Ross's *Real Love: In Pursuit of Cultural Justice* (New York: New York University Press, 1998).

65 Kimberlé Williams Crenshaw, "Beyond Racism and Misogyny: Black Feminism and 2 Live Crew," in *Words That Wound: Critical Race Theory, Assaultive Speech, and the First Amendment*, ed. Mari J. Matsuda, Charles L. Lawrence III, Richard Delgado, and Kimberlé Williams Crenshaw (New York: Routledge, 1993), 111–32.

66 Most of the stuff I know about Miami Bass has been worked out on dance floors and in conversation with women (friends, sisters, cousins) who lived and danced to it. For other forms of critical literature, see Dave Tompkins, who has an ecology of publications around Miami Bass and a forthcoming book about it. For the most current, see Dave Tompkins, "An Oral History of the Miami Mobile DJ Scene," September 23, 2019, accessed December 2019, https://daily.redbullmusicacademy.com/2019/09/miami-bass-mobile-djs-regulating-oral-history. Dave Tompkins, "In a World of Hz: Nat Moore, the Dolphins, and the History of Miami Bass in One Big Hit," *Grantland*, August 8, 2012, accessed September 13, 2012, https://grantland.com/features/nat-moore-dolphins-history-miami-bass; Dave Tompkins, "The Bass Mechanic's Field Guide to Florida While Videodromed in Brazil," *Miami Rail*, March 1, 2013, accessed on June 21, 2013, https://miamirail.org/performing-arts/the-bass-mechanics-field-guide-to-florida-while-videodromed-in-brazil. For a great overview of the history and actual mechanics behind bass, see David

Font-Navarette, "Bass 101: Miami, Rio, and the Global South," *Journal of Popular Music Studies* 27, no. 4 (2015): 488–517. Joe Gonzalez (aka "Papa Wheelie") is considered the go-to resource on all things Bass with his original "Miami Bass History" project (and Miami Bass Multimedia Group), active since 2000 in the virtual reaches of Facebook, YouTube, tumblr, etc. His website miamibasshistory.com is no longer available as such, but his well-circulated 2005 "Miami Bass: The Primer" can be found here: http://stylusmagazine.com/articles/weekly_article/miami-bass-the-primer.html. See also Jacob Katel, "Ten Best Miami Booty Bass Acts of All Time," *Miami New Times*, August 22, 2013, www.miaminewtimes.com/music/ten-best-miami-booty-bass-acts-of-all-time-6393093. There are many who have compiled "Best of Miami Bass" playlists that are easily available on the internet.

67 I was thrilled to stumble across a recent interview that puts on the record the something of what girls who came of age with Miami Bass took with them. See this interview with electronica artist Jubilee (Jessica Gentile), who was influenced deeply by both Luke and Anquette: Ben Hindle, "Jubilee's Guide to Miami Bass," *DJ Mag*, March 24, 2020, https://djmag.com/longreads/jubilees-guide-miami-bass. See also this one to verify the commonality of the underage club experience for girls and young women: Kat Bein, "How Jubilee's Time in Miami's Underage Club Scene Sparked Her Adventurous Productions," *Vice*, October 19, 2016, www.vice.com/en_us/article/pg8mqb/jubilee-after-hours-mixpak-miami-interview-crate-expectations.

68 Leah Jackson and Gwen McRae, in discussion with the author, July 3, 2020. McCray discussion, December 29, 2020.

69 The combined racial-sanitary-health panic (Mohl's "public health argument") that worked to overtly repress Blacks in Miami and set the proprieties for the model Black community in Liberty Square (and the state's first public housing project for Black residents in 1937) is explored in Chanelle N. Rose's *The Struggle for Black Freedom in Miami*, especially in chapter 2. Rose quotes the building manager James E. Scott's regulations: "Residents dress better and deport themselves in keeping with their new surroundings. Indeed the smartness and cleanliness of the place itself, and the consistent decency of its occupants since its completion, has made it one of Greater Miami's outstanding showplaces." N. D. B. Connolly's *A World More Concrete* is also required reading on how uplift in the hands of some Black property owners cooperated with white real estate interests.

70 Dave Tompkins in discussion with the author, December 2014.

71 Earl Lovelace, *The Dragon Can't Dance* (New York: Persea Books, 1998), 14.

72 For a deeply moving account of McDuffie, those who loved him, and the afterlives of the rebellions, see the incredible documentary *When Liberty Burns*, directed by Dudley Alexis and Femi Folami-Browne (2020). A must-read on McDuffie is Antonio López's unforgettable "Around 1979: Mariel, McDuffie, and the Afterlives of Antonio," in *Unbecoming Blackness: The Diaspora Cultures of*

Afro-Cuban America (New York: NYU Press, 2012). Listen to López's take in Ella Washington's moving performance of "The Ballad of Arthur McDuffie," which he hears as "an indictment of the city's form, Miami's built environment, in the production of this racialized killing."

73 Campbell, *The Book of Luke*, 58.

74 This quotation and the compressed history of Pac Jam here are from Campbell, *The Book of Luke*, 59–68.

75 McKittrick, *Demonic Grounds*, xiv. Thanks to McKittrick's work, to imagine the connections between Hurtson and Anquette are all the more material and deeply historical. And as for their sonic connections it is Daphne Brooks, of course, whose lightening fast ability to hear song-in-song offered a perfect association. Brooks pointed me to the 1939 recording of Zora Neale Hurston singing and enacting "Let's Shake It," a track-lining song sung by northern Florida railroad workers as they laid the rail. You can hear her performing this for Stetson Kennedy and Herbert Halpert here: Stetson Kennedy, Herbert Halpert, and Zora Neale Hurston, "Let's Shake It," Jacksonville, Florida, 1939, audio, www.loc.gov/item/flwpa000004.

76 These questions, like this, are taken from Eudora Welty's *On Writing* and are answered, bountifully, by Anquette who anticipated them. To me Anquette's text is required listening/reading for southern arts and letters. Here is a more complete quote from Welty: "It is by the nature of itself that fiction is all bound up in the local. The internal reason for that is surely that *feelings* are bound up in place . . . fiction depends for its life on place. Location is the crossroads of circumstance, the proving ground of 'What happened? Who's here? Who's coming?'—and that is the heart's field." Eudora Welty, *On Writing* (New York: Modern Library, 2002), 41–42.

77 Brooks, *Liner Notes for the Revolution*, 2.

78 Here is where Miami's City Girls (the musical duo Yung Miami and JT) come in as the clear inheritors and the transformative next of this whole chapter. But I want and need to leave this work to another.

AFTERWORD

1 Theodor W. Adorno, *Letters to his Parents: 1939–1951*, ed. Christoph Gödde and Henri Lonitz, trans. Wieland Hoban (Cambridge: Polity, 2006), 26–64. In this selection of correspondence you can read Adorno trying to suss out the United States (Miami, Daytona Beach, New York, New Orleans) and Havana, as he works out, from a difficult afar, fascism.

BIBLIOGRAPHY

Abreu, Christina D. *Rhythms of Race: Cuban Musicians and the Making of Latino New York City and Miami, 1940–1960*. Chapel Hill: University of North Carolina Press, 2015.

Adorno, Theodor W. *Essays on Music*. Selected, with Introduction, Commentary, and Notes by Richard Leppert. Translated by Susan H. Gillespie. Berkeley: University of California Press, 2002.

Adorno, Theodor W. *Letters to His Parents: 1939–1951*. Edited by Christoph Gödde and Henri Lonitz. Translated by Wieland Hoban. Cambridge: Polity, 2006.

Agawu, Kofi. *The African Imagination in Music*. Cambridge: Oxford University Press, 2016.

Aja, Alan A., Gretchen Beesing, Daniel Bustillo, Danielle Clealand, Mark Paul, Khaing Zaw, Anne E. Price, William Darity Jr., and Darrick Hamilton. *The Color of Wealth in Miami*. 2019. https://insightcced.org/wp-content/uploads/2019/02/The-Color-of-Wealth-in-Miami-Metro.pdf.

Allman, T. D. *Miami: City of the Future*. Gainesville: University Press of Florida, 2013.

Bacareza Balance, Christine. *Tropical Renditions: Making Musical Scenes in Filipino America*. Durham, NC: Duke University Press, 2016.

Backhouse, Paul N., Brent R. Weisman, and Mary Beth Rosebrough, eds. *We Come for Good: Archaeology and Tribal Historic Preservation at the Seminole Tribe of Florida*. Gainesville: University Press of Florida, 2017.

Barnes, Germane. "Black Miami's Resiliency: A Photographic Essay." *Anthurium* 16, no. 1 (2020): 3. http://doi.org/10.33596/anth.404.

Barton, Eric. "The Quiet Demise of Florida's Room." *Flamingo Magazine*, September 15, 2020. www.flamingomag.com/2020/09/15/the-quiet-demise-of-floridas-room.

Bartram, William. *Travels and Other Writings*. New York: Literary Classics of the United States, 1996.

Bein, Kat. "How Jubilee's Time in Miami's Underage Club Scene Sparked Her Adventurous Productions." *Vice*, October 19, 2016. www.vice.com/en_us/article/pg8mqb/jubilee-after-hours-mixpak-miami-interview-crate-expectations.

Blackman, E. V. *Miami and Dade County, Florida: Its Settlement, Progress and Achievement*. Washington, DC: Victor Rainbolt, 1921.

Bordman, Gerald Martin. *American Musical Theater: A Chronicle*. Oxford: Oxford University Press, 1978.

Brady, Mary Pat. *Scales of Captivity: Racial Capitalism and the Latinx Child*. Durham, NC: Duke University Press, 2022.

Brady, Mary Pat. *Extinct Lands, Temporal Geographies: Chicana Literature and the Urgency of Space*. Durham, NC: Duke University Press, 2002.

Brock, Hanson. *Down Miami*. Miami: Tropic Press, 1920. http://hdl.loc.gov/loc.gdc/scd0001.00022293497.

Brooks, Daphne A. *Bodies in Dissent: Spectacular Performances of Race and Freedom*. Durham, NC: Duke University Press, 2006.

Brooks, Daphne A. *Liner Notes for the Revolution: The Intellectual Life of Black Feminist Sound*. Cambridge, MA: Harvard University Press, 2021.

Bruegmann, Robert. "Introduction." In *Paul Rudolph: The Florida Houses*, edited by Christopher Domin and Joseph King, 15–16. New York: Princeton Architectural Press, 2002.

Bush, Gregory W. *White Sand, Black Beach: Civil Rights, Public Space, and Miami's Virginia Key*. Gainesville: University Press of Florida, 2016.

Campbell, Luther. *The Book of Luke: My Fight for Truth, Justice, and Liberty City*. New York: HarperCollins, 2015.

Capó, Julio, Jr. *Welcome to Fairyland: Queer Miami before 1940*. Chapel Hill: University of North Carolina Press, 2017.

Capouya, John. *Florida Soul: From Ray Charles to KC and the Sunshine Band*. Gainesville: University Press of Florida, 2017.

Carr, Robert S. *Digging Miami*. Gainesville: University Press of Florida, 2012.

Casals, Elena. *Elena Casals: Mis Cajas de Carton/Elena Casals: My Cardboard Boxes*. Edited by Armando Suárez Cobián. Translated by Jodi Marr and Desmond Child. Nashville: Deston, 2021.

Cattelino, Jessica. "Florida Seminole Housing and the Meaning of Sovereignty." *Comparative Studies in Society and History* 48, no. 3 (2016): 699–726.

Cattelino, Jessica. *High Stakes: Florida Seminole Gaming and Sovereignty*. Durham, NC: Duke University Press, 2008.

Césaire, Suzanne. *The Great Camouflage: Writings of Dissent (1941–1945)*. Edited by Daniel Maximin. Translated by Keith L. Walker. Middletown, CT: Wesleyan University Press, 2009.

"Chico O'Farrill." In Radamés Giro, *Diccionario enciclopédico de la música en Cuba*, vol. 3, 167–68. Habana: Letras Cubanas, 2007.

Chuh, Kandice. *The Difference Aesthetics Makes: On the Humanities "After Man."* Durham, NC: Duke University Press, 2019.

Chuh, Kandice, Joshua Javier Guzmán, Ricardo Montez, Tavia Nyong'o, Alex Pittman, and Jeanne Vaccaro. "Being with José: An Introduction." *Social Text*, no. 4 (2014): 1–7.

Colbert, Soyica Diggs. *Black Movements: Performance and Cultural Politics*. New Brunswick, NJ: Rutgers University Press, 2017.

Congdon, Kristin G., and Tina Bucuvalas. *Just above the Water: Florida Folk Art*. Jackson: University Press of Mississippi, 2006.

Connolly, N. D. B. "Colored, Caribbean, and Condemned: Miami's Overtown District and the Cultural Expense of Progress, 1940–1970." *Caribbean Studies* 34, no. 1 (2006): 3–60.

Connolly, N. D. B. *A World More Concrete: Real Estate and the Making of Jim Crow South Florida*. Chicago: University of Chicago Press, 2014.

Connolly, Nathan. "Speculating in History." *Anthurium* 16, no. 1 (2020): 9 https://anthurium.miami.edu/articles/10.33596/anth.364/.

Covington, James W. *The Seminoles of Florida*. Gainesville: University Press of Florida, 1993.

Craton, Michael, and Gail Saunders. *Islanders in the Stream: A History of the Bahamian People*, vol. 1, *From Aboriginal Times to the End of Slavery*. Athens: University of Georgia Press, 1992.

Crenshaw, Kimberlé Williams. "Beyond Racism and Misogyny: Black Feminism and 2 Live Crew." In *Words That Wound: Critical Race Theory, Assaultive Speech, and the First Amendment*, edited by Mari J. Matsuda, Charles L. Lawrence III, Richard Delgado, and Kimberlé Williams Crenshaw, 111–32. New York: Routledge, 1993.

Cresswell, Tim. *Geographic Thought: A Critical Introduction*. Malden, MA: Wiley-Blackwell, 2013.

Curtis, Kurt. *Florida's Famous and Forgotten: History of Florida's Rock, Soul, and Dance Music the First 30 Years: 1955–1985*, vols. 1 and 2. Altamonte Springs, FL: Florida Media, 2005.

Danticat, Edwidge. *Brother, I'm Dying*. New York: Knopf, 2007.

Díaz Balsera, Viviana, and Rachel A. May, eds. *La Florida: Five Hundred Years of Hispanic Presence*. Gainesville: University Press of Florida, 2014.

Didion, Joan. *Miami*. New York: Simon and Schuster, 1987.

Dilley, Carrie. *Thatched Roofs and Open Sides: The Architectures of Chickees and Their Changing Role in Seminole Society*. Gainesville: University Press of Florida, 2015.

Dixon, Jacqueline Eaby, Kyla Simons, Loretta Leist, Christopher Eck, John Ricisak, J. A. Gifford, Jeff Ryan. "Provenance of Stone Celts from the Miami Circle Archeological Site, Miami, Florida." *The Florida Anthropologist* 53, no. 4 (2000): 328–41.

Dodd, Dorothy. "Jacob Houseman of Indian Key." *Tequesta* 1, no. 8 (1948): 3–20.

"Dorothy Fields (The HistoryMakers A2006.024), Interviewed by Tracey Lewis, February 17, 2006." HistoryMakers Digital Archive. Session 1, tape 5, story 6.

Dungy, Camille T. "Before the Fetus Proves Viable, a Stroll Creekside in the Sierras." *Callaloo* 34, no. 3 (2011): 787.

Dunn, Marvin. *Black Miami in the Twentieth Century*. Gainesville: University Press of Florida, 1997.

Elgart, Alison A. "The Animal Interments at the Miami Circle at Brickell Point Site (8DA12)." *Florida Anthropologist* 59, nos. 3–4 (2006): 179–90.

Federal Writers' Project of the Works Progress Administration for the State of Florida. *Florida: A Guide to the Southernmost State*, American Guide Series. New York: Oxford University Press, 1939.

Fondation pour l'Architecture. *Miami: Architecture of the Tropics*. New York: Princeton Architectural Press, 1993.

Font-Navarette, David. "Bass 101: Miami, Rio, and the Global South." *Journal of Popular Music Studies* 27, no. 4 (2015): 488–517.

Francis, Donette, and Allison Harris, eds. "Looking for Black Miami." Special issue, *Anthurium* 16, no. 1 (2020). http://doi.org/10.33596/anth.408.

Frank, Andrew K. *Before the Pioneers: Indians, Settlers, Slaves, and the Founding of Miami*. Gainesville: University Press of Florida, 2018.

Friend, Craig Thompson. "Editor's Preface." *Florida Historical Quarterly* 81, no. 3 (2003): 253.

Gänzl, Kurt. *The Encyclopedia of the Musical Theater*, vol. 2. 2nd ed. New York: Schirmer, 2001.

García, Maria Cristina. *Havana U.S.A.: Cuban Exiles and Cuban Americans in South Florida, 1959–1994*. Berkeley: University of California Press, 1997.

"Garth Reeves (The HistoryMakers A2013.183), interviewed by Larry Crowe, June 5, 2013." HistoryMakers Digital Archive. www.thehistorymakers.org/digital-archives.

Gates, Henry Louis, Jr. "2 Live Crew, Decoded." June 19, 1990. www.english.upenn.edu/~jenglish/Courses/gates.htxx.

Gay, Ross. *The Book of Delights*. Chapel Hill, NC: Algonquin, 2019.

George, Paul S. "Colored Town: Miami's Black Community, 1896–1930." *Florida Historical Quarterly* 56, no. 4 (1978): 432–47.

Gilroy, Paul. *The Black Atlantic: Modernity and Double Consciousness*. Cambridge, MA: Harvard University Press, 1993.

Glassman, Steve, and Kathryn Lee Seidel, eds. *Zora in Florida*. Orlando: University of Central Florida Press, 1991.

Goldman, Danielle. *I Want to Be Ready: Improvised Dance as a Practice of Freedom*. Ann Arbor: University of Michigan Press, 2010.

Goodison, Lorna. *To Us, All Flowers Are Roses*. Urbana: University of Illinois Press, 1995.

Gordon, Ed. "Bobby Caldwell: Perfect Island Nights." NPR, May 19, 2005. Accessed May 1, 2019. www.npr.org/templates/story/story.php?storyId=4657970.

Gosin, Monika. *The Racial Politics of Division: Interethnic Struggles for Legitimacy in Multicultural Miami*. Ithaca, NY: Cornell University Press, 2019.

Griffin, Farah Jasmine. *Harlem Nocturne: Women Artists and Progressive Politics during World War II*. New York: Civitas, 2013.

Griffin, Farah Jasmine. *"Who Set You Flowin'?": The African-American Migration Narrative*. New York: Oxford University Press, 1995.

Hailey, Charlie. *Spoil Island: Reading the Makeshift Archipelago*. Lanham, MD: Lexington, 2013.

Hamilton, Virginia. *The People Could Fly: American Black Folktales*. New York: Knopf Books for Young Readers, 1993.

Harris, Laura. "What Happened to the Motley Crew? C. L. R. James, Hélio Oiticica, and the Aesthetic Sociality of Blackness." *Social Text* 30, no. 3 (2012): 49–75.

Harris, Wilson. *The Selected Writings of Wilson Harris*. Edited by Andrew Bundy. London: Routledge, 1999.

"Helene Smith." *Sir Shambling's Deep Soul Heaven*. www.sirshambling.com/artists_2012/S/helene_smith/index.php.

Hindle, Ben. "Jubilee's Guide to Miami Bass." *DJ Mag*, March 24, 2020. https://djmag.com/longreads/jubilees-guide-miami-bass.

Hine, Albert C. *Geologic History of Florida: Major Events That Formed the Sunshine State*. Gainesville: University Press of Florida, 2013.

Hurston, Zora Neale. *Go Gator and Muddy the Water: Writings by Zora Neale Hurston from the Federal Writers' Project*. Edited by Pamela Bordelon. New York: W. W. Norton, 1999.

Hurston, Zora Neale. *A Life in Letters*. Collected and edited by Carla Kaplan. New York: Anchor, 2002.

Hurston, Zora Neale. *Seraph on the Sewanee: A Novel*. Harper Perennial Modern Classics. New York: HarperCollins, 2008.

Hurston, Zora Neale. *Their Eyes Were Watching God*. New York: HarperCollins, 2006.

Jenkins Fields, Dorothy. "The Origin of the Miami Times." *Update* 5, no. 5 (June 1978).

Jenkins Fields, Dorothy. "Tracing Overtown's Vernacular Architecture." *Journal of Decorative and Propaganda Arts* 23 (1998): 323–33.

Johns, Willie, and Stephen Bridenstine. "'When Is Enough, Enough?': Willie Johns on Seminole History and the Tribal Historic Preservation Office, the Creek Perspective." In *We Come for Good: Archaeology and Tribal Historic Preservation at the Seminole Tribe of Florida*, edited by Paul N. Backhouse, Brent R. Weisman, and Mary Beth Rosebrough, 1–19. Gainesville: University Press of Florida, 2017.

Johnson, Barbara. *A World of Difference*. Baltimore: Johns Hopkins University Press, 1987.

Johnson, Howard. "Bahamian Labor Migration to Florida in the Late Nineteenth and Early Twentieth Centuries." *International Migration Review* 22, no. 1 (1988): 84–103.

Jumper, Betty Mae Tiger, and Patsy West. *A Seminole Legend: The Life of Betty Mae Jumper*. Gainesville: University Press of Florida, 2001.

Justilien, Christian. "Musicians and Entertainers in the Bahamas." Bahamas Entertainers, www.bahamasentertainers.com/copy-of-featured-artists.

Katel, Jacob. *A People's History of Overtown*. Self-published, 2016.

Katel, Jacob, and Henry Stone. *The Stone Cold Truth: Inside the Music Biz*. Henry Stone Music USA Inc., 2016.

Kennedy, Stetson. "Florida Folklife and the WPA: An Introduction." Florida Memory State Library and Archives of Florida. Accessed January 15, 2020. floridamemory.com/learn/classroom/learning-units/zora-neale-hurston/stetsonkennedy.

Kersey, Harry A., Jr. *An Assumption of Sovereignty: Social and Political Transformation among the Florida Seminoles, 1953–1979*. Lincoln: University of Nebraska Press, 1996.

Kersey, Harry A., Jr. "Florida's Indians: Their Journey from Backwoods to Big Time." *Forum: The Magazine of the Florida Humanities Council*, January 31, 2007. https://issuu.com/flahum/docs/forum_2007spring.

Kersey, Harry A., Jr. "The Havana Connection: Buffalo Tiger, Fidel Castro, and the Origin of Miccosukee Tribal Sovereignty, 1959–1962." *American Indian Quarterly* 25, no. 4 (2001): 491–507.

Kersey, Harry A., Jr. *The Seminole and Miccosukee Tribes: A Critical Biography*. Bloomington: Indiana University Press, 1987.

Kincaid, Jamaica. "Gardens: Dances with Daffodils." *Architectural Digest* 64, no. 2 (April 2007): 78–82.

Kincaid, Jamaica. *Lucy: A Novel*. New York: Farrar, Straus and Giroux, 2002.

King, Joseph. "Twitchell and Rudolph." In *Paul Rudolph: The Florida Houses*, edited by Christopher Domin and Joseph King, 22–56. New York: Princeton Architectural Press, 2002.

Laferrière, Dany. *The Enigma of the Return*. Translated by David Homel. London: Quercus, 2011.

Laguna, Albert. *Diversión: Play and Popular Culture in Cuban America*. New York: New York University Press, 2017.

Lamb, Andrew. *150 Years of Popular Music Theatre*. New Haven, CT: Yale University Press, 2001.

Lee, Donna J., and Anafrida B. Wenge. "Estimating the Benefits from Restoring Coastal Ecosystems: A Case Study of Biscayne Bay, Florida." In *Coastal Watershed Management*, edited by Ali Fares and Aly I. El-Kadi, 283–96. Southampton, UK: WIT Press, 2008.

Leigh, Devin. "Between Swamp and Sea: Bahamian Visitors in Southeast Florida before Miami." *Florida Historical Quarterly* 93, no. 4 (2015): 511–37.

Leitch Wright, J. *Creeks and Seminoles*. Lincoln: University of Nebraska Press, 1986.

León, Christina A. "Trace Alignment: Object Relations after Ana Mendieta." *Post45*, December 9, 2019. https://post45.org/2019/12/trace-alignment-object-relations-after-ana-mendieta.

Linzee, Jill Inman. *A Reference Guide to Florida Folklore from the Federal WPA Deposited in the Florida Folklife Archives*. Tallahassee: Florida Department of State, Division of Historical Resources, Bureau of Florida Folklife Programs, 1990.

Lipsitz, George. "World Cities and World Beat: Low-Wage Labor and Transnational Culture." *Pacific Historical Review* 68, no. 2 (1999): 213–31.

López, Antonio. *Unbecoming Blackness: The Diasporic Cultures of Afro-Cuban America*. New York: New York University Press, 2012.

Lovelace, Earl. *The Dragon Can't Dance*. New York: Persea Books, 1998.

Mahon, John K. *History of the Second Seminole War, 1835–1842*. Gainesville: University of Florida Press, 1967.

Mahon, John K., and Brent R. Weisman. "Florida's Seminole and Miccosukee Peoples." In *The New History of Florida*, edited by Michael Gannon, 183–206. Gainesville: University Press of Florida, 1996.

Manucy, Albert C., and St. Augustine Historical Society. *The Houses of St. Augustine: Notes on the Architecture from 1565 to 1821*. St. Augustine, FL: St. Augustine Historical Society, 1962.

McAlister, Elizabeth. "Rara: Vodou, Power, and Performance." *Smithsonian Music*, March 2016. https://music.si.edu/story/rara-vodou-power-and-performance.

McInnis, Tatiana Danielle. "Missing Miami: Anti-blackness and the Making of the South Florida Myth." PhD diss., Vanderbilt University, 2017.

McDonogh, Gary W., ed. *The Florida Negro: A Federal Writers' Project Legacy*. Jackson: University Press of Mississippi, 1993.

McKittrick, Katherine. *Demonic Grounds: Black Women and the Cartographies of Struggle*. Minneapolis: University of Minnesota Press, 2006.

McKittrick, Katherine, ed. *Sylvia Wynter: On Being Human as Praxis*. Durham, NC: Duke University Press, 2015.

McLeod, Yanela G. *The Miami Times and the Fight for Equality: Race, Sport, and the Black Press, 1948–1958*. Lanham, MD: Lexington, 2019.

Mestas, María del Carmen. *Pasión de Rumbero*. Barcelona: Puvill Libros, 1998.

Milanich, Jerald T. *Florida's Indians: From Ancient Times to the Present*. Gainesville: University Press of Florida, 1998.

Milano, Gary R. "Island Restoration and Enhancement in Biscayne Bay, Florida." In *Proceedings of the Twenty Sixth Annual Conference on Ecosystems Restoration and Creation*, edited by P. J. Cannizzaro, 1–17. Tampa: Hillsborough Community College, 2000.

Mohl, Raymond A. "Black Immigrants: Bahamians in Early Twentieth-Century Miami." *Florida Historical Quarterly* 65, no. 3 (1987): 271–97.

Mohl, Raymond A. "An Ethnic 'BOILING POT': Cubans and Haitians in Miami." *Journal of Ethnic Studies* 13, no. 2 (1985): 5–74.

Mohl, Raymond A. "Miami, Florida." In *The Great Migration: A Historical Encyclopedia of the American Mosaic*, edited by Stephen A. Reich, 206–9. Santa Barbara: Greenwood, 2014.

Mohl, Raymond A. "Race and Space in the Modern City: Interstate-95 and the Black Community in Miami." In *Urban Policy in Twentieth-Century America*, edited by Arnold Richard Hirsch and Raymond A. Mohl, 100–158. New Brunswick, NJ: Rutgers University Press, 1993.

Mohl, Raymond A. "Trouble in Paradise: Race and Housing during the New Deal Era." In *The Making of Urban America*, edited by Raymond A. Mohl, 214–27. Wilmington, DE: SR Books, 1988.

Moraga, Cherríe, and Gloria Anzaldúa, eds. *This Bridge Called My Back: Writings by Radical Women of Color*. 4th ed. Albany: State University of New York Press, 2015.

Moreno, Gean. "Writing the Glyph." In *Purvis Young*, edited by Juan Valadez, 36–49. Miami: Rubell Museum, 2018.

Mormino, Gary R. *Land of Sunshine, State of Dreams: A Social History of Modern Florida*. Gainesville: University Press of Florida, 2008.

Toni Morrison, *Song of Solomon*. New York: Knopf Doubleday, 2004.

Muir, Helen. *Miami, U.S.A.* New York: Henry Holt, 1953.

Muñoz, José Esteban. *Cruising Utopia: The Then and There of Queer Futurity*. New York: New York University Press, 2009.

Muñoz, José Esteban. *Disidentifications: Queers of Color and the Performances of Politics*. Minneapolis: University of Minnesota Press, 1999.

Muñoz, José Esteban. *The Sense of Brown*. Edited by Joshua Chambers-Letson and Tavia Nyong'o. Durham, NC: Duke University Press, 2020.

Nancy, Jean-Luc. *Being Singular Plural*. Translated by Robert Richardson and Anne O'Byrne. Stanford, CA: Stanford University Press, 2000.

National Park Service. *Miami Circle: Special Resource Study*. Washington, DC: US Department of the Interior, 2007.

Navakas, Michele Currie. *Liquid Landscape: Geography and Settlement at the Edge of Early America*. Philadelphia: University of Pennsylvania Press, 2017.

Oré, Luis Jerónimo de. *Account of the Martyrs in the Provinces of La Florida*. Edited and translated by Raquel Chang-Rodríguez and Nancy Vogeley. Albuquerque: University of New Mexico Press, 2017.

Ortiz, Ricardo. *Cultural Erotics in Cuban America*. Minneapolis: University of Minnesota Press, 2007.

Owens, Imani. "Toward a 'Truly Indigenous Theater': Sylvia Wynter Adapts Federico García Lorca." *Cambridge Journal of Postcolonial Literary Inquiry* 4, no. 1 (2017): 49–67.

Panken, Ted. "For Saxophonist-Composer Yosvany Terry's 45th Birthday, a Jazziz Feature from 2014, Two Interviews from 2013, and a Downbeat Profile (and the Interview for that Profile) from 2013." *Today Is the Question: Ted Panken on Music, Politics, and the Arts* (blog). May 31, 2017. https://tedpanken.wordpress.com/2017/05/31/for-saxophonist-composer-yosvany-terrys-45th-birthday-a-jazziz-feature-from-2014-two-interviews-from-2013-and-a-downbeat-profile-and-the-interview-for-that-profile-from-2013.

Parish, Susan Scott. "Zora Neale Hurston and the Environmental Ethic of Risk." In *American Studies, Ecocriticism, and Citizenship: Thinking and Acting in the*

Local and Global Commons, edited by Joni Adamson and Kimberly N. Ruffin, 21–36. New York: Routledge, 2013.

Parks, Arva Moore. *The Forgotten Frontier: Florida through the Lens of Ralph Middleton Munroe*. Miami: Centennial, 1977.

Patrin, Nate. "A Tribute to Graphic Designer Shusei Nagaoka." Red Bull Music Academy, August 4, 2015. https://daily.redbullmusicacademy.com/2015/08/shusei-nagaoka-feature.

"Paul Rudolph—A Life of Art and Architecture." Paul Rudolph Heritage Foundation. Accessed January 13, 2020. www.paulrudolphheritagefoundation.org/biography.

Peatross, C. Ford. "Preface." In *Paul Rudolph: The Florida Houses*, edited by Christopher Domin and Joseph King, 9. New York: Princeton Architectural Press, 2002.

Perrine, Henry E. *A True Story of Some Eventful Years in Grandpa's Life*. Buffalo, NY: Press of E. H. Hutchinson, 1885.

Pexa, Christopher J. *Translated Nation: Rewriting the Dakhóta Oyáte*. Minneapolis: University of Minnesota Press, 2019.

Pisani, Fabien, dir. *Return to Havana*. Cuban Joint Production, 2020.

Portes, Alejandro, and Ariel C. Armony. *The Global Edge: Miami in the Twenty-First Century*. Berkeley: University of California Press, 2018.

Prieto, Dafnis. *A World of Rhythmic Possibilities: Drumming Lessons and Reflections on Rhythms*. Miami: Dafnison, 2016.

Quashie, Kevin. *The Sovereignty of Quiet: Beyond Resistance in Black Culture*. New Brunswick, NJ: Rutgers University Press, 2012.

Quintana, José Luis, and Chuck Silverman. *Changuito: A Master's Approach to Timbales*. Los Angeles: Alfred, 1998.

Quiroga, José. *Cuban Palimpsests*. Minneapolis: University of Minnesota Press, 2005.

Retman, Sonnet H. *Real Folks: Race and Genre in the Great Depression*. Durham, NC: Duke University Press, 2011.

Riley, Sandra. "Mariah Brown." In *Bahamas Trilogy*, 79–136. Miami: Parrot House, 2017.

Riley, Sandra. "Mariah Brown and Coconut Grove's African-Bahamian Village on the Bay." *Journal of the Bahamas Historical Society* 29 (2007): 33–41.

Robinson, T. Ralph. "Henry Perrine, Pioneer Horticulturalist of Florida." *Tequesta* 1, no. 2 (1942): 18–19.

Rodrigue, Matthew. "The Search for Anti-racial Exoticism: Black Leisure Travel, the Caribbean, and Cold War Politics, 1954–1961." MA thesis, Temple University, 2010.

Rommen, Timothy. *Funky Nassau: Roots, Routes, and Representation in Bahamian Popular Music*. Berkeley: University of California Press, 2011.

Rose, Chanelle N. *The Struggle for Black Freedom in Miami: Civil Rights and America's Tourist Paradise, 1896–1968*. Baton Rouge: Louisiana State University Press, 2015.

Sarduy, Severo. *For Voice*. Translated by Philip Barnard. Pittsburgh: Latin American Literary Review Press, 1985.

Scott, David. "The Re-Enchantment of Humanism: An Interview with Sylvia Wynter." *Small Axe* 8 (2000): 119–207.

Scott, Emmett Jay. *Negro Migration during the War*, rev. ed. New York: Arno, 1969. Originally published 1920.

Shell-Weiss, Melanie. "Coming North to the South: Migration, Labor and City-Building in Twentieth-Century Miami." *Florida Historical Quarterly* 84, no. 1 (2005): 79–99.

Shell-Weiss, Melanie. *Coming to Miami: A Social History*. Gainesville: University Press of Florida, 2009.

Slate, Claudia S. "Florida Room: Battle for St. Augustine 1964: Public Record and Personal Recollection." *Florida Historical Quarterly* 84, no. 4 (2006): 541–68.

Spillers, Hortense J. *Black, White, and in Color: Essays on American Literature and Culture*. Chicago: University of Chicago Press, 2003.

Spillers, Hortense J. "A Tale of Three Zoras: Barbara Johnson and Black Women Writers." *diacritics* 34, no. 1 (2004): 94–97.

Stepick, Alex, Guillermo Grenier, Max Castro, and Marvin Dunn. *This Land Is Our Land: Immigrants and Power in Miami*. Berkeley: University of California Press, 2003.

Sturtevant, William C. "Chakaika and the 'Spanish Indians': Documentary Sources Compared with Seminole Tradition." *Tequesta* 2, no. 13 (1953): 35–74.

Sturtevant, William C., and Jessica Cattelino. "Florida Seminole and Miccosukee." In *Handbook of North American Indians*, vol. 14, *Southeast*, edited by Raymond D. Fogelson, 429–49. Washington, DC: Smithsonian Institution, 2003.

Sullivan Sealey, Kathleen, Ray King Burch, and P.-M. Binder. *Will Miami Survive? The Dynamic Interplay between Floods and Finance*. Cham, Switzerland: Springer International, 2018.

Swilly-Woods, Graylyn Marie. "Glocalizing Community Heritage Tourism in Two African-American Communities in Miami." PhD diss., Antioch University, 2019.

Tiger, Buffalo, and Harry A. Kersey Jr. *Buffalo Tiger: A Life in the Everglades*. Lincoln: University of Nebraska Press, 2002.

Tompkins, Dave. "The Bass Mechanic's Field Guide to Florida While Videodromed in Brazil." *Miami Rail*, March 1, 2013. Accessed June 21, 2013. https://miamirail.org/performing-arts/the-bass-mechanics-field-guide-to-florida-while-videodromed-in-brazil.

Tompkins, Dave. *How to Wreck a Nice Beach: The Vocoder from World War II to Hip Hop*. Chicago: Stop Smiling, 2011.

Tompkins, Dave. "In a World of Hz: Nat Moore, the Dolphins, and the History of Miami Bass in One Big Hit." *Grantland*, August 7, 2012. Accessed September 13, 2012. https://grantland.com/features/nat-moore-dolphins-history-miami-bass.

Tompkins, Dave. "An Oral History of the Miami Mobile DJ Scene." Red Bull Music Academy, September 23, 2019. https://daily.redbullmusicacademy.com/2019/09/miami-bass-mobile-djs-regulating-oral-history.

Valadez, Juan, ed. *Purvis Young*. Miami: Rubell Museum, 2018.

Vargas, Deborah R. "Punk's Afterlife in Cantina Time." *Social Text* 31, no. 3 (2013): 57–58.

Vazquez, Alexandra T. "Can You Feel the Beat? Freestyle's Systems of Living, Loving, and Recording." *Social Text* 28, no. 1 (2010): 107–24.

Vazquez, Alexandra T. "How Can I Refuse?" *Journal of Popular Music Studies* 23, no. 2 (June 2011): 200–206.

Vazquez, Alexandra T. "Learning to Live in Miami." *American Quarterly* 66, no. 3 (September 2014).

Vazquez, Alexandra T. *Listening in Detail: Performances of Cuban Music*. Durham, NC: Duke University Press, 2013.

Vazquez, Alexandra T. "You Can Bring All Your Friends." *Small Axe* 49 (March 2016): 185–93.

Vickery, W. E. *The Economics of the Negro Migration: 1900–1960*. New York: Arno, 1977.

Victoria, Carlos. "Comentarios De Un Oidor o Lorenzo García Vega En Su Florida Room." *Encuentro De La Cultura Cubana* 21/22 (2001): 48–51.

Vieux-Chauvet, Marie. *Dance on the Volcano*. Translated by Kaiama Glover. New York: Archipelago, 2016.

Vieux-Chauvet, Marie. *Love, Anger, Madness: A Haitian Triptych*. Translated by Rose Myriam-Réjouis and Val Vinokur. New York: Modern Library, 2009.

Vizenor, Gerald. "Aesthetics of Survivance: Literary Theory and Practice." In *Survivance: Narratives of Native Presence*, edited by Gerald Vizenor, 1–24. Lincoln: University of Nebraska Press, 2008.

Vogel, Shane. *The Scene of Harlem Cabaret: Race, Sexuality, Performance*. Chicago: University of Chicago Press, 2009.

Vogel, Shane. *Stolen Time: Black Fad Performance and the Calypso Craze*. Chicago: University of Chicago Press, 2018.

Wallis, Neill J., and Asa R. Randall, eds. *New Histories of Pre-Columbian Florida*. Gainesville: University Press of Florida, 2014.

Weidman, Dennis. "Global Marketing of Indigenous Culture: Discovering Native America with Lee Tiger and the Florida Miccosukee." *American Indian Culture and Research Journal* 34, no. 3 (2010): 1–26.

Weisman, Brent Richards. *Unconquered People: Florida's Seminole and Miccosukee Indians*. Gainesville: University Press of Florida, 1999.

Welty, Eudora. *On Writing*. New York: Modern Library, 2002.

West, Patsy. "Abiaka, or Sam Jones, in Context: The Mikasuki Ethnogenesis through the Third Seminole War." *Florida Historical Quarterly* 94, no. 3 (2016): 393–94.

West, Patsy. *The Enduring Seminoles: From Alligator Wrestling to Casino Gaming.* Gainesville: University Press of Florida, 1998.

West, Patsy. *Seminole and Miccosukee Tribes of Southern Florida.* Charleston, SC: Arcadia, 2012.

West, Patsy, and Lee Tiger. "'Tiger Tiger': Miccosukee Rock 'n' Roll." *Southern Cultures* 14, no. 4 (2008): 127–40.

Wheeler, Ryan J., and Robert Carr. "It's Ceremonial Right? Exploring Ritual in Ancient Southern Florida through the Miami Circle." In *New Histories of Pre-Columbian Florida*, edited by Neill J. Wallis and Asa R. Randall, 203–22. Gainesville: University Press of Florida, 2014.

Whiteis, David. "Latimore: Some Things You Can't Fake." *Living Blues* 49, no. 5 (2018): 10–20.

Wickman, Patricia R. "Introduction to the 2003 Edition." In William A. Read's *Florida Place Names of Indian Origin and Seminole Personal Names*, vii–xiv. Tuscaloosa: University of Alabama Press, 2004.

Wickman, Patricia R. *The Tree That Bends: Discourse, Power, and the Survival of the Maskoki People.* Tuscaloosa: University of Alabama Press, 1999.

Wright, James M. "The Wrecking System of the Bahamas Islands." *Political Science Quarterly* 30, no. 4 (1915): 618–44.

INDEX

Page numbers followed by f indicate figures.

2 Live Crew, 145, 147, 154; *As Nasty as They Wanna Be*, 198n59; "Throw the D," 150

Abakuá, 104
Abiaka, 191n9
Adorno, Theodor, 157, 201
aeration, 31, 39; in chickees, 11; in the Mariah Brown House, 16, 18
Africa, 25, 39, 109, 111, 189n48, 191n9; West, 90
African Square Park, 150, 152
Afro-Cuban music, 103–5, 114
Afro-Cuban Roots, 114
Agawu, Kofi, 82, 85, 89, 107
Alabama, 125, 130, 152, 170n26; Birmingham, 180n23; Muscle Shoals, 32
Alaimo, Steve, 29, 32, 136, 175n74
Albury, Arnold, 134
Alexander Graham Bell family, 16
Allen, Anquette, 150–55, 201nn75–76. *See also* Anquette
Allen, Myshjua, 141
Allman Brothers Band (Duane and Gregg), 29, 33, 136; "Please Be with Me," 156
Alston, 136
Amadeo Roldán (conservatory), 115
Ambrose, Sammy, 29
Anka, Paul: "My Way," 61

Anquette, 153–55, 201nn75–76; "Janet Reno," 151; "Shake It (Do the 61st)," 151–52; "Throw the P," 150
Antilles, 149
Apfelbaum, Peter, 93
Aranov, Michael, 3
Arkansas, 130; Forrest City, 34
Artic Records, 195n37
Astaire, Fred, and Adele Astaire, 181n31
Atco Records, 136
Atkins, Juan, 154
Atlantic Ocean, 25, 123, 149, 172n44
Atlantic Records, 38, 64
Atlantic Starr, 143

Bacharach, Burt, 147
Bahamas, 25, 41, 44, 123, 131, 145, 171n34; Bahamian Conch houses, 14–18; Bahamian musicians, 119–22; Nassau, 117, 121–22, 125–26, 146–47, 192n12; Upper Bogue (Eleuthera), 15; and wrecking, 122, 191n7, 191n9
baile funk, 150
Baker, Ruby, 100
Banda Macho, 35
baroque style, 22, 25, 39, 158
Barrett, John Charles. *See* Child, Desmond (John Charles Barrett)
Barry University, 188n34
Bauhaus, 5

Bayfront Park, 158
Beauty-Rama, 147, 149
"Because Florida," 47
"being with," 10–11, 86
Beluthahatchee, 24, 173n57
Benitez, John, 187n24
Berroa, Ignacio, 105
Berry, Chuck, 77
Bidney, Beverly, 184n61
Big Maybelle, 34
Bike Week, 158
Billboard, 32; top 40, 30, 65, 100–101
Billie, Frank J., 52
Billie, Henry John, 52
Billie, James E., 11–13, 52
Bird Bowl, 158
The Birdwatchers, 136
Biscayne Bay, 8, 51
Blackman, Ethan, 49–53, 55–56, 58, 70, 178n12
Blanco, Richard: "El Florida," 3
Blowfly. *See* Reid, Clarence (Blowfly)
Bogdon, Ron, 32, 34–35
Bohemian Trio, 114
Bokamper's Sports Bar, 146
boleros, 33, 39, 59, 61–62, 121, 182n45, 183n47, 188n32
Bon Jovi, Jon, 62; "Livin' on a Prayer," 66
Bounty, 151
Bradley-Hobbs, Tameka, 194n25
Brahms, Johannes, 56
Brill Building pop, 182n45
British West Indies, 25
Brooks, Daphne, 26, 154, 174n62, 197n49, 201n75
Brown, James: "Get into It," 154; "Get on Up," 154
Brown, Mariah, 15, 18. *See also* Mariah Brown House
Brownsville, FL, 123, 128–29, 195n34
Brownsville Junior High, 195n34
Bruegmann, Robert, 7
Bryant, Althea, 125
Buckskin Declaration, 71

Bueno, Descemer: "Bailando," 115, 190n65
Bunny D, 150
Byrd, Bobby, 154; "I Know You Got Soul," 152

Cabrera León, Lydia, 112
Caldwell, Bobby, 141, 197n55
Calhoun, Cynthia, 141
California, 185n70; Bay Area, 115; Los Angeles, 34, 77, 133, 154; Santa Ana, 154
Calle Ocho, 158
Calvaire, Fritz, 97–98, 188nn33–34
Calvaire, Gerda Meley, 97
Calvaire, Obed, 84, 95f, 96–100, 102, 104–9, 115–16, 187n27, 188n35; "Good Hope," 101, 103
calypso, 121, 148
Camacho, Juanito, 91
Campbell, Luther (DJ Luke Skyywalker), 43, 144, 147–50, 183n46, 198n61; *The Book of Luke*, 145–46. *See also* Luke Skyywalker Records; *Luther Campbell v. Acuff-Rose Music Inc.*
Campbell, Stanley, 145, 149
Campbell, Yvonne, 145–47, 149, 198n63
Capó, Julio, Jr., 181n28
Capouya, John, 131, 134, 175n73, 195n31, 195n36
Cara, Irene, 143
Carcasses, Roberto, 115
Caribbean, x, 116, 153; and Obed Calvaire, 98; and Luther Campbell, 198n61; climate, 178n14; "Come to the Caribbean" (song), 117–21, 153, 190n3; and exoticism, 181n28; and the Miami Circle, 9; music cultures, 64, 98, 188n34, 190n6; and Yosvany Terry, 109; and Sylvia Wynter, 116, 185n2. *See also individual countries*
The Caribbean Dancers, 185n2
Carol City, FL, 139, 152
Carr, Robert S., 8–9
Casals, Elena, 63f, 66, 182n44; "Magic City," 59–61, 64, 67, 182n42; "Muchísimo," 61–62; "Noches de Maracaibo," 59; "Que seas feliz con tu dinero," 61–62

cáscara, 85, 96
Casey, Harry Wayne, 140
Castro, Fidel, 71
CBGBS, 66
Central America, 25
"ceremonial trash," 8
Cesaire, Suzanne, 119
Cetera, Peter, 143
Chakaika (cakâykico:bî), 51, 178n15
Chalmers, Charles, 29
Chappotín, Felix, 113
Charles, Ray, 195n31
chekeré, 109–15, 187n24
Chicago (band): *Chicago VII*, 80
Chicago, IL, 19, 39, 41, 45, 101, 130, 195n35
chickees, 10–14, 71, 75, 160, 169nn23–24, 170n26
Child, Desmond (John Charles Barrett), 62–64, 77, 182n42, 182n45; "I Was Made for Lovin' You," 65–66; "Livin' on a Prayer," 66
Children's Environmental Group of Coconut Grove, 79
Chile, 39, 115, 189n62
Chopin, Frédéric, 56
Christ Episcopal Church, 171n34
Christianity, 5, 49, 97
citrus, 55, 135–36, 149. *See also* key limes; oranges
City Girls, 201n78
Civil War (US), 49. *See also* Confederacy
Clarke, Willie, 37, 125, 129–33, 152–53, 196n46. *See also* Deep City Records
clave, 85, 87–88, 96, 106, 148, 154, 189n59
climate, 2, 5, 48, 102, 117, 125, 167n11, 178n12, 178n14
climate change, 31, 48
Coast Arts Center, 5
Coconut Grove, 18, 46, 128, 177n1; Village West, 15–17, 159, 171n33
Coconut Grove Cemetery, 17
Coconut Grove Historical Cemetery Association, 18

Coconut Grove Village West Neighborhood Conservation District (NCD-2), 16
Cohen, Larry, 195n37
Colas, Roger, 97–98, 105, 188n32
Coleman, Steve, 115
colonialism/imperialism, xii, 9, 117–18, 131, 147, 170n26, 187n19; anticolonialism, 104; settler colonialism, 10, 50–54, 71–72, 75, 122, 169n24, 178n15
Coltrane, John, 100
Columna B, 115
Company B: "Fascinated," 30
composition/composers, and Anquette, 153; and Descemer Bueno, 190n65; and Desmond Child, 66; and "Good Hope," 101; and Augustín Lara, 188n32; and "Let's Straighten It Out," 33–35; and Eloise Lewis, 123; and "Magic City," 59–62, 182n42; and Arturo "Chico" O'Farrill, 165n2; and "Old Folks at Home," 180n25; and "On Miami Shore (Golden Sands of Miami)," 56, 58; and Dafnis Prieto, 84–85, 88–89, 93–94; and Yosvany Terry, 109, 114–15. *See also individual composers*
Conch houses, 14–18
Confederacy, 40
congas, 61, 80
Connecticut: New Haven, 142
Connolly, N. D. B., 129, 172nn44–45, 172n49, 180n24, 192nn13–14, 193n23, 194n25, 200n69
Coochie Crew, 147
Cooke, Billy, 190n3
Cooke, Sam, 37, 128; *Live at the Harlem Square Club*, 126, 193n21
Coral Gables Senior High, 16, 171n40
counterculture, 153; and Eloise Lewis, 120; and Tiger Tiger, 68
COVID-19 pandemic, 86, 89, 97, 116, 144, 159, 186n17
Crandon Park Zoo, 63f, 123
Craton, Michael, 122, 191n9
creative salvage, 48, 122–23, 144

Cree nation, 78
Crenshaw, Kimberlé Williams, 147
criollo theory, 25
Crist, Charlie, 180n25
Cross River, 104
Cruz, Celia, 39, 158, 196n41
The Crystal Parrot, 18
Cuba, x, 25, 50, 62, 65, 90, 120; Buffalo Tiger in, 71, 184n61; Caibarién, 47; Camagüey, 109, 111–15; Cuban music, 34, 39, 61, 64, 66, 88, 95–97, 103–16, 165n2, 182n45, 189n59; Florida (city), 113; Jovellanos, 108–9; Matanzas, 108; Oriente, 113; Pinar del Río, 59, 61; and return narratives, 91–93; role in Miami, 165n4; Santa Clara, 85, 88–89; US relations with, 71, 146, 184n61. *See also* Habana (Havana), Cuba
Cuban-Ecuadorians, 104
Cuban Revolution, 71
Cult Cargo, 132
cumbia, 26
Cuní, Miguelito, 113
curation, 120, 128, 131–32, 188n33; and Buffalo Tiger, 75; and Clyde Killens, 128; curated foreignness, 51; curated lifestyles, 7; and Jazz Cubano (Yosvany Terry), 95, 113; and Juan Valadez, 20; and the local, xi; and tourism, 117, 120. *See also individual curators*
Curtis, Kurt "K.O.T.O.," 34, 39, 140; *Florida's Famous and Forgotten*, 27–30
Cypress, Jeanette, 168n20

Dade County, 15, 18, 49–53, 151, 158, 170nn31–32, 178n15
Dade County Public School Board, 53
Dade County Youth Fair, 158
Dadeland, 158
dance music, 27–29, 34, 38, 65
Danza Española, 56
Davis, Miles, 100–101
Day, Doris: *Sings Her Great Movie Hits*, 70
Daytona Beach, 33, 158, 201n1

Dean, Snoopy, 136
Decca Records, 121
Deep City Records, 125, 131–32, 134, 136, 141, 145
Deep City: The Birth of the Miami Sound, 132
Department of Public Works (Cuba), 39
Desmond Child & Rouge, 63f, 66; "Our Love Is Insane," 65
Diddley, Bo, 77
Dinner Key Marina, 46, 67
"disciplined plurality," 82, 85, 94
disco, 29, 65, 147, 158
displacement, x, 10, 26, 46, 58, 95, 118, 139; and Indigenous Peoples, 51–52, 179n18; and race, 18, 48, 128–29, 194n26, 197n52
Dixon, Jean, 9
DJs, 27, 39–45, 132, 145, 149–50, 158. *See also individual DJs*
DJ Uncle Al (Albert Leroy Moss), 43; *Liberty City*, 43–45
Dorsey Public Library, 128
drums/drummers, xii, 64, 66, 81–115, 117, 125, 136, 141, 187n24, 188n43; goombay drum, 120, 121, 148; and the lapse, 85–86; in "Let's Straighten It Out" (Latimore), 32, 34; in "Mega Mix" (Sama), 45; at Musa Isle, 72, 73f, 75; steel pan drum, 148; tambores arará, 108; tenor drum, 131; and time travel, 25. *See also individual drummers*
Dumas, Alexandre, 181n31
Dungy, Camille, 27
Dunn, Marvin, 170n31, 171n32, 193n16, 193n18
Dustin, Elizabeth, 3–5, 8, 22, 167n7

Earth, Wind & Fire, 40; *Helios*, 68
Eatonville, FL, 23
Eccentric Soul, 132
Echoes of Joy, 196n44
ecology: and Dafnis Prieto, 94; and Dave Tomkins, 199n66; fragile, x, 31; and Kurt Curtis, 30; and Zora Neale Hurston, 25, 174n66

Eden Roc Hotel, 64
Egan, John, 50
elders, 23, 52, 75, 85, 98, 101, 112, 116, 131, 168n20
electronic music, 154, 200n67
Eleguá, 111, 113
Elgart, Alison A., 8
Ellison, Ralph, 174n65
El Nuevo Herald, 79
England, 18, 25, 71; London, 58, 185n2. *See also* Great Britain; United Kingdom
English, William, 50
Epic Records, 140
Escambray Mountains, 93
Estefan, Gloria, 141; "Coming Out of the Dark," 143; *Into the Light*, 142–43
Europe, 9, 25, 38, 56, 58, 115. *See also individual countries*
Everglades, xii, 25, 30–31, 183n51; and Indigenous Peoples, 12, 52–53, 71–72, 76f, 76–78, 169n21
Everheart, Dennis, 141
exoticism: and botany, 54, 171n35; "exotica records," 190n3; in Florida room representations, 2; and the "Magic City" moniker, 54; and race, 180n24, 181n28; and tourism, 56, 117

Fagan, Donald, 3
Fairchild, David, 16, 171n35; "Poinciana," 186n13
Fania Records, 176n88, 196n41
Federal Writers' Project (FWP), 23; *The Florida Negro*, 24, 173n57
Felix and Jarvis: "Jam the House," 154
Ferguson, Robert, 34
Fernández, Roberto G.: "Wrong Number," 3
Ferrer, Frank, 66–67
Fields, Dorothy Jenkins, 128, 172n45, 192n12, 194n26
filin movement, 61, 66
Finch, Rick, 140

First Born Church of the Living God, 196n44
Firth, Vic, 102
Flanigan's Bar, 27
flight, 7; and Obed Calvaire, 96, 108; and "On Miami Shore (Golden Sands of Miami)," 59; and Dafnis Prieto, 92, 96, 108; role in African folklore, 189n48; and Yosvany Terry, 109, 114
Floral Heights Elementary School, 123
Flores, Charles, 93
"Florida (Where the Sawgrass Meets the Sky)," 180
Florida Agricultural and Mechanical University (FAMU), 99, 131, 134
The Florida East Coast Homeseeker, 53–54, 54f
Florida East Coast Railroad, 53
Florida Historical Quarterly, 3
Florida Humanities Council, 76, 76f
Florida room (in homes), xii, 19–24, 32–34, 40, 84, 98, 144, 167n7, 167n11; history of, 1–9, 13, 16, 18
Flynn, Frank Emilio, 39
folk culture, 24, 26, 108, 120, 173n58
Font-Navarette, David, 199n66
Foster, Stephen: "Old Folks at Home," 180n25
France, 32, 71, 114, 121, 181n36, 187n29; Paris, 115, 189n63
Frankfurt school, 156–57
Franklin, Aretha, 64, 125, 134, 182n45; "Respect," 151
Franklin, Kirk, 99, 103
Frank Williams and the Rocketeers, 34
Freestyle music, 43, 141, 158
funk music, 103, 125, 158; baile funk, 150

Gainesville, FL, 59, 156
Galloway, Yvonne, 145
Gänzl, Kurt, 58, 181n36
Garber, Jan, 115
Gates, Henry Louis, Jr., 147
Gatica, Lucho, 39
Gay, Ross, 167n10

gender, 131; and chickees, 169n24; in *Deep City*, 132; and Miami Bass, 146–55, 199n64, 199n66, 200n67; and migration, 122–23; and Overtown music scene, 135–44; and "race record" labels, 135, 196n41
General Services Administration, 197n47
gentrification, 18, 129
Georgia, x, 16, 129, 134, 148, 154, 170n26, 193n18; Atlanta, 9, 31, 152; Cairo, 135, 196n44; Cochran, 29; Fort Gaines, 129; Piedmont, 9; Thomasville, 37; Valdosta, 125
Germany, 154, 157
Ghetto Style DJs, 149–50
Gibbs, Joe, 141
Gilberto, João, 134
Gismonti, Egberto, 115
Glades I period, 8
Glades Records, 32
Glam Slam, 158
Glen St. Mary Nurseries, 24
global South, 9
God's Property, 99
Goldman, Danielle, 138
Gonzalez, Eladio "Don Pancho" Terry, 109, 111
Gonzalez, Joe ("Papa Wheelie"), 199n66
Good Bread Alley, 172n45
Goodison, Lorna: "Deep Sea Diving," xi
Goodnough, Abby, 48
Goombay (club), 125
goombay (music), 44, 120–21, 132, 148
Gore, Robin, 18, 171n40, 172n42
Gore, Tipper, 198n59
Gosin, Monika, 194n25
gospel music, 37, 97–100, 103, 136, 188n34, 196n44
Grasselli, Diana, 65
Great Britain, 25, 31, 101, 122. *See also* England
Great Migration, x, 125
Gropius, Walter, 5

Guillot, Olga, 61; "Doña Tristeza," 182n44
Gulf Coast, 25, 30
Gulf Stream, 120, 122–23
Guns N' Roses, 66
Guthrie, Woody: *Seeds of Man*, 24
Guzmán Gonzalez, Dionisio "Tanguito," 111

Hailey, Charlie, 46
Haithman, Bessie Thompson Williams, 16–17, 17f
Haiti, x, 25, 96, 107–9, 112–13, 117, 188n33–34, 197n55; Baradé, 97, 102, 187n29; Cap-Haïtien, 97; Little Haiti (Miami), 98, 102, 105, 152, 153; Port-au-Prince, 97, 103
Hale, Willie "Little Beaver," 34–35, 38, 141; "I Love the Way You Love," 136; "Party Down," 156
Hall, Lancelot "Sir Lancelot," 141
Halpert, Herbert, 173n58
Hamilton, Roy, 125
Hargrove, Roy, 187n24
Harlem Square Club, 126, 128, 193n21
Harris, Wynonie, 195n31
Harvard University, 5, 116
Havana, Cuba, 45, 67, 99, 117; and Theodor Adorno, 156–57, 201n1; Atarés, 84; and Obed Calvaire, 108; and Luther Campbell, 147; and Changuito (José Luis Quintana), 106; and Elena Casals, 61; Little Havana (Miami), 152, 153; and María del Carmen Mestas, 84; and Dafnis Prieto, 91, 93; and Felix Sama, 39; and Yosvany Terry, 113–16
Hawkins, Minnie Lee Mosely, 37
Hayes, Isaac, 142
Healy Guest House (Cocoon House), 5
Henderson, Joe, 32
Hendrix, Jimi, 77; "Rainy Day, Dream Away," 64
Hialeah, FL, 97, 158
Hialeah Hospital, 97
High, Robert King, 59

Hill, Erica, 8
Hillside Church of God, 98–99
hip-hop, 43, 148, 153
Hobbs, David (Mr. Mixx), 154
Holder, Boscoe, 185
Holiday, Jennifer, 143
Holland, Dave: "Good Hope," 101–3
Holliday, Billie, 125
Hollywood, FL, 86–87, 87f
Homestead, FL, 34, 150
Honorat, Peter, 98
Horne, Chickie, 125
horticulture, 50–51, 178n15
Hot 105 FM (radio station), 41
Hot Wheels Roller Rink/Skating Center, 41, 42f, 158
house music, 43
House of Chapel Church, 37
Housman, Jacob, 178n15
Hungary, 56, 181n36; Budapest, 58, 67
Hurricane Andrew, 142, 151
hurricanes, 3, 30, 91, 142, 151
Hurston, Zora Neale, 29, 39, 129, 154–55, 165n1, 174nn61–63, 174nn65–66, 199n64; and *The Florida Negro*, 23, 173n57; "Let's Shake It," 201n75; "Negro Mythical Places," 24, 173n57; "Proposed Recording Expedition into the Floridas," 24–27, 152, 173n58
Hyman, Phyllis, 142

i:laposhni:cha thli:, 10, 13, 53, 71–79, 168n20, 170n26. *See also* Miccosukee Tribe of Indians of Florida; Mikasuki language; Seminoles; Seminole Tribe of Florida
The Impacs: "Forever and a Day," 30
Indian Key, 51, 178n15
Indian Pride, 77
Indigeneity, xi, 10, 52, 179n18, 193n24. *See also individual Indigenous Peoples*
Inner Circle, 141
Instant Attraction, 100
Interstates 95 and 395, 19, 126, 145

Jackson, Leah, 36, 148
Jackson, Millie, 147
Jackson Memorial Hospital, 79–80, 97
Jackson Toddle Inn School, 123
Jacksonville, FL, 121
Jacobi, Victor: "On Miami Shore (Golden Sands of Miami)," 56–59, 61; *Szibill (Sybil)*, 58
Jafee's Printing Company, 40
jalousie windows, 15. *See also* Florida room (in homes)
Jamaica, x, 93, 117, 120, 145–46, 148, 185n2, 197n55; Kingston, 81–82, 141, 147; Montego Bay, 141; Ocho Rios, 41
James E. Scott housing complex, 152, 196n44
Jamie Records, 195n37
Jarreau, Al, 141
Jay-Z, 35
jazz, 37, 61, 99–100, 102–3, 110–11, 115, 125, 187n24; big-band, 165n2; Cuban, 95, 108–9, 113; Latin, 95, 186n13
Jazz Gallery, 115, 187n24; Jazz Cubano, 95, 108–9, 113
Jazz Plaza festival, 108
Jazz Standard, 93
Jim Crow, 125
John, Elton, 62
Johnny's Records, 131, 195n34
Johns, Mary G. Frances, 52
Johns, Willie, 169n24
Johnson, Barbara, 174n63, 174n65
Johnson, Howard, 41, 191n7
Johnson, James Weldon, 121
Jordan, Louis: "Saturday Night Fish Fry," 130
JT (Jatavia Shakara Johnson), 201n78
Jubilee (Jessica Gentile), 200n67
Jumper, Alan, 52
Jumper, Betty Mae Tiger, 168n20, 179n18, 193n24
junkanoo, 121

Kaempfert, Bert: *Strangers in the Night*, 70
Kahn, Chaka, 142

Katel, Jacob, 125, 130, 176n88, 192nn15–16
KC and the Sunshine Band, 33, 140, 158
Kebo, 15, 170n32
Kendall Skating Rink, 158
Kennedy, Stetson, 23, 201n75; *Palmetto Country*, 24; *Southern Exposure*, 24
Kennedy Pier, 79
Kersey, Harry A., Jr., 72, 168n20
key limes, 51
Key West, 14–15, 47, 178n15, 191n7
KidEthnic. *See* Reshamwala, Saleem (KidEthnic)
Killens, Clyde, 128–30, 149, 193n22; *Knight Beat*, 32, 34, 125–26, 127f, 192n16
Kincaid, Jamaica, 187n19
KISS, 62; "I Was Made for Lovin' You," 66
Kraftwerk: "Numbers," 154
Kreisler, Fritz, 180n27; *Apple Blossoms*, 56, 181n31
Kreyol language, 112

Lady Tigra, 150
La ENA (National Art Schools), 92, 100, 108, 115
La Fábrica de Arte Cubano, 91–92, 108, 116
Laferriére, Dany: *Enigma of Return*, 187n29
Lake Okeechobee, 168n20
lapse: and Dafnis Prieto, 85–86, 89, 91–92, 186n9; and José Luis Quintana (Changuito), 106
Lara, Augustín, 188n32
Latimore, Benny, 23, 136, 140, 176n89; "Let's Straighten It Out," 32–39, 175n73, 176n90; *More More More*, 32–33, 33f, 175n74
Latin music, 43, 115, 182n42, 182n45, 197n55; Latin jazz, 95, 186n13
LeBaron, William, 180n26; *Apple Blossoms*, 56, 181n31; "On Miami Shore (Golden Sands of Miami)," 56–59, 61
Ledesma, Roberto: "Muchísimo," 61–62; "Que seas feliz con tu dinero," 61–62; "Triste," 61
Legba, 157

León Charles, Basilia, 112
Leroy, Alfred, Jr., 43
levitation/levitación/levitado, 88, 94, 107
Lewis, Eloise, 126, 130, 133, 149, 153–54; "Come to the Caribbean," 119f, 119–23, 190n3
Lewis, Mike, 36
Liberty City, FL, 18–19, 59, 62, 123, 125, 144, 146, 149, 152, 182n45, 196n44; El Portal, 136, 196n44; *Liberty City* (DJ Uncle Al album), 43–44, 44f, 177n94; and Overtown, 128–29, 131–41, 145, 148, 150, 197n52, 197n54, 198n63, 200n69
Liberty Square, 136, 197n52, 200n69
Library of Congress, 7, 173n58
Lipsius, Harold, 195n37
Little, Robert, 5
Little Haiti (Miami), 98, 102, 105, 152, 153
Little Havana (Miami), 152, 153
López, Antonio, 194n25, 200n72
Lord Calvert, 192n16
Los Angeles Times, 3
Los Chikos del Maíz, 35
Los Van Van, 105, 113; "Soy Todo," 156
Louisiana: New Orleans, x, 130–31, 133, 152–53, 201n1
Lovelace, Earl, 149
L'Trimm: "We Like the Cars That Go Boom," 150
Lucayan archipelago, x, 149
Lucumís, 109, 111
Luke Skyywalker Records, 150
Luther Campbell v. Acuff-Rose Music Inc., 145, 198n59
Lyman Wheeler Beecher Elementary School, 142
Lyric Theater, 125

Machito, 165n2
Madison Square Garden, 66
Madison Square Park, 116
"Magic City" moniker, 53–55, 58, 67; Elena Casals song, 59–61, 64, 182n42
Mane, Gucci, 180n23

mangos, 51, 92
mangroves, 166n6; and musical relationships, 67, 107; and reading method, xii, 31; and spoil islands, 47
Manhattan School of Music, 96
Marerro, Zoraida, 33
Mariah Brown House, 15f, 15–18, 170n31, 171n38
Marlboro, DJ, 150
Marley, Bob, 197n55; "Buffalo Solider," 141; "Natural Mystic," 68
Martin, Ricky: "Livin' la Vida Loca," 62; "She Bangs," 62
Martin, Tony, 180n27
Martinez, Aledaida, 154
Martinez, Eddie, 136
Martínez, Pedrito, 104, 187n24
Martinique, 25
Mar-vells, 125
Masa, Carlos, 115, 189n62
Maskókî ("Creek") language, 168n20, 169n24. See also Seminoles
Massachusetts: Boston, 85, 90; Cambridge, 116
Matthews, Dhaima, 141
McAlister, Elizabeth, 187n29
McCrae, George, 37, 176n85; "Rock Your Baby," 176n87
McCrae, Gwen, 148; Gwen McCrae, 38; Let's Straighten It Out (album), 36, 36f; "Let's Straighten It Out" (song), 36–39, 176n90; On My Way, 38; "Rockin' Chair," 37; "You Were Always on My Mind," 37
McCraney, Tarell Alvin: Head of Passes, 3
McCray, Namphuyo Aisha, 137, 142, 144f, 196nn43–44
McDuffie, Arthur, 150
McInnis, Tatiana, 194n25
McKeithan, Willie, 18
McKittrick, Katherine, 152, 190n1
McNair, Barbara, 138
mega mixes, 43–45
Mendelsohn, Felix, 56
merengue, 121

Mestas, María del Carmen, 84
Metro Zoo, 158
Mexico, 51, 117, 182n45, 188n32; Monterrey, 35. See also Yucatán Peninsula
Miami (film), 180n27
Miámi (operetta), 58
Miami Bass, 26, 145, 147–53, 199n66, 200n67
Miami Beach, 3, 62, 64, 126, 128, 139, 171n35, 183n36
Miami Beach High School, 62, 64, 183n46
Miami Circle, 8–9, 22, 149, 168n14
Miami Dade Community College, 59, 65, 141
Miami Department of Housing and Urban Development, 197n47
Miami Gardens, 18
Miami Homeless Services, 79
"Miami interdisciplinarity," 103
Miami Parks and Recreation, 79
Miami Pop Festival, 64, 77
Miami River, 8, 50, 76
"Miami sound," 31, 132, 134, 138–39, 176nn87–88
Miami Springs, 40
Miami studies, x, 165n1
Miami Times, 123–28, 145, 192nn13–14, 193n23
Miami Waterfront Advisory Board, 48
Miccosukee Music Festival, 78
Miccosukee Tribal School, 78
Miccosukee Tribe of Indians of Florida, x, 67, 71–73, 75–79, 168n20, 179n18, 183n51, 184n61; Bird Clan, 11, 14, 14f. See also Seminoles
Michigan, 9; Detroit, 134, 154
Midway Travel Service, 117–18, 118f
Mikasuki language, 10, 14, 51, 52–53, 168n20, 178n15, 179n18, 180n19. See also Chakaika (cakâykico: bî); i:laposhni:cha thli:; Seminoles
Mills, Stephanie: "I Never Knew Love Like This Before," 40, 44
Millinder, Lucky, 130, 195n31

Miramar, FL, 146
misogyny: in *Deep City*, 132; and Miami Bass, 146–55, 199n64, 199n66, 200n67
Mix, Eddie, 158
Modern Drummer, 83
modernism, 5–6
Mohl, Raymond A., 128, 170n32, 193n18, 194n25, 200n69
Montaner, José, 47–50, 55, 67, 79–80, 178n4
Moore, Sam, 192n16, 193n18
Moreno, Gean, 20
Morrison, Toni, 123
Mosely, George Washington, 37
Moss, Albert Leroy. *See* DJ Uncle Al (Albert Leroy Moss)
Motown, 29, 41, 176n88, 182n45, 196n41
Ms. B and Miami Spice Publishing Co., 140
The Mummers, 34
Munnings, Freddy, 190n3
Muñoz, José Esteban, 70, 165n4, 168n19
Murdoch, Shirley, 143
Murphy, Bob, 115
Musa Isle Seminole Indian Village, 72–77, 184nn63–64. *See also* Miccosukee Tribe of Indians of Florida; Seminoles
music journalism, 83
musicking, 61, 67
Mustafa, Melton, Jr., 99–100, 105
Mustafa, Melton, Sr., 99
Mutiny on the Bounty, 151

N. G. La Banda: "Los Sitios Entero," 156
Nagaoka, Shusei, 68
Nassau Guardian, 192n12
Nautilus Junior High School, 62
Navakas, Michelle Currie, 165n3
Negro Women's Club, 18
Nelson, Willie, 37
Neville, Aaron, 134
New Jersey, 66–67, 154, 156–57; Englewood, 40; New Brunswick, 178n10
New Order, 158

New World School of the Arts, 99–100, 104–5, 108, 116, 188n35
New York City, 15, 34, 67, 97, 100, 154, 176n89, 187n23; Bed-Stuy, 40; Brooklyn, 116, 154; Obed Calvaire in, 96, 109, 115; Desmond Child in, 65–66; and the Florida room, 2; Victor Jacobi in, 58; and Miami music cultures, x, 45; José Montaner in, 47; Dafnis Prieto in, 93–94, 96, 109, 187n24; Queens Village, 188n33; Yosvany Terry in, 109, 111, 113, 115–16, 187n24; Tiger brothers in, 77, 185n70; West Village, 102; Betty Wright in, 142
New York State: North Pitcher, 49; Woodstock, 77
New York Times, 5–7, 7f, 48, 147
New York University (NYU), 65
NIGHTCHILD, 62, 65
Norris, McArthur, 135, 196n43
North Miami, 40–41
North Miami Senior High School, 40, 41
Northwestern Senior High, 123
Northwest Miami, 147
Numero Group, 132, 195n35
Nyro, Laura, 64

Obama, Barack, 146
obscenity, 147, 199n64. *See also* Parents Music Resource Center
Ochehachee, Daniel Tommie, 11–14, 168n20, 169n23
O'Farrill, Arturo "Chico": "Gone City," 165n2
O'Hara's, 100
Okeechobee Canal, 40–41
Olga Alonso School of Fine Arts, 186n9
Opa-locka, FL, 128–29, 139, 158
oral history, xiii, 72, 178n15, 185n2
"The Orange Blossom Song," 55
oranges, 4, 50, 55
Orbison, Roy: "Oh, Pretty Woman," 145
Organization of Black American Culture: Wall of Respect, 19
Orientalism, 54
orishas, 111

Ormond Beach, FL, 156
Orquesta Aragón, 113
Orquesta de Cuerdas de Pepe Delgado, 182n44
Orquesta Maravillas de Florida: "Búscame el abanico," 116
Orquesta Ritmo Oriental, 113
Osceola, Pete, Sr., 53
Overtown, 19–20, 152–53, 172n44, 197n54, 198n63; destruction of, 18, 126, 128–29, 139, 143, 145, 171n33, 172n45, 194nn25–26; music scene in, 32, 124–45, 148–50, 192n15, 196n44. See also Sir John Hotel

Pac Jam II, 150
Pac Jam Teen Disco, 150–51
Pancoast, Lester, 16, 17
Pantry Pride, 40
Paredes, Osmany, 104, 189n61
Parents Music Resource Center, 198n59
Peace in da Hood, 43
Peacock Inn, 15
Pearsall, Johnny, 131, 133, 135–36, 195n34. See also Deep City Records
Peatross, C. Ford, 167n11
Pendergrass, Teddy, 39
Pensacola, FL, 37, 176n85
Pepis, Betty, 5–7
Perdomo, Luis, 187n24
Perrine, FL, 135
Perrine, Henry, 4, 50–52, 178n10, 178nn14–15, 196n42
Philadelphia, x, 34, 132–34; Bridesburg, 34
Phil-L.A. of Soul, 132–33, 133f
Pisani, Fabien: Return to Havana, 108, 189n54
Playboy Club, 41
Poison Clan, 43
Poland, 101–2
Poleo, Helena, 79–80
polyrhythm, 82–84, 101
Pompano Beach, 37
Potter, Chris: "Good Hope," 101–3
Power 96 FM (radio station), 41, 42f

practice-based theory (Wynter), 81, 93. See also Wynter, Sylvia
Pretty Tony, 33: "The Party Has Begun," 158
Prieto, Dafnis, 95–97, 99–100, 102, 104–9, 115–16, 122, 186n17, 187n24, 189n63; collaborators, 189n61; and polyrhythm, 84, 88; Rhythmic Synchronicity, 87, 89, 186n14; on songo, 189n44; and Stick Control for the Snare Drummer, 85–86, 90, 93, 186n11; "Thoughts," 93–94; Triangles and Circles, 91
Prince, 158
public health, 35, 48, 126–28, 149, 193n24
Puerto Rico, 117, 120, 182n42, 187n24

Quintana, José Luis "Changuito," 105; Changuito: A Master's Approach to Timbales, 106

Rabin, Sam, 192n16
racial integration, 16, 128, 192n12, 192n16
racial segregation, 126
racism, 18, 20, 39–40, 123, 139, 149, 180n24. See also Jim Crow
rake-and-scrape, 121
Rara, 97, 187n29
Rastafarianism, 148
Ray Ray, 150–51
R&B, 29, 100, 133, 136, 195n37, 197n55
RCA Records, 77
RCR, 29
Real Roxanne, 154
Red, Keia, 150
Redding, Otis, 64
Reeves, Garth, 192n12
Reeves, Henry Ethelbert Sigismund, 123, 192nn12–13, 193n23, 199n63
reggae, 141, 197n55
reggaeton, 26
Reid, Clarence (Blowfly), 29, 36–37, 136
Reinig, Mike, 34
Renegades, 77
Repo Crew, 147
reservations, 12, 12f, 71, 179n18

Reshamwala, Saleem (KidEthnic): *Regresar: Back to Cuba*, 92
Retman, Sonnett H., 173n56
Rhodes, Donna, and Sandra Rhodes, 29
Rhodes Brothers, 29
Riepe, Samantha, 178n4
Riley, Sandra, 18, 170n32, 171n40
rockabilly, 182n45
rock and roll, x, 27–28, 35, 70, 93, 130; classic rock, 158; and Desmond Child, 64–67, 182n45; disco rock, 29; pop-rock, 66; rock en español, 26; and Tiger Tiger, 67–68, 72, 75, 77–78
Rodilles, Guillermo García, 79–80
Rodney, Red, 101
Rodríguez, Alfredo, 115, 189n63
Rodriguez, Mike, 104, 108, 116
Roop, John, 184n63
Roosevelt, Blind, 34
Rosa, Draco: "She Bangs," 62
Rosado, Marlow, 182n42
Rose, Chanelle N., 194n25, 200n69
Rose's Bar, 158
Ross, Diana, 196n41
Roundtree, Cynthia, 141
Rourke, Mickey, 62
Royal Palm Hotel, 52
Rudolph, Paul, 5–8, 22, 167n11
Rufus, 142
rumba, 64, 84, 121

Saadia Records, 35
Sainte-Marie, Buffy, 78
salvage, 48, 122–23, 144. *See also* wrecking
Sama, Caridad, 39
Sama, Felix, 39–45
Sama Brothers (store), 39
Sambora, Richie: "Livin' on a Prayer," 66
Sam & Dave, 34, 125, 138, 192n16
Sánchez, Grisel, 50, 61
Sanford and Son, 41
Santana, 158
Sarasota School of Architecture, 5
Sarduy, Severo: playas concept, xii, 154

Saunders, Gail, 122, 191n9
saxophone, 34, 93, 101, 109, 111, 114, 187n24
Scott, David, 81
Scott, James E., 200n69
Secada, Jon, 143
"See It Like a Native" slogan, 78
Seminoles, 10, 51–53, 70, 72, 168n20, 170n26, 179n18, 184nn63–64, 193n24; Trail Seminoles, 71. *See also* i:laposhni:cha thli:; Maskókî language; Miccosukee Tribe of Indians of Florida; Mikasuki language; Musa Isle Seminole Indian Village; Seminole Tribe of Florida
Seminole Tribe of Florida, 10–11, 13, 168n20; Bird Clan, 10, 70, 74; Panther Clan, 11; Wildcat Clan, 169n24. *See also* Seminoles
Seminole Wars, 14, 14f, 51, 169n24, 178n15, 191n9
service economies, 118, 122, 125. *See also* tourism
settler colonialism, 10, 50–54, 71–72, 75, 122, 169n24, 178n15
SF Jazz Collective, 102–3
Shake-A-Leg Foundation, 47, 79
Shalimar, 41
Shell-Weiss, Melanie, 194n25
Shepp, Archie: "Invitation," 156
Shipley, Ken, 195n35
Sinatra, Frank, 41, 142
Si O Si Quartet, 93–94
Sir John Hotel, 136–38, 197nn47–48; Knight Beat, 32, 34, 125–26, 192n16
Skin, Evelyn "Champagne," 41
slavery: in "Come to the Caribbean," 120; and Cuba–Haiti relation, 108–9; enslavers, 50; in Purvis Young's work, 20, 22
Smith, Helene, 135, 145, 149, 153, 195n34, 195n36, 196n41; "A Woman Will Do Wrong," 132–34; "The Clean Up Woman," 136; "Good Lovin'/Paralyzed," 136; "Mr. Lucky/Thank You Baby," 136; "Willing and Able," 134

Smith, James Merrick, 5
Smith, Patti: "Because the Night," 68
Sol 95 (radio station), 100
songo, 105, 189n44
son music, 121
Sorg, Stuart, 48
soul music, 27–29, 125, 132–33, 154
South Beach, FL, 158
South Carolina, 101, 125, 154
South Florida, 13, 25, 32, 39, 100–101, 116, 136, 172n42, 176n88, 186n13, 198n61; Bahamian migration to, 15–16, 170n32; horticulture in, 50–51; Indigenous Peoples in, 67, 70, 77, 178n15, 179n15, 193n24; race in, 123, 125, 180n24, 192n13, 194n25
South Miami Junior High, 158
Spain, 25, 35, 39, 50, 71
Spec's Music, 40
Spillers, Hortense, 174n63, 174n65
spirituality, 12, 31, 38, 43, 55, 104, 108, 143, 148, 156
spoil islands, 46–49, 55, 67, 79
Springsteen, Bruce: "Because the Night," 68
Stanford Jazz Workshop, 115
Stanley, Paul: "I Was Made for Lovin' You," 65–66
Steely Dan, 3, 141
Stewart, Billy: "Summertime," 121, 136
Stone, George Lawrence: *Stick Control for the Snare Drummer*, 85–86, 90, 93, 103, 186n11
Stone, Henry, 27, 37, 136, 176n88, 196n41
Stone, Joss, 141, 143
St. Petersburg, FL, 28
St. Petersburg Times, 167n7
Straits of Florida, 122–23
"The Streets of Cairo, or the Poor Little Country Maid," 121
Streisand, Barbra, 64
Strickland, E. J., 100
Sturtevant, William C., 178n15, 179n18
Suárez-Cobián, Armando, 91, 116

Sugarhill Gang: "Rappers Delight," 40
Sun Country, 77
Sun Ra, 180n23
Sunshine Club, 195n31
Sunshine Roller Rink, 150
Super Q FM (radio station), 158
"survivance," 70
Suwannee River, 180n25
Swilly-Woods, Graylyn Marie, 171n33
Symphonie Angelique, 98, 105

Tallahassee, FL, 131, 134, 168n20
Tamiami Trail, 53, 71, 78
Tampa, FL, 173n58
Tampa Bay, 30
Tarpon Springs, 14
Teatro La Mella, 92
Tennessee: Charleston, 32; Memphis, 29
Tequesta, 8, 10
termination era, 71
Terry, Yosvany, 84, 95, 106, 108–11, 115–16, 187n24, 187n27, 189n54, 189n61; *Ancestral Memories*, 114; "Erzulie," 114; *New Throned King*, 112; "Ojun Degara," 112; "Summer Relief," 104, 113; *Today's Opinion*, 104
Terry, Yunior, 104, 110f, 111–12, 114
Thomas, Timmy, 38, 140
Thomas Jefferson Middle School, 99
Thunder, Lightening and Rain: "Super Funky," 35
Tiger, Buffalo (Heenehatche), 10, 70–77, 118, 168n20, 169n21, 170n26, 184n61, 185n70; "My Heart Is with Nature," 78–79
Tiger, Lee, 67, 70, 72, 75–78, 168n20, 183n51, 185n70
Tiger, Stephen, 67–70, 72, 77, 168n20
Tiger Tiger, 67, 77; "Because the Night," 68; *Eye of the Tiger*, 68–70, 78; "My Heart Is with Nature," 78–79; "Taste My Love," 70
Tiki Lounge, 128
Titus, Libby, 3
Tommie, Jimmy, 11

Tommie, Ruby, 11–12
Tommie, Shonayeh Shawnie, 13–14
Tompkins, Dave, 149, 177n5, 198n60, 199n66
tourism, 5, 15, 53, 139; Black, 146; and botany, 51; and "Come to the Caribbean," 117–22; and commodification, 55, 61; heritage tourism, 171n33; and Indigenous Peoples, 72–77, 184n63; and labor, 14; and race, 180nn24–25; tourist attraction economy, 72; tourist gaze, 173n56. *See also* Musa Isle Seminole Indian Village
Trail Seminoles, 71
Trax, 66
Trick Daddy, 143
Trinere, 33, 43
Tropical Park, 158
Trotignon, Baptiste, 114
Trucks, Butch, Jr., 136
Tucker, Johnny, 11, 169n23
Turre, Steve, 187n24
Tuttle, Julia T., 50
Twitchell, Ralph, 5

United Kingdom, 38, 121. *See also* England
University of London, 185n2
University of Miami, 64, 89, 116
Upstairs (nightclub), 158
US Congress, 51, 71
US Supreme Court, 198n59

Valadez, Juan, vif, 20
Valera, Manuel, 93
Valle, Myriam, 65
Vargas, Deborah, 38
Vaughan, Sarah, 61
Venezuela, 59, 187n24
vernacular architectures, 10, 167n9; and Paul Rudolf, 5, 8
Vidal, Maria, 65
Virgin Islands, 117
Vizenor, Gerald, 70

wade-ins, 192n12
Wagmarlove Online Music Store, 188n33
Walstein, Deborah, 62
Warwick, Dionne, 138; "I'll Never Fall in Love Again," 147
Washington, Baby, 134
Washington, Dinah, 126, 127f
Washington, Ella: "The Ballad of Arthur McDuffie," 200n72
Watts, Jeff "Tain," 100, 114
WBAI, 65
Wells, Mary, 134
Welty, Eudora, 201n76
West, Patsy, 68, 72, 77, 168n20, 191n9, 193n24
West Indies, 25, 117
West Palm Beach, FL, 37
Wexler, Jerry, 64
Wexler, Lisa, 64
Wheeler, Ryan, 8, 167n13
White, Barry, 39, 141
"Who Threw Whiskey in the Well?," 130, 195n31
Wickman, Patricia R., 52
Williams, Alfred, 16
Williams, Frank, 34–35
Williams, Linda, 16–18, 171n34, 171n40, 171nn37–38, 172n42
Williams, Noel "King Sporty," 141
Willie, Charlie, 184n63
Willie, Willie, 184n63
Wilson, Flip, 136, 138
Wilson, Jackie, 138
Winnicott, D. W., 64
Wonder, Stevie: *Hotter Than July*, 140
Wordsworth, William, 92, 187n19
Works Progress Administration (WPA), 23. *See also* Federal Writers' Project (FWP)
wrecking, 44, 122–23, 154, 178n15, 191n7, 191n9
Wright, Betty, 37–38, 132, 135, 137–39, 145, 149, 152–53, 195n36, 196n41, 196n44, 196n46; *Betty Wright*, 140; *Danger High*

Voltage, 140; *I Love the Way You Love*, 136; *Mother Wit*, 140f, 140–43; *My First Time Around*, 136; "No Pain, No Gain," 140; "So Many Ways," 143–44, 144f; "Tonight Is the Night," 140; *Wright Back at You*, 140
Wright, Charles, 143
Wright, James M., 191n9
Wright, Rosa Lee "Nana," 135–36, 196n44
Wurlitzer pianos, 59
Wynter, Sylvia, 81–83, 93–94, 101, 103, 114, 116; *The Hills of Hebron*, 185n2

Yale Art and Architecture building, 5
Yellow Brick Road (nightclub), 65
Yerba Buena, 190n65
Young, Purvis, 20, 22, 172n49; *Good Bread Alley*, 18–19, 19f; *Untitled*, 21f
Youngstown, FL, 167n10
Yucatán Peninsula, 50, 178n14
Yung Miami (Caresha Romeka Brownlee), 201n78

Zadymka (Lotos) Festival, 101–2
Zenón, Miguel, 187n24

www.ingramcontent.com/pod-product-compliance
Lightning Source LLC
Chambersburg PA
CBHW070841160426
43192CB00012B/2266